SEXUALITY AND PHYSICAL DISABILITY

Personal perspectives

SEXUALITY AND PHYSICAL DISABILITY

Personal perspectives

Edited by

DAVID G. BULLARD, Ph.D.

Assistant Clinical Professor of Medical
Psychology (Psychiatry) and Director,
Intensive Training Project in Sexuality
and Disability, Human Sexuality Program,
Department of Psychiatry,
University of California,
San Francisco

SUSAN E. KNIGHT, M.S.W.

Director, Sex and Disability Unit,
Human Sexuality Program,
Department of Psychiatry,
University of California,
San Francisco

The C. V. Mosby Company

ST. LOUIS • TORONTO • LONDON   1981

MOSBY

1906 **75** 1981
YEARS

A TRADITION OF PUBLISHING EXCELLENCE

Editor: Pamela L. Swearingen
Manuscript editor: Jean Kennedy
Design: Suzanne Oberholtzer
Production: Stella Adolfson

Printed in the United States of America

The C.V. Mosby Company
11830 Westline Industrial Drive, St. Louis, Missouri 63141

Library of Congress Cataloging in Publication Data

Main entry under title:

Sexuality and physical disability.

   Bibliography: p.
   Includes index.
   1. Physically handicapped—Sexual behavior—
Congresses.   2. Physically handicapped—Rehabilitation
—Congresses.   I. Bullard, David G., 1945-
II. Knight, Susan E., 1950-   . [DNLM: 1. Handi-
capped.   2. Sex.   3. Sex behavior. HQ 54 S518]
RD798.S49   613.9′5′0880816   81-11008
ISBN 0-8016-0861-9   AACR2

C/D/D 9 8 7 6 5 4 3 2 1   03/A/301

CONTRIBUTORS

VICTOR ALTERESCU, R.N., E.T.
John Muir Memorial Hospital, Walnut Creek, California

TONI AYRES, R.N., D.A.
School of Nursing, University of California, San Francisco

ROBERT S. BADAME, Ph.D.
Human Sexuality Program, Department of Psychiatry, University of California, San Francisco

ELLE F. BECKER
Lewis and Clark College, Portland, Oregon

HANK BERMAN, M.A.
Catholic Social Services, San Francisco, California

SHELDON BERROL, M.D.
Department of Physical Medicine and Rehabilitation, Ralph K. Davies Medical Center, San Francisco, California

JANE ELDER BOGLE, M.P.A.
U.S. Public Health Service, Seattle, Washington

DAVID G. BULLARD, Ph.D.
Human Sexuality Program, Department of Psychiatry, University of California, San Francisco

ELIZABETH BURGER, R.N.
DES Action Group
California

HOWARD BUSBY, M.A.
Arizona State School for the Deaf and the Blind, Tucson, Arizona

MARY S. CALDERONE, M.D., M.P.H.
Sex Information and Education Council of the United States (SIECUS), New York, New York

BARBARA CAPELL
United Cerebral Palsy Association, Fresno, California

JOSEPH CAPELL, M.D.
Leon S. Peters Rehabilitation Center, Fresno, California

BERNADETTE CHAVES
Robert Lenz Associates, Merced, California

EMANUEL CHIGIER, M.D.
Israel Society for Rehabilitation of the Disabled, Tel Aviv, Israel

SOPHIA CHIPOURAS, M.A.
Prince Williams Mental Health Center, Manassas, Virginia

SUSAN M. DANIELS, Ph.D.
Rehabilitation Counseling, Louisiana State University Medical Center, New Orleans, Louisiana

MICHAEL DUNN, Ph.D.
Spinal Cord Injury Service, Veterans Administration Medical Center, Palo Alto, California

REESE N. EPSTEIN, M.A., M.P.A.

Petaluma, California

LORETTA J. FERRIS

Women in Transition, Inc., Santa Cruz, California

PAMELA FINKEL

Disabled Students Services, San Diego State University, San Diego, California

MELANEE FISHWICK, M.A.

Rehabilitation Institute, Detroit, Michigan

ROBERT C. GEIGER, M.D.

Departments of Orthopedic Surgery and Ambulatory and Community Medicine, University of California, San Francisco

ELIZABETH HALL

Planned Parenthood, Sherman Oaks, California

GEORGE W. HOHMANN, Ph.D.

Department of Psychology, University of Arizona, Tucson, Arizona

JOANNE JAUREGUI

Center for Independent Living, Berkeley, California

LIZABETH KATZ

Planned Parenthood, Sherman Oaks, California

SUSAN E. KNIGHT, M.S.W.

Human Sexuality Program, Department of Psychiatry, University of California, San Francisco

REGINA KRISS, M.A.

Stanford University Medical Center, Stanford, California

ROBERT LENZ, M.A.

Robert Lenz Associates, Merced, California

E. ELAINE LLOYD, R.N., M.S.

Spinal Cord Injury Service, Veterans Administration Medical Center, Palo Alto, California

KATHRYN L. NESSEL, M.Ed.

Jewish Family Service Agency, Tucson, Arizona

JOSEPH K. NOWINSKI, Ph.D.

Human Sexuality Program, Department of Psychiatry, University of California, San Francisco

LILLIAN PASTINA

Center for Independent Living, Berkeley, California

GRAHAM H. PHELPS, M.S.W.

Spinal Cord Injury Service, Veterans Administration Medical Center, Palo Alto, California

MARY M. RODOCKER, R.N., M.S.

Human Sexuality Program, Department of Psychiatry, University of California, San Francisco

ELLEN RYERSON, M.S.W.

Y.W.C.A. Rape Relief, Seattle, Washington

SUSAN L. SHAUL, Ph.D.

Elliott Bay Health Associates, Seattle, Washington

DON SMITH

Disabled Students Program, Sonoma State University, Sonoma, California

DEBRA SOLIZ, M.S.W.

Disabled Students Services, San Diego State University, San Diego, California

JEAN M. STOKLOSA, R.N., M.S.

Nursing Services, Veterans Administration Medical Center, San Francisco, California

TERRIANNE STRAW, M.A.

Employment Project of the Disabled, United Cerebral Palsy Association of San Francisco, Inc., San Francisco, California

CARLA E. THORNTON, R.N., M.S.

Human Sexuality Program, Department of Psychiatry, University of California, San Francisco

VICTORIA A. THORNTON

Center for Independent Living, Berkeley, California

DOUGLAS H. WALLACE, Ph.D.

Human Sexuality Program, Department of Psychiatry, University of California, San Francisco

BARBARA F. WAXMAN

Planned Parenthood, Sherman Oaks, California

JULIE A. WYSOCKI, M.Ed.

Elliott Bay Health Associates, Seattle, Washington

To the memory of

Catherine A. Valdez

(1945-1981)

I'd rather learn from one bird how to sing
than teach ten thousand stars how not to dance

e.e. cummings

From "you shall above all things be glad and young."
In Complete poems, 1913-1962,
New York, 1972, Harcourt Brace Jovanovich, Inc.

PREFACE

As sex educators and therapists for the past several years, we have learned a great deal from persons with physical disabilities about their personal perspectives on sexuality. A wide variety of health professionals and educators have similarly reported that hearing directly about personal experiences concerning sexuality and disability greatly increased their own understanding of human sexuality. We have therefore selected contributors for this volume who are knowledgeable and sensitive to the issues; a majority of them are disabled. Several of the authors presented this information at the First and Second Annual National Symposia on Sexuality and Disability (1979 and 1980), which were sponsored by the Department of Continuing Education in the Health Sciences, University of California, San Francisco; the Sex Information and Education Council of the United States (SIECUS); and the Israel Society for Rehabilitation of the Disabled. Cosponsors for these symposia included regional and national organizations such as the Paraprofessional Manpower Development Branch of the National Institute of Mental Health.

It is unlikely that a single book could ever give a broad enough or deep enough perspective on human sexuality. Certainly many disabilities, medical conditions, and sexual life-styles are not represented in this collection. For example, we did not include the vital issues of aging, emotional disability, and mental retardation. Gay and lesbian issues are addressed to some extent, but we hope others working in the field of sexuality and disability will explore more fully these and other important life-style orientations in the future.

A great number of people have contributed in various ways to the preparation of this book, and we thank them all. We are especially indebted to our longtime friends and co-workers Mary Rodocker and Bob Geiger. Their warmth, good humor, and intelligence have been important to us over the past several years. Pamela Swearingen, our editor at The C.V. Mosby Company, was influential in the book's development from its original proposal to completion. Her unstinting enthusiasm and wise counsel were crucial ingredients. Our typists Ken Jones and Kathy Kavanagh (our gentle critic) are tireless workers who have our gratitude.

Our work since 1976 has been funded primarily by grants from the National Institute of Mental Health and from the Bureau of Education for the Handicapped, U.S. Department of Education. We have especially appreciated the assistance and support of Jack Weiner, Ralph Simon, Sam Silverstein, Don Fisher, and Vernon James (NIMH); Herman Saettler and Thomas Behrens (BEH); and Evalyn Gendel and Douglas Wallace (The University of California, San Francisco).

Susan would like to express her special thanks to John King, Jay Mann, Gini Geiger, and the late Herbert Vandervoort for their encouragement when she was not only young but also untried in this new field of sexuality and disability. She also wants to acknowledge her parents for their unconditional love and support.

David wishes to thank his friends and teachers, especially Harvey Caplan, Rebecca Black, Lonnie Barbach, Manny Chigier, and Jerry Nims, for all they have shared, and, most of all, his wife Jean and his family for their love.

Finally, we wish to thank the men and women who share so much of themselves in these pages.

David G. Bullard   Susan E. Knight

CONTENTS

PART I

PERSONAL PERSPECTIVES

Susan E. Knight

When I began working in the field of sex and disability in 1972, health professionals were talking as if those of us with disabilities were somehow separate and different from "normal," able-bodied people. Now, 8 years later, many people with disabilities are sharing their experiences and knowledge and are experts about their own sexuality. Not infrequently, they are also teaching able-bodied people that they may not be using their full sexual potential. I believe this is a major breakthrough.

In the early 1970s the study of human sexuality became popular and acceptable. Masters and Johnson's publications, *Human Sexual Response* and *Human Sexual Inadequacy*, were the new "bibles" of helping professionals. On the other hand, the civil rights movement of the disabled was in its infancy. People with disabilities were only beginning to see that, along with racial minorities and women, we, too, were a legitimate minority group. We also were denied access to economic and social opportunities.

I believe that a process of empowerment has happened in those 8 years. Webster defines "empower" as "to give official authority or legal powers to." The following discussions of personal perspectives demonstrate the authority and legitimacy of individual experience as well as the knowledge base within sexuality and disability. What is particularly important to acknowledge is that disabled people themselves have taken the initiative to gain credibility in the sexuality field rather than being given it by "the powers that be" in fields such as medicine and social service.

This process of "taking" rather than "being given" has been a gradual but persistent force in this field during the past decade. The message people with disabilities have been saying is, "I don't only want my political rights, I want my human rights as well." To be able to get into a restaurant or business establishment or to have a job for the first time is a hollow victory if those around you see you as not quite human, sexual, attractive, or having the same basic needs and abilities to share closely with others. Those of us who have been working in this field have been able to point out to the able-bodied society that, "It isn't enough to allow me a job or an education. I want you to realize I'm a sexual person, too."

Interestingly, this message has created opportunity for people who are not disabled as well. By understanding that having a disability does not mean you are less than human, able-bodied people have the chance to see that physical impairments which they may face in the future need not exclude them from love and life. We have not only empowered ourselves, we have also opened up possibilities to those who are not disabled with whom we share our lives.

As I write this introduction, I look around me and see that "sex and disability" is no longer just a concept or an idea. There are a substantial number of persons working in the field, many of us disabled. There are conferences, workshops, training programs, and journals on the topic. I am happy to have been able to be a part of this growth. This book on personal perspectives, and especially this discussion of people's individual experiences, is important to me personally because it is a hallmark in people speaking for themselves and determining their own life's course. I feel honored to have had the opportunity to facilitate a process that I strongly believe is important to all of us, whether disabled or not.

I want to share an early experience that may have lead me into this field. When I was 18 years old, some of us in my high school visited Vietnam veterans at a nearby hospital. One young man, sitting alone in a room, motioned for me to come talk with him. He told me his feelings about the war. He had enlisted the year before and was now recovering from severe shrapnel wounds to both legs sustained in combat. At that time, I was shocked because we were the same age. He had experienced a tragic and terrifying part of life at an age when I was trying to decide what clothes to wear the next day and what college to attend.

I listened to him intently. At one point, he asked me if he could show me his legs. I agreed and he briefly showed me the many scars that covered him from ankle to hip. I looked at them with interest and responded to him with respect for what he had gone through and this "badge of courage" he would carry for the rest of his life. That day I saw him as someone who was trying to impress me with his manliness and courage.

With a few more years of life behind me, I saw him in a different light. Here was a young man who had faced the horrors of war and returned disfigured. He was talking to a woman, his same age, about his experience and his loss. I realized that he probably was wondering, "Will a woman ever see me as attractive when I look like this? If I show her my legs, will she reject me?"

This section on personal perspectives is dedicated to this man and all of us who have dealt with the fear that we are not desirable or lovable in the eyes of others. To all who read the personal contributions that follow, I urge you to recognize that we each have a tremendous amount to contribute because we no longer need to hide our bodies or our minds.

INDIVIDUAL PERSPECTIVES

1 Critical issues in sexuality and disability

Susan M. Daniels

I have some dreams about the future that I would like to share. Ten years ago lack of access to sex information was a serious problem. If you were a disabled person and you wanted to know something about your sexuality, you had two choices: (1) give up or (2) go to a urological journal stuck in the back of some medical library. If you were able to get that journal down from the shelf, you might have found out a few things about how genital organs behave under specific circumstances. This is interesting but probably not very helpful information. This is what you had access to if you wanted to know about your sexuality and you were disabled.

Today we see improvement in three specific areas. One, professionals are better trained. They are less afraid of disabled people and of sexuality. They are also more willing to open up and share with us, the disabled, the information they have. Secondly, more information is available. There are now books that we can read and films that we can see. We can discuss these issues with each other. Ten years ago we didn't have access to each other and couldn't share information. And, finally, the media have changed. Several years ago I considered retiring from my career in sex and disability after seeing the movie "Coming Home." I didn't think there was anything further to say after that film. The media have portrayed disabled people in a variety of uncomplimentary ways in the past and now are beginning to portray us as healthy, interesting, sexual people. Our access to information has changed in the last 10 years from almost nothing to quite a bit. I am very pleased about that.

In future years, I think we will have a different view of disability and thus a different concept of sexuality and disability. We may see disability as part of the developmental process. The truth is that when we are born we are all on our way to death. On that road we encounter various problems, situations, and crises. Those are our disabilities. How we react to these as human beings, male and female, is part of our sexuality. I hope that people won't continue to look at information about sexuality and disability as something separate from other human and sexual knowledge. Hopefully, all boys and girls will learn about the disabilities associated with aging, illness, blindness, and deafness, as well as disabilities associated with pregnancy, loneliness, or isolation. Perhaps we will see disability not as a special and unique problem but as one of many life issues with which we all must expect to deal, just as we all expect to face crises and change in our lives. Disability is only a severe and inconvenient change that happens to us.

Limited access to information about sexuality was a major problem that we encountered as disabled people. Another problem, perhaps the most serious problem we all face as human beings, is finding opportunities to form partnerships and loving relationships with other people. For years disabled people were excluded from schools, recreational activities, other people's homes, and jobs. Yet most people meet their sexual partners where they learn, play, or work. That is the reason we did not meet people to be close to. Because we were not *where* the other people *were.* It was not because we were intrinsically unattractive or uninteresting. It was because we were not where the action was. Now we *are* where the action is and are becoming more and more so. The rejection our society heaped on us 10 years ago was tremendous. Our society was often not even aware of the problems existing for us. We were rejected indirectly. Architectural barriers said, "You don't belong here; go home. You don't belong in my school. You don't belong in my church. You don't belong in my swimming pool, and you certainly don't belong in my nightclub. Please go home."

These barriers and attitudes made us feel strange if we were any place but in rehabilitation centers or what I call the "handiworld." The handiworld is where you have a handicapped building, with handicapped access, with handicapped cars, with handicapped people going to a handicapped school. We *were* in the handiworld, but now we are escaping. From that major change, our access to partners and opportunities to form loving relationships has grown tremendously.

But there are many disabled citizens who are still very lonely and isolated. I find it difficult in my occupation to hear that there is a young disabled person in a nursing home. I want to run into a closet and cry. But there are *many* of us who are still in nursing homes or at home without opportunities to gain the love and support of other people. This is the problem no one wants to talk about. This is the most difficult problem in the area of sexuality and disability. We professionals allude to this problem as the need for "social skills training." We also call it "learning how to get along with others" or "reaching out to the community." What we are really talking about is overcoming the intense personal loneliness that a disability can impose on a person. If there is any single major problem in the area of sexuality and disability, it is the one killer called loneliness.

The future looks much better to me. I see us participating in the same neurotic problems our fellow able-bodied Americans have: problems of "Who next?" "What now?" and "Where do I belong in this ever-changing society?" Not, "How do I get in it?" These problems will not be any less or any more frightful than they are now for nondisabled men and women. The opportunities to form partnerships are a very important changing dimension in sexuality and disability.

Of course, the one thing that all writers have written about are the effects of specific conditions on sexual functioning. We now have several books on this. By the way, 10 years ago we didn't even have those books. We did not even talk about the specific disabilities and their specific effects on sexual functioning. This is the third problem.

It is obvious that some people will not swing from a chandelier, as they will not ski down the slopes, or run the mile in under 5 minutes. But 10 years ago we were told in a popular song, "Ruby, don't take your love to town." The lyrics say that "It is hard to love a man whose legs are bent and paralyzed." I take it that the songwriter never tried.

Today we are realizing our physical *capabilities*. We are beginning to understand how specific disabilities affect sexual functioning. We are beginning to understand spinal cord injury a little better and how various neurological impairments impinge on sexual functioning. We are learning how heart conditions affect sexuality and how renal dialysis can affect a person's sexual well-being. The future will continue to generate new knowledge in those areas. I think that that will be wonderful because I am a growing person, too. I want to know what is going to happen to me when I am 50 and my hormones change.

But there may be even bigger changes. Hopefully, we will begin to discover that each human being has an unlimited potential for sexual well-being that is not related to neurology, the cardiovascular system, or the skeletal-muscular system. We will find out that we all have an unlimited capacity to give and receive, to belong in the world and to each other, to respect ourselves as sexual persons, and to enjoy the pleasure that life gives us, be that with ourselves or with other people. We will begin to see the effects of disability not as how they impinge on certain neurological conditions or how certain muscles respond, but how they might limit or change the way we respond to other people. If we begin to understand those issues, we might begin to see sexuality as part of the total person as opposed to limiting it to the genital area.

Ten years ago I saw three major areas of problems in sexuality and disability. The first was limited access to even more limited information. That is now changing. The second and the most desperate problem is lack of opportunities to form partnerships and loving relationships. The third is knowing effects of specific disabilities on sexual functioning. Those problems are still with us, but we have a better future ahead. We have a better future because we had the courage 10 years ago to say we wanted to belong, we wanted to participate. We will have to strive for some new goals, not just more information, not just more opportunities to be with other people, and not just a better understanding of specific disabilities and their effect on sexual functioning. We will have a different mission.

There are five points I would like to share with you: The first is that those of us who study and work in the area of sexuality are called "softies." It is said that we don't change anybody. We don't fix any systems. We don't put any prostheses in, order wheelchairs, or teach people any particular skills. How do we know what we do makes any difference? We are the people in the rehabilitation centers. You can find us at the bottom line of the budget. If anybody is going to go, it will probably be us. Well, I want to tell you that we are here to stay. Some good research is beginning to back us up. And our first job will be to let people know that we are important to the total well-being of disabled people. We, as sex counselors and educators, are as important as the physician, the rehabilitation nurse, the physical therapist, the sign language teacher, and the mobility instructor.

I would like to share with you one piece of research. Mary Capone, Raphael Good, and their co-workers did a follow-up study 3, 6, and 12 months after genital surgery for women with cancer.[1] They used a control group and an experimental group in a research design that any "hard scientist" would appreciate. Theirs was a very simple intervention strategy—a crisis counseling model. The counseling that the people in the experimental group got lasted no longer than 4 hours. It was brief, nonintensive, and very goal directed. One year later, of those women who received the counseling, 84% had resumed their usual level of sexual activity or more. Of those who did *not* receive the counseling, only 42% had resumed such activity levels. With counseling, twice as many resumed the level of sexual functioning that they had before genital cancer surgery. "Okay," you might say, "that's very nice, but sexuality counseling doesn't pay for itself, right?" Consider this: of those who got 4 hours of sexuality counseling, 70% returned to work; of those who did not, 35% returned to work. Again, there was a 2-to-1 ratio. Now what does that tell us? That tells us something very important—sexuality is not just between the legs. Our interventions work in many areas. They need not be complex and elaborate, but can be simple and straightforward. I recommend that you look up this study.

In addition to showing that sexual counseling can be important to the well-being of disabled people, we must continue the fight against the oppressive myth of perfection. We are still told that if we are not perfect, we are not good enough. We must continue our assault on that notion of perfection because none of us, visibly disabled or able-bodied, is perfect. All of us know that. I think it would be interesting to do a study with nondisabled people to find how poor their self-image is, how much they distrust their own sexual feelings. Although none of us is perfect, the myth of perfection hurts everyone. We must particularly fight this myth among our health care professionals.

I had polio when I was a 6-month-old baby, so I grew up disabled. I have a 33-to 42-degree scoliosis. One hip is dislocated and I have a total hip replacement. I've had several hip transplants. My legs and arms don't work right, and my back is crooked. For my entire first 23 years, I can't remember hearing even one doctor say to me that my eyes were a beautiful sea green or my hair a lovely strawberry blonde. No one ever mentioned those things to me then. I don't recall hearing one nice thing about myself in terms of my rehabilitation. Not one complimentary remark. I think that the first thing we need to teach everyone who works with disabled people is to walk in with a smile and say something nice.

The next issue, something I learned most recently, is that we need to bring the lessons we have recently learned about sexuality and disability to our nondisabled brothers and sisters. We have not yet fulfilled our own potential to be loving sexual partners, nor have they. They believe that a perfect body (in its mid-twenties) is what they need to be sexual. We know they don't. We have found that our nondisabled brothers and sisters see sexuality as depending on a certain body configuration. We know better; they don't. We need to reach out to our nondisabled brothers and sisters to help them. We have, in effect, explored the frontier. We have stepped forward and cleared the field. Now we need to bring them along with us. I think there are times when we feel resentment, jealousy, and anger. It is normal to feel that way given the barriers we face. But I also think that our nondisabled brothers and sisters may not have the security of knowing that sexuality does not exist in the perfect body but in the pleasing body. We can help them overcome their handicaps.

We must also continue our assault against sexism. It should be addressed in every talk about sexuality. Our country is not free of sexist notions and stereotyping. It is a tremendous handicap for most people, and it is one that we can overcome. So we must continue to fight. We must fight it in our society, in our legal system, in our legislation, and we must fight it in ourselves. When I expect men to be what they are not, and when men expect me to be what I am not, we all lose. We must fight this on a personal and on a political level. It is very important that we strive to be full human beings as well as full men and women.

Ten years ago, I would not have written or given talks about sexuality and disability. Back then, I had no disabled friends. I thought that being with disabled people would be stigmatizing and would draw attention to me. My father once introduced me to one of his colleagues who had a disability and who subsequently asked me out. I refused the date. I said that I was busy but I lied. I didn't want to go out with him because of the possible stigma.

Our last and greatest task is to be proud of our maleness and our femaleness. Our disabilities are outstanding inconveniences—they are not to be glorified, and they are not to be honored; they are to be fought whenever possible. But our maleness and femaleness is gorgeous. It is God given, and we need to love that in each other.

We also have to reach out to our other disabled brothers and sisters and help them become actively involved in this society. It is very hard because we know that disability is compounding. It seems that one disabled person is a disabled person, two disabled people are a field trip, and three disabled people are a rehabilitation center. But our society needs rehabilitation, and we might as well get to it and do it with them. We are sometimes ashamed because of our disabilities, and that is almost tolerable. We must be sure that we are not ashamed of our maleness and our femaleness. Together we can bring the others in. We can do that, and it may be one of our most important tasks in the future: to be proud of ourselves as sexual people.

REFERENCE

1. Capone, M.A., Good, R.S., Westie, K.S., and Jacobson, A.F.: Psychosocial rehabilitation of gynecologic oncology patients, Arch. Phys. Med. Rehabil. **61**:128-132, 1980.

♀ **ABOUT THE AUTHOR** ♀

Susan M. Daniels, Ph.D., is the head of the Department of Rehabilitation Counseling at the Louisiana State University Medical Center, School of Allied Health Professions. She received her Ph.D. from the University of North Carolina at Chapel Hill in 1976. Dr. Daniels was the former acting director of the Regional Rehabilitation Research Institute on Attitudinal, Legal and Leisure Barriers at the George Washington University, Washington, D.C. and project director for the Sexuality and Disability Project granted by the Rehabilitation Services Administration. She is the editor of the journal *Sexuality and Disability* and pursues interests in clinical practice and teaching.

2 Spinal cord injury

Don Smith

Everyone with a disability is going to adjust to the disability differently. It's as individual as the personality is. To give you an idea of how disability has affected me, I will describe briefly how I was *before* my disability. It is important to realize that I was disabled at age 19; someone who is disabled at an earlier age might have very different experiences.

When I was 19, I was living in a very middle-class neighborhood in southern California. I had a poor self-image; I didn't like myself and felt unworthy of love and figured that if people really knew me they wouldn't like me. I felt like I was on the bottom of the list. I said yes to everybody because I wanted them to like me. Talk about disabilities, right? I hadn't even broken my back yet!

I thought I knew all the facts—a man's sex was in his penis; if a man was a *man* he tried to "score" whether he was interested or not. If he got a "no," he still persisted. Sex was definitely just between men and women, and when people got to bed they naturally had sex. The thought of them just sleeping together with their clothes off seemed unreasonable, so I always had a goal in mind. Other guys would talk about their conquests or their experiences. Most men exchanged their information about sexuality in competitive environments like the locker room. They would say, "I did this and that," and I would nod my head like I knew what was going on; to admit that I *didn't* know what was going on was to admit I wasn't a man.

Then I broke my back body surfing in 1968. What this did for me was to confirm all the feelings I had that I wasn't worthy of love. I was sure I wasn't worthy of love now. I was sure I was somebody who couldn't give love now. I was sure that I was somebody whom no one would be interested in. So whatever feelings of self-doubt that I had before were intensified after the accident. At first I continued pretty much to deal with people as I had before. I went to a hospital in southern California to be rehabilitated. That means getting up in the morning if you want breakfast and having to be at physical therapy, occupational therapy, and dinner on time. The doctor tells you when you are supposed to eat, and the nurse tells you when you are supposed to take your pills, and the aide tells you when you are supposed to go

12

to the bathroom. There was total denial of my responsibility for my life; the hospital took it over completely, and I cooperated completely. I figured that they knew the answers, so I just followed. The "white coat brigade" would come in and say, "Do this and this," and I'd say yes without asking any questions. I think my disability has since taught me to ask a lot more questions. What they taught me in the hospital was how to get around in the wheelchair, how to take care of my daily needs, a bowel and bladder program, how to "pop wheelies," and how to get my chair out of the car. These are all important things to learn; but they didn't give me any idea about the attitudes people have about disability.

Many people in the helping professions treated me like a medical condition rather than as a person. They would check up on the bone disease that I have in my hips and looked at x-ray pictures of my back to see how it had curved. Whenever I was touched, it was for a medical reason. No one asked about my feelings. I would have liked to have been treated as an individual. If I could go back and be treated differently, I would have liked them to give me a little more. Instead of just being 80591, bed 6, room 213, I could be treated as Don Smith, for example.

If I think back before my disability, I had a stereotype of a disabled person as being dependent and needy; as someone who was asexual and into his head more than his body; the kid watching the other kids play through the window instead of being outside participating; being the observer; the poster child with big, sad eyes appealing to you to send money: "make me walk." I had all negative ideas of what disabled persons were. After I was disabled, I accepted that stereotype just as I had accepted the stereotype of what a man was supposed to be.

Also, I come from a family that didn't talk about sex. I didn't have much information about sexuality, and I had been acting like I knew what was going on all along, anyway, so why blow my cover? My family didn't touch; I didn't have much experience in knowing how to reach out and touch somebody. The thought of putting my hand on a friend's shoulder was about as frightening as my first sexual encounter. I was very self-conscious about what the other person was going to think of me touching them and was really worried about their reaction, fearful of rejection because of it. So I didn't have any real experiences to plug into. My experiences before my injury were with boys my same age. After all, sex was within the confines of marriage, and sex was between man and woman only. There was also an automatic connection between penis and vagina—a man automatically knows how to please a woman without being told. I had this idea that a man was supposed to orchestrate the whole sexual contact. With no previous experiences and a new body after the accident, I was pretty confused.

My level of sensation is at my nipples. The top half of my nipples have typical tactile sensation and below my nipples it starts getting numb and I can feel only pressure on my body. I feel pleasure from feeling my partner's weight on my body. I knew I was the same person but everybody treated me a little differently. My family let go of some of the expectations they had for me in very subtle ways; they figured I wasn't going to be a track star. I also let go of expectations I had had for myself. I thought I would have a lesser role in life; after all, people with disabilities worked at Salvation Army and Goodwill. Those were the only places I saw people with disabilities. How many of you have employees with disabilities where you work? It seems to me that having such a limited viewpoint of what a disabled person is and can be really is itself a disability. It limited my perception of who I could be. There were no role models. I knew I wasn't like the television character "Ironsides." I knew I didn't live up to many of my images of what a man was supposed to be. I had feelings of being tender and feelings of being hurt, and I wanted to cry, but a man was not supposed to cry.

Some people have asked me what kind of sexuality counseling would have been helpful to me. That is a difficult question because people in this culture are not given much permission to talk about sexuality. You know, sex is not often spoken about seriously in this culture. It is something that many of us do not feel open about, so it is often difficult to approach people after a disability and open up the subject of sexuality to them. They all come from different backgrounds. Some of them might be from a religious background. Some of them might have had a wonderful background, but as far as approaching them is concerned, it is going to be pretty much of an individual thing. Now that I do counseling, I leave the door open and let patients know that there is information available and then let them approach me. They should be told that there are books available about their body in general if they want to read. Those books should include a section on sexuality.

When I was going through rehabilitation, they asked me if I wanted to speak to a psychologist about sex. To me, women went to psychologists, not men. So going to a psychologist was just another admission of not being a man. The door of therapy was open to me then, but I was not ready. Maybe the hospital should have a support group of people who have already dealt with their disabilities. That would have helped me.

When I think back to when I broke my back—that tremendous hurt and anger and emotion that you feel at the time—I swallowed it all because I was a "man." When I think about it now, it makes me angry that my feelings were bottled up like that. I spent about 4 years after my injury being asexual, but feeling very needy, not having any way to get that good human contact. That luxurious feeling of having someone lay next to you in bed—having someone to hug, someone to go home and hold, was missing in my life. I really felt that I needed it.

I got to the point where I was suicidal so I decided I would go to see a counselor. I went specifically for sex counseling. At that time they had one psychologist on a ward of 120 beds to deal with the sexual concerns of the patients and clients. I talked for 3 months about how the world was crummy and I couldn't see how I was playing a part in how things were turning out. And I felt like I wanted to get some sexual contact with somebody, because when I broke my back my sexual urges did not turn off automatically. It seems absurd that some people feel that when you have an injury to your body, all of a sudden you are not sexual or you don't need to be held or touched. Basically, I had strong needs to be close, but no way to get these needs met.

So I approached the safest person I knew to possibly get involved with in a sexual encounter—a friend's girlfriend, so we had to be discreet. All this time I was talking with my counselor and she was giving me lots of support and encouragement to go out and take a risk. My self-image built up a little bit during the 3 months of counseling, and I was feeling better about myself and more confident. This is how confident I was: I think I was saying things like "Did you see the sunset last night? I'd like to have sex with you; nice day today." Well, this woman friend of mine was really sharp and she caught it, and she said she'd think about it. A few days later I got a phone call saying, "George is going to be at work tonight so come on over." I went over and I talked and I talked and talked. It was so frightening to make the first move. Men are supposed to be aggressive; they are the initiators, and I was shy, so it felt really awkward to make the first move.

Finally, she said she was tired, and I excused myself and went into the bathroom and came back into the room to find her standing there naked. Every romantic image I had was of the couple standing, walking down the beach in the moonlight, etc. Here was this woman standing next to me, and I couldn't figure out what to do. What *do* I do? Grab her leg and kiss her hip? Nothing fit. Finally she said, "Let's lie down." So we lay down in bed and I took my pants down to my ankles; I didn't take them all the way off because it was hard for me to get them back on and I didn't want her to see me struggle.

We lay down and she taught me how to kiss and we were rolling around and I was touching her everywhere: here, there, like, A, B, C, D, E, F, G, A, B, C, D, E, F, G . . . It was so much a head trip that I really couldn't appreciate touching her. And I was up in my head wondering what she was thinking about me, how I compared with the men she'd been with, what it was like for her to be with a man with a disability. I couldn't tell where she was touching me. In the course of us rolling around I got an erection and she said, "Guess what? You've got a hard-on." I said, "Far out!" But I did not want to attempt intercourse, it was scary enough for me to be lying down in bed rolling around.

That was pretty much the evening. I left early in the morning before George got home, and I remember feeling charged up even though when I think back on it, it was relatively awkward and miserable, but I felt *sexual.* I remember yelling joyfully in the car on the way home. So I went back to my therapist and she said, "Great, great, do it again." I had also talked to her about my feelings of wanting to be sexual with a man as well. She gave me a lot of support for this, too. She allowed me to direct my own course and meet my needs the way that I needed to. She had no hang-ups about a person's chosen affectional choice, so I went ahead. This was about 2 weeks after I had had sex for the first time. I was talking to a good friend about what I had talked to my therapist about and mentioned that I wanted to have sex with a man, and he replied, "Well, do you want to have sex right now?" I wasn't expecting that because in my circle of friends it wasn't accepted for men to relate to each other sexually, and I had spent many years denying any feelings like that. This was finally the chance where I gave myself the go ahead to experience those feelings. He and I managed to play with each other's genitals, but kissing or hugging and holding each other was too threatening, so it was pretty much just mutual masturbation. It wasn't very sensual but it was another first step, and I really felt good about it.

A lot of my focus with my first partners was on pleasing them; I figured if I could please them, then I'd be a good lover and things would be all right. But this was dissatisfying in the long run. I wanted to get something for myself.

I felt asexual for a long time because a man's sex was supposed to be in his penis, and I couldn't feel my penis. So that contributed to my feelings of being asexual; it didn't occur to me that it felt good to have the back of my neck licked, or that it felt good to have my arms stroked lightly. Stroking the wrists, then to the arms, then up the arms, is a sequence that I've since learned can be very exciting.

A lot of my first sexual contacts were just to gain experience. I wanted to find out what was going on and what I liked. With the help of two really excellent lovers, I learned about my body. I learned to take goals out of my lovemaking; I don't have to have intercourse or any kind of penetration if I'm going to have sex. I don't even have to do anything with the genitals if I'm going to have sex. I can take my time; I feel less pressure and less performance anxiety. That's not to say it's all gone, because it's there; I want to be there for my partner.

I did happen to have a relationship with a woman who was a call girl who made money by going out with men; she didn't necessarily sleep with them, but she did make money by going out and being seen with them. A lot of times they just wanted to be seen with her: a woman that was nice and had nice clothes, and a nice car; all they needed was this other accessory to go along with their image. Someone was taking care of her car, decorating her apartment, and paying for her rent. It was tremendously flattering for me that she chose to be with me because she liked me when she could have other men pay for her. So I think if I ever needed any boost over the top that said that "you are someone that can be loved, you are someone that is worthy of love," it was that relationship with that woman.

I'm presently living with a man and am going to school. I feel that we have a very equal relationship; I don't feel like I have to be the initiator all of the time. And it's an unusual relationship because most of the men that I've met unfortunately don't openly talk about their feelings; women have many more opportunities to talk about their feelings. So it feels really good; it's a warm, close relationship, and right now that's what's happening in my life.

♂ ABOUT THE AUTHOR ♂

Don Smith was trained as a sexuality and disability educator through the Sex and Disability Unit of the Human Sexuality Program, Department of Psychiatry, University of California and has been actively involved in sexuality workshops throughout the United States since 1977. Don draws from his own experience as a person with a disability and from the experiences of others in his teaching. He presently conducts a course in sexuality and disability at Sonoma State University in northern California.

3 Sexuality and the spinal cord—injured woman

AN INTERVIEW*

Elle F. Becker

On February 25, 1975 I was involved in a riding accident. I was thrown from my horse and sustained a compression fracture of the seventh thoracic vertebra. My injury resulted in severe, permanent damage to my spinal cord, so I have no sensation or voluntary function below the level of T6.

After my injury, I had many questions regarding my sexuality. I had married my husband 4 years prior to my accident. Since the sexual aspect of our relationship had been, up to the time of my injury, a very integral and rewarding part of our union, I immediately became concerned about how the injury might change this.

Some of my questions were answered completely and competently by professionals in the fields of neurology, psychology, psychiatry, and urology. However, many of my questions were left unanswered because, as I discovered much to my consternation, there was very little information available on the subject of the sexuality of spinal cord—injured women. For this reason I went to the paraplegic and quadriplegic women in my community and asked them about their lives as sexual beings. I also sent questionnaires to women in different parts of the country.

I tape-recorded all of the conversations for accuracy. All the spinal cord—injured women's real names have been changed; however, their life stories are true. Most of the women I talked to for the case histories have learned what they know today from experimentation. Perhaps it will help a newly injured person to read what someone else with a spinal cord injury has experienced, although this should be used to supplement, not replace, sensitive, understanding, and knowledgeable sexual counseling.

I share in the collective anger of many spinal cord—injured women who labor under the destructive impact of negative labels such as "crippled," "handicapped," and "disabled." I realize that in the literal definition of the words, I must fit the

*Permission has been given to reprint this excerpt from Becker, E.F.: *Female sexuality following spinal cord injury*, 1978, Bloomington, Accent Special Publication, Cheever Publishing, Inc., P.O. Box 700, Bloomington, Ind. 61701. The excerpt was also published in Sexuality and Disability 2:278-286, 1979.

description, but somehow our society has also often found these words to mean "paralyzed from the neck up," as a friend of mine would say. We are first and foremost sensitive human beings with a terrific sense of accomplishment after all of the horrible but challenging experiences we have been through. Second to this, I consider myself a woman, and third, a paraplegic (which is the only word I have no objection to). I hope I haven't chosen words objectionable to other disabled women.

I can't help but cringe in my chair when the medical profession makes references to paralegics' or quadriplegics' sexual "alternatives" as if, by implication, we cannot enjoy normal sex.

It has been demonstrated clearly by research in the fields of psychology and sociology that people with the most extensive and accurate information regarding their own sexuality have fewer emotional problems emerging from sexual conflicts. They will also make a better adjustment to life in general than those with insufficient data about sex. However, the lack of any extensive information regarding sexuality in the spinal cord–injured woman is astounding. The few articles that are available rarely deal with the physical aspects of sex. If they do, it is only to mention intercourse as the only means of sexual expression and, of course, the woman is in the passive missionary position. Most of the films and books I am aware of are primarily concerned with male sexuality as if women do not exist, or worse yet, as if we are expected to completely accept the traditional passive role and not ask any questions.

The following is representative of the 19 in-depth interviews and questionnaire replies from spinal cord–injured women. There are, of course, limitations in transcripts of interviews. The full meanings are often lost, since written words cannot show facial expressions, tone of voice, eye contact, and so on. Even so, it is remarkable how alive the words, and, therefore the women, become. In my initial contact with them I always disclosed personal information about myself so a woman would know I was there to share as well as to learn. For this reason the personal interviews and questionnaire responses contained a great deal of detailed information.

Finally, the following primarily reflects one person's approach to her sexuality. Rather than setting any standards or goals for others, I hope it will serve to increase the understanding that we are all sexual beings and that we experience and express our sexuality uniquely.

In May, 1976 I received the answers to my questionnaire from Ann, who was 42 years old. Born in Japan, she has an incomplete spinal cord injury.

Elle: Was your spinal cord severed?
Ann: My spinal cord was damaged, but not severed. I have complete bowel and bladder control. My sensation is somewhat erratic and unpredictable, however it has in-

creased somewhat over the years. I have only partial sensation in my vaginal area and no sensation at all between my navel and pubic hair line. I have no sensation in one buttock, but am very sensitive in the other. I have completely normal sensation from my navel up.

Elle: How do men react to you when you first meet them and later on as your relationship matures?

Ann: This certainly depends on the man. I find it difficult to generalize. Men are usually attracted to my intellect and somewhat curious and hesitant about my sexual potential. I have a great number of platonic friends, "brothers," and gay male friends. I find that I am often suspicious of the motives of men who are attracted to me sexually. That is, some men want to be caretakers; some men can't find able-bodied partners (and assume that disabled women are also unable to find partners). Other men are sexually intrigued with disabled women, believing they will have a "kinky" experience; some men want a "strong mother confessor" figure they can depend on or want a woman who will be totally dependent on them. I don't intend to do a general indictment of the whole male race, but do believe disabled women must be very selective in choosing partners.

Many of my relationships have matured into strong relationships with sexual dimensions, some of my partners have been "affairs," flings, one-night stands, etc. During my sexually active years, I have had several different partners; among them three long-term relationships. I have had one sexual experience with a gay woman.

Elle: Do you feel that men are attracted to you?

Ann: I believe that men are usually attracted to me, but my disability is an impairment to immediately considering sexual possibilities, and as I previously indicated, I am somewhat cautious. I move somewhat awkwardly, have a somewhat peculiarly shaped body, and am obviously very independent.

It seems that most of the population is much more used to dealing with people in wheelchairs and that it is somehow more graceful or feminine than using the crutches and brace. It also fits our stereotype of the "helpless, dependent" woman.

I've spent some short periods of time in a chair and was amazed at how differently people reacted to me. They know what to do, how to categorize or stereotype a "typical cripple," and are more comfortable with initial interaction. Women using crutches do not fit our stereotype, and people have even less idea how to react. Women in chairs don't usually have to contend with unattractive braces, which can really distort one's sense of "body integrity."

There are obviously many advantages to crutches. However, they really take a toll on your hands and arms, require superhuman amounts of energy, are cumbersome, wear out your clothes, etc., etc. I have also developed very broad shoulders and gigantic muscles. But in the long run, to walk, bear weight, exercise, etc., is far superior to a chair.

There is not enough effort in rehabilitation centers to explore the possibility of crutches and braces. A chair is so much easier. If you want to explore this, there are some absolutely revolutionary orthodists (brace makers). They believe that anyone with good arms who is willing to wear a hip band for stabilization (if necessary) has some bracing potential.

I also sometimes think that men want to become involved with me, but don't want to be seen "dating" me. (The implication being they can't get an able-bodied partner.)

Elle: Have any men ever indicated these feelings to you verbally?

Ann: Yes, especially that they are very concerned with "appearance." One time I foolishly allowed a friend to set me up on a blind date without telling the man I was paraplegic. He arrived and in summary refused to take me out (lamely explaining it was some horribly inaccessible function where all anyone would do is dance). Blind dates are usually purely masochistic.

In spite of all of this, in general my sex and social life has been full and active.

Elle: On a scale of 1 to 10 (10 being the highest) how would you rate the importance of your sexuality to you?

Ann: This varies tremendously. At times I would rate it at 8, other times I'd rate it at 2. When all my energies are committed to other pursuits, that is, my work, music, platonic relationships, I become almost asexual. I almost constantly want the security of knowing that I am loved and desired but often don't want the sex. Many times "cuddling" is more fulfilling to me.

Elle: This often is true for me, also. Who helped you the most with your sexual feelings?

Ann: The most influential person on my sexual outlook and life was my first sexual partner. He really enjoyed the "uniqueness" of my body and really transformed me from a "neuter" to a sexual person. He was very sexually creative, experimented with various positions, and really unlocked a lot of my subsequent potential.

Elle: Did any doctors or family members help you with your sexual feelings?

Ann: My family behaved as if I were "neuter" and never dealt with any sexual issues and certainly never acknowledged my sexuality enough to seek any professional expertise.

Elle: How did you feel about that while you were growing up; how do you feel about that now?

Ann: I was unaware of this attitude as I assumed that I was, in fact, neuter. So I did not perceive them denying any needs. I don't blame them as they too bought the myth that disability implies asexuality. They did the best they knew how.

Elle: Has your sexual preference changed?

Ann: My sexual preference has changed somewhat in that I now believe women are a viable option, but not at the exclusion of men certainly. This is probably an outgrowth of some feminism. I also feel that masturbation is an extraordinarily important option for disabled people. Not as a kind of substitute, although it certainly is an alternative outlet if one is without a partner, because it helps one learn or relearn about the potential of one's body, and I believe it is very healthy to be "your own best lover." Then sexuality does not become a privilege of partnership. It seems that the disabled body is so often a source of such negatives, that is, pain, impairment, and bowel and bladder hassles and that masturbation can become one really positive, pleasuring experience making you feel a lot better about your body in general. It is also important to do some experimenting and exploring on your own so you can communicate to your partner what feels best.

Elle: Right. I had no opportunity to do any of this type of exploring before I came home, due to the lack of privacy. What do you mean by the term "privilege of partnership"?

Ann: I mean that your sexual expression and opportunity (or your sexuality in general) does not simply vanish or should not vanish when you are nonpartnered. "Sexualness" should not be dependent on a partner. So there are really viable sexual activities one can engage in alone, that is, fantasy, masturbation, or dreams.

Along this line, it has recently been learned that vibrators can be dangerous for those with impaired sensation, as they may damage vaginal tissue or become too hot.

Elle: Do you ever dream about sex? If so, do you ever achieve orgasm in your dreams?

Ann: I have dreamed about sex and think (although I am not sure) that I have achieved orgasm in the dreams.

Elle: What method of birth control do you use or have you tried?

Ann: I have taken the pill, had an IUD, used a diaphragm, and also foam and condoms. I am planning on having my tubes tied this summer.

Elle: Why are you considering this?

Ann: I don't wish to have children of my own. A pregnancy would be very difficult (although not impossible) because of my scoliosis. I have professional and life-style goals which are not compatible with children, at least at this stage. If I do decide to have a family, I will adopt. I have given this a great deal of thought and feel that a tubal ligation is a reasonable solution.

There are complications with both the pill and IUD. Disabled women are more likely to have circulatory problems that the pill can exacerbate, and often women who have impaired sensation in their uterine areas will not feel the pain indicating problems with them and the IUD. The IUD also increases the likelihood of vaginal infection, which can spread to the urinary tract.

Elle: What causes this?

Ann: The likelihood of infection is increased because the strings on the IUD tend to collect bacteria, and vaginal infection can easily spread to the urinary tract just because of proximity. This is especially true for the women with catheters.

Elle: How did you feel the first few times you tried sex?

Ann: It was sort of a comical nightmare. I always believed my body would behave somewhat normally, which was hardly the case. It was very difficult to find a good position, my partner was in an incredible hurry. I found that I couldn't detect when his penis had actually penetrated and that I didn't know how to "thrust." It was difficult at best.

Elle: How have your feelings changed?

Ann: I have learned a great deal about my own limitations and potentials, educated my future partners, and developed a lot more sensitivity in my vaginal area.

Elle: Do you enjoy sex now?

Ann: I usually enjoy sex now if I'm having intercourse because I want to, not out of expectation or duty. At times, I find myself bored with it and wishing it were over.

Elle: I used to feel that way sometimes, but now I have learned how to focus more attention on the sensation I do have and how to utilize fantasy. That has increased my enjoyment 95%. What positions have you tried?

Ann: Some positions are very uncomfortable for me. I also find I can really throw my left hip out of whack if we are too active. I also believe I have a tendency to try to "please" in a sort of overcompensating way, probably really believing that sex is not as good with me as it would be with an able-bodied woman.

Elle: Does your partner enjoy sex?

Ann: I think all of my partners (with the exception of one) enjoyed sex. Temporary impotence has been a problem several times because there has to be a lot of plotting out of positions and some experimenting. When a man has to become a mechanical engineer it can quickly extinguish passion. However, once we have worked out the initial logistics, the problem usually abates. I am always apprehensive with a new partner and probably assume a lot of guilt about "causing" the impotence. I have had an orgasm while masturbating, but never with a partner. This occurred after believing that it was neurologically impossible. I saw a woman obstetrician-gynecologist who had specialized in working with preorgasmic women. She examined me and discovered that my clitoral area was only partially sensitive and encouraged me to stimulate other areas of my body while using fantasy. Also, to concentrate on trying to breathe way down into my vaginal area, sort of deep yoga breathing. I used a lot of rectal, breast, and shoulder stimulation, and it suddenly happened. It was an incredibly intense, almost violent experience, and went on forever. I was thrashing around, my teeth chattering, heart racing, etc. The next day I was exhausted and ached all over. Subsequent orgasms have been less intense and more pleasurable. The emotional experience provides enormous relief and tremendous affirmation of my "wholeness."

Elle: That is wonderful. I had the same impression you did about the "neurological impossibility" aspect until I had experienced orgasm myself. Could you explain the yoga breathing more?

Ann: In yoga, the breathing tends to "turn on" any part of your body you direct it to, if you know how to do it. I think yoga is a really good tool for disabled people to have for many reasons (i.e., relaxation of muscle spasms, muscle toning, exercise, calming). It unlocks a lot of potential. But you must be taught by a competent yoga teacher. There are a lot of charlatans around. Physiologically, by breathing into your vaginal area, you actually are sending a rush of blood there which of course stimulates response. Try breathing into your big toe. See if you get any sensation. It may surprise you.

Elle: Have you ever experienced a loss of bowel control during sex?

Ann: This happened only once when I had diarrhea for 2 days resulting from the flu. The sexual thrusting caused a small accident.

Elle: Have you ever experienced a loss of bladder control during sex?

Ann: I urinated a bit during the first orgasm but now I don't lose control of my bladder.

Elle: Do you do anything before sex to prevent an accident?

Ann: No.

Elle: How did you and your partner react to your accident?

Ann: I was really surprised and slightly embarrassed, but my partner and I had been together for so long, it was pretty comfortable. We laughed a lot and he claimed he sort of got off on the whole experience in a unique way.

Elle: Do spasms bother you during sex?

Ann: I've had two partners say that my spasms intensify their sexual experience, something about the spasm making my vagina contract sharply. They don't bother me at all.

Elle: During sex, have you found ways to move your vaginal area?

Ann: I seem to have good control of my vaginal muscles and have done some contracting exercises, which have really helped.

Elle: I've tried exercises for one very weak muscle that has partial function (no sensation) in my stomach, but it doesn't seem to move the vaginal barrel at all. However, I have found that my spasms move my vagina, but this doesn't happen often. Do you lubricate during sex?

Ann: I seem to lubricate normally.

Elle: So do I. It was (and is) very difficult for me to be assertive sexually. I am becoming more able to say what I would like *when* I would like, but I wondered if this could possibly carry over into everyday experiences. I sometimes find that I don't always ask for something I need in everyday situations. Do you ask for something if you need it? If so, will you ask right away?

Ann: This seems to be the only pragmatic approach to one's life. I ask immediately when I need something. I find that people ask me for things that I can assist them with.

Elle: Do you find that sometimes people will help you when you don't need any help? If so, how do you feel about this?

Ann: I am simply firm but courteous. Sometimes people need to feel that they have helped you. It is important to be sensitive to their feelings; however, not at the expense of your own.

♀ **ABOUT THE AUTHOR** ♀

Elle F. Becker is the author of *Female Sexuality Following Spinal Cord Injury*. She has worked as the sexuality and disability education counselor at Kaiser Rehabilitation Center, Vallejo, California, as well as vocational counselor, Sho-Craft, a sheltered workshop for the disabled in Vancouver, Washington. Elle is a paraplegic as a result of a horseback riding accident in 1975.

4 Growing up with cerebral palsy

Victoria Thornton

My disability is cerebral palsy, which I've had since birth. It is classified as the spastic type, which means that I have tight muscles and some limited range of motion that has affected my walking; from the age of 2 to almost 17 I wore leg braces from the waist down. In terms of my current sexual functioning, my disability limits my mobility when I make love. I have a different range of positions to choose from than some other people; the missionary position is not one of my options. These physical restrictions have been of relatively minor concern to me.

For me, the real issue is how to feel good about myself as a whole person: body, mind, emotions, and spirit. I find that my sexuality, communicating sexually, acting sexual, and being attractive to people all have much to do with how I feel about myself and how I conduct myself in the world. I draw people to me very easily when I am out there "doing my thing" and feeling good. When I am depressed and feel that I am not worthy to be loved, people move away. That is probably true for almost everyone, but I do think that there are specific issues related to my disability that impede the process of coming to feel like a whole person and like a person worthy of being loved. Two concerns I have dealt with are (1) my body image, and (2) social isolation that I had because of my disability.

I would like to talk about body image first, because that involves the mechanics of my disability and the medical treatment I received. When I was put in braces at the age of two, I also began physical therapy. I had physical therapy for 20 years. It brought a lot of benefit in terms of my ability to walk better, but it brought a lot of confusion and a lot of pain in other areas. I was in the care of doctors, physical therapists, and an overprotective family from the beginning, and so I never really felt my body quite belonged to me. It never did quite what I wanted it to. I could not run across the street with the other kids. I had to do a variety of exercises to try to strengthen weak muscles and to try to loosen tight ones. It was a frustrating time.

And then there were the clinical examinations. I can remember going for diagnostic tests when I was 3 or 4 years old, as well as the weekly physical therapy, and no one ever asked me, "How do you feel about my touching you?" I didn't have the connection between my mind and body that all people need to express themselves sexually.

I learned very early to put my mind and my body in separate places. The first physical therapy I had involved stretching tight muscles. It was painful, and I resolved to be very brave about it, so I just clenched my teeth and pretended I was not there. For the first 9 years I had this type of therapy, and it was not really doing me too much good. So my parents got fed up and took me to a physical therapist who used a more sensory approach. With cerebral palsy there is a miscommunication, as it were, between the brain and the motion of the muscles—the neuromuscular coordination. This therapist tickled my skin or rubbed it with ice cubes so that my nerves would jump and then my muscles would move. All this touching was going on but it was intrusive and very clinical.

In California, where I grew up, education for disabled persons has often been segregated. Until high school I went to special schools for the physically handicapped. At that time we had monthly clinic visits by an orthopedist who would come, like a circuit judge, to the schools. I remember how painful these visits were for me in terms of my body image. I would get out there in my underwear in front of the doctor, the physical therapist, a couple of teachers, maybe the principal, other kids, and parents. I'd be paraded around and had to listen to my "case" being discussed. For many kids this is a painful experience because they understand what is going on, and I can remember hearing my fate decided in such a public setting innumerable times.

I finally got to the point where I had some privacy with my doctor. We shared information about procedures that were going to happen in advance. Because of this sharing of information early and privately, I no longer had to fear that, for example, the decision to have surgery would be read into a dictaphone before a crowd of people while I was present, when I had no previous knowledge that such a decision had been made.

For me, one of the important things that I have realized is that I am no longer a child. I think that children have a rougher time with the medical profession in terms of not knowing how to be assertive or not knowing how to ask questions. I remember asking questions and getting laughed at because I was just a kid. I grew up to become pretty feisty about my medical rights. Some people did help me along the way, counselors for example. One particular gynecologist was a great support after I had had some negative experiences with my first pelvic exams. I became assertive and found her, and she helped me a lot. Counseling helped me, as did good social relationships, so I could feel like a human being, independent of professionals. I reached the point where I knew more about my body and what was going on with me than any doctor or anyone else that I could contact. My body was unique and different, and I could not be put into a particular category. When I moved to northern California, I had to find out what my needs were and then I had to communicate them to my new physicians.

But on the whole I thought my body was "yucky." It was connected with all those unpleasant experiences, so I began to concentrate on my mind and became a typical, academic bookworm kid. I was quite happy with that, or so I thought. But that led to a lot of social isolation at school. The other kids more or less thought of me as a snob, and I pretty much played the part. I really did not have any good role models to help me be who I wanted to be. I went to high school and left special school, and that meant going from a school of about 100 students to a school of 3000. That was a real challenge. For the first time I had the chance to choose who I wanted to be with. I began to make friends, and I began to learn how to be social with people. This was a really fine experience for me. All of a sudden people were treating me as an equal. I did not feel like I was being put in a special place because I could not cut it in the outside world.

However, at this time I was also going through my adolescence, and I did not have disabled peers to help me deal with questions of being social and being sexual. I was stuck with able-bodied kids that had never seen a kid in braces before. I wasn't being treated as a girl. This was very painful for me, because I hung around with a group of guys who were really my good friends. They treated me like one of the fellows, and I did not feel like one. I had not learned any way to communicate that, and I walked around with an agonizing crush on one boy for 2 years. I felt that it was my noble duty not to share it, not to let the other person know, because I thought he'd be embarrassed. The sexual feelings I had, I saw others having also, but they were not disabled. I thought, "I have these feelings, too, but I am ashamed because I realize I am not supposed to have them." So I walked around with a lot of emotional pain.

My parents did not understand how to help in this process; instead, as is common, they were overprotective. They talked to me about the biology of sex, but they were afraid that I would be hurt in relationships, and they did not know how to deal with my feelings of pain. When I was going through that crush in high school, I would come home pretty depressed and low. My mother could not listen to these feelings. She would start changing the subject or chattering about something else. It was not until recently that I learned that she knew perfectly well what was going on, and she felt it was her duty to cheer me up when I was depressed. So, instead of having someone to listen, I felt I could not bring these feelings up.

Also at that time, perhaps 12 years ago, there was not much written about sex and disability. Even sex for able-bodied people was not in the press as much as it is now. *The Joy of Sex** had not been published. I had a lot of questions such as, "Will I actually be able to have intercourse if I can't move my legs the way I'm

---

*Comfort, A., New York, 1971, Fireside, Simon & Schuster.

supposed to?" I did not have any books to refer to, and I was really too embarrassed to ask questions. Then, around this time, something very dramatic happened. I went through some experimental surgery which enabled me to get out of braces. I can remember a case conference before the operation in which my surgeon sat down with his colleagues. I was in the room, a very nervous 16-year-old in her bathing suit with loose shoulder straps, trying to make sure it did not fall off, and he gave a brief talk about what he was going to do. Then he put me up on the table and invited his colleagues to proceed. There were about eight of them examining me all at the same time with their rubber hammers and their blunt instruments and sharp tools, saying, "Is this sharp? Is this dull? Move this," and "Move that." I stared at the ceiling, trying to pretend that I was not there.

I described this to another disabled woman last year. I told her that at that time I felt like a sack of potatoes lying on the table, and she said to me, "It's really funny that you should use that phrase to describe your body, because that's what I used to call my body, too." So it is not that uncommon an experience for many of us to have.

But I especially remember one doctor's comment. When she watched this examination, she said, "My, you've been so well trained!" This remark, as anyone can imagine, made me very angry and hurt. When I did get out of my braces and stood alone without them for the first time, in some ways it was a reward, but it scared me to death in other ways. I had no way to relate to my body anymore. It was no longer familiar to me. I used to know what it could do. Now all of a sudden it was ground zero, and I had to start all over again. That was very scary at first, but as time went on I learned.

I also learned the social skills to begin to form relationships, and that was a process that took much longer. I did some dating in college. I was still living at home with Mom and Dad, and did not meet guys that I liked that much. I was pretty shy and withdrawn and did not know how to reach out, at least not until my last year. I remember going out on dates occasionally, and I remember once when this one guy and I were in a car together, starting to make out. I can remember feeling absolutely terrified: "Oh, my God, what do I do next?" We were in a parking lot, and my car was nearby. I jumped out of his car and went to my own car and drove home in a panic.

About 4 years later, after my first sexual experiences, and after I was feeling pretty comfortable sexually, I had the same experience while making out with somebody. I experienced the same feeling, the same panic, but I went to bed with him anyway. What I discovered was not that I was hung up or afraid of sex, and it was not, "Oh, my God, what do I do now?" but that the person was *wrong* for me and that I did not really want to have sex with him. I had not learned how to discriminate my feelings.

Sex had a huge mystique for me. Either you did it or you didn't. And if you did not do it, there was something wrong with you. Remember, this was the late 1960s with James Bond, Twiggy, and short skirts. I began to realize gradually that it was also okay for me if I chose not to be sexually active. I had the right to choose who I wanted to be with. I also needed to feel comfortable with people before I could enjoy being sexual with them.

Partly because my disability does make sex a little awkward for me in positioning myself, I feel much more comfortable if I can talk with my partner explicitly, either in the course of getting ready to make love or beforehand. I find that for me this is absolutely essential as a prerequisite to becoming involved sexually. I find that I get a lot more out of sex when I do that. I feel good, and I enjoy it and feel like I am really participating. I feel like my partners enjoy it also. I was lucky to have a first partner who was very verbal and versatile. He talked a lot about what he wanted and so I felt permission to go ahead and do the same thing. If people do have questions, it is a good idea to encourage them to talk with each other.

Occasionally, partners have told me, "You are the first woman that I've ever been with who talked about sex." This surprises and saddens me. They missed the ability to really get as much as they could from the experience. For me, sex is a way for people to get closer, and it can be pretty earthy.

I walked around with my head in the clouds most of my early life because I was trying to avoid my body and I did not associate earthiness with sexuality at all. I did not associate sexuality with my body. I associated it with my emotions and with my spirit. I still have some wonderful platonic relationships. But it is through my sexual relationships that I find a greater acceptance of my whole person, body and mind.

♀ ABOUT THE AUTHOR ♀

Victoria Thornton is currently peer counselor coordinator for the Center for Independent Living, Berkeley, California. She is also a graduate student in social work at San Francisco State University. Her special career interest is in medical social work, particularly as it applies to family planning and family health care. She has been disabled since birth with cerebral palsy.

5 The impact of genetic disability

Lillian Pastina

There is a great deal of clinically written material on the subject of genetics but virtually nothing written from the personal perspective. Before I go into my experience with genetic counseling, I will provide some background information about my experiences with the medical profession.

I was born in 1951 with a birth defect that affects my joints and connective tissues, leaving them unstable and weak. I have spent several years in hospitals and therefore have had a great deal of exposure to medical personnel.

While growing up I was often pushed, pulled, prodded, and poked by teams of doctors. This was a very dehumanizing experience and one that seems to be shared among many in the disabled community. Rarely was I spoken to directly during these examinations. I was given instructions and was asked to speak up only when it hurt. I didn't hear many positive comments about my body. It was mostly things like "her joints are a mess." This doesn't do much for a person's self-esteem. Frequently there was pain during these examinations. I learned to withdraw, to pull out of myself so I would not feel.

Generally by the midteens, most of what can be done medically is accomplished, and the disabled person may be cared for by one physician. This was true in my case, and I was able to start building an adult patient/physician relationship.

In 1973, at the suggestion of my orthopedic surgeon, my husband and I went to the medical center of the local university for genetic counseling. This advice surprised me because I distinctly remember having asked my doctor several times during my teen years if having children would be a problem. I was told I would have to deliver by cesarean section but otherwise all would be well.

We set up an appointment with the genetics clinic, and they sent out a nurse to take our family medical histories. She spent 3 hours talking with us, and I remember feeling reassured when she left.

The morning we arrived at the clinic, we were ushered into a small room with an examining table. This is where we were to spend the next 3 hours. We were introduced to two staff physicians and a medical student. There was some time spent discussing our family medical histories; then I was told the medical student would examine me. I was asked to remove my clothes, and the exam began. I interrupted and asked for a gown. For the first time in my life, I felt I was being examined by someone who was loathe to do so. It was clear that the medical student was uncomfortable with me, which made me angry. Next, four or five physicians were brought in to see if my disability resembled anything they were researching. Once again, after all those years, I found I was being spoken about, not spoken to. I was an object being discussed, not a person. Somehow I felt helpless to do anything about it.

I do not know if it was the insensitivity of the situation or having my husband there, but I had never before felt such humiliation or violation. It was as though I was no longer my own person, no longer in control. I burst into tears, and they finally cleared the room, where we waited for almost 2 hours while the staff consulted. No one said, "Get dressed and have lunch"; no one offered coffee. We just waited alone in that room.

When the two staff physicians and the medical student returned, we were given the results. The disability was hereditary, and there was a 50% chance with each pregnancy that the child would be born disabled. There was no way of knowing how severe the disability would be. They said that if I became pregnant, I should come in for tests; goodbye and good luck. I have difficulty calling this counseling.

There was no place to go, no one to talk to. But the anger! The rage at the unfairness. The feelings of hurt and loss. During this time my husband withdrew. He kept saying he didn't mind, that everything was okay. But it wasn't. It was almost a year before we were really able to talk about it.

It seems ludicrous, after that experience, that it was called genetics counseling. We were never counseled, just given information. I was handled, fed through the computer, and spewed out.

My point isn't that the results of the counseling were bad, but that the way the program at the clinic was set up was very nonsupportive. Anyone going for genetics counseling is going in with, at the very least, feelings of apprehension. There should be something done to try to alleviate the tension somewhat. There wasn't even any follow-up done. No one gave us the opportunity to process the feelings that were a direct result of the clinic experience.

This most certainly would have been helpful to me. I went through a long period of time not feeling sexual or desirable, feeling that something had been taken from me, which it had. I needed reassurance, and getting it from my husband was not enough. I felt my friends didn't understand, and I resented them for their carefree attitudes in starting a family.

There are a number of things that could be done as part of the clinic program that would be supportive of the client, such as having the person who did the initial interview follow through the case to the end. In other words, the interviewer could be in the examining room with the clients. Since rapport with the clients has already been established, the interviewer could act as a buffer. There most definitely should be a follow-up visit a short time after the initial clinic visit. This allows the clients time to assimilate the information and to formulate questions. The clinic should act as a resource for follow-up should counseling be desired by a couple.

The responsibility for all the counseling need not fall on one person. Although each member of the staff need not be a professional counselor, he or she should have some training in counseling skills. There are also some things that come under the heading of consideration. There should be some acknowledgment, verbal or nonverbal, that this is not necessarily a wonderful experience the client is going through. An apology for being the fifth physician to rotate a joint or whatever in half an hour, or maybe even asking permission would be helpful. Give the client back some control over the situation. And finally, some eye contact and a smile truly helps. These are all things that are simple and require very little time, but they show that you are human and caring.

♀ ABOUT THE AUTHOR ♀

Lillian Pastina is an independent living skills teacher and counselor at the Center for Independent Living in Berkeley, California. She has been trained at the Sex and Disability Unit of the Human Sexuality Program, Department of Psychiatry, University of California, San Francisco, and is currently teaching a human sexuality class for mentally retarded men and women in Oakland, California. Ms. Pastina has been disabled since birth with a syndrome that affects her musculoskeletal system.

6 Visual impairment

Terrianne Straw

I am the peer counseling coordinator for an independent living program for the disabled and am also the director of a job-seeking assistance program for disabled people. My disability is called retinitis pigmentosa or, more affectionately, RP. It is congenital, progressive, and hereditary, involving nearsightedness, night blindness, and tunnel vision. Although I was born with it, it really did not become a significant problem in my life until the last 10 years and especially so in the last year, since I initiated divorce from my husband after 15 years of marriage. As a 34-year-old single parent of two teenage boys, a whole new life-style has opened up for me.

I hope that you are not waiting to read about all of the exotic sexual techniques that blind people use—I don't think there are any. That is not to say that I don't have exotic sex; sometimes I do, and I hope sometimes you do! It's just that I don't think the sexual act itself is any different because I am blind.

LACK OF SIGHT AND ITS EFFECT
ON SEXUALITY

I have normal sexual responses. The only difference is that I don't have access to visual stimulation. I do not see bodies anymore. But I have to say that physical appearance has never been that important to me. What makes people attractive to me is personality.

I can still see enough to have a sense of what somebody's shape is like, and I have my own biases about what body shapes I do and do not like. I am not afraid to admit that. I can tell a great deal by a person's movements and posture.

I don't see erotic photographs or movies now, and they are not important to me. I enjoy my other senses a lot, however; I enjoy touching other people, and I like other people that are that way, too. I have difficulty with people who keep themselves at a distance, people who have a wide private base around themselves. I feel personally distant from them and often have a communication problem with them.

COMMUNICATION AND SOCIAL SKILLS

The differences between blind and sighted people are not what goes on in bed, but what happens before that. Two important areas to consider are communication barriers and social skills. Blind people may have unique difficulties both in initially meeting someone and then in maintaining that relationship. People who participate mainly in sighted activities (like many sports) might not want to relate to a person who is blind. For example, a man who wants a partner to play tennis or go to art museums with him would probably not be interested in me. These individual interests have to do with the maintenance of a relationship.

When I am trying to meet a person for the first time, I do not have access to eye contact. For example, I can't flirt with my eyes anymore. I may still do it unconsciously because I grew up having that available to me. But now I am less conscious, and I don't notice when I'm doing it.

I am in an awkward situation because I pass unintentionally as being sighted, since I used to be. This is different from someone who is blind from birth. I used to work very hard at passing for being sighted. Now I don't work on it at all. But being mistaken for a sighted person happens and can be awkward.

Since my remaining vision is constantly changing, I have to learn new techniques to deal with situations. For example, one might extend his or her hand to me, and, since I don't see it, I don't shake hands. I might later be told by an observer that the person felt rejected and embarrassed, so now I put my hand out first. If somebody tries to hand something to me and I don't see it, that's also awkward, so I've learned to put my hands up there first in that situation.

Many times people do not even know that I am disabled. If I am sitting down, there is nothing apparent by facial expression or my eyes that makes it obvious that I am blind. Even sometimes when I have my white cane, people don't notice. It really creates a lot of awkwardness. Somebody tries to make contact with me and I just walk past them. They think, "Oh, isn't she stuck-up."

Going to parties is particularly difficult for me. If the party is in a friend's house, I don't usually walk around with my cane because I feel comfortable and familiar there. People who don't know me might think that I am drunk when I go stumbling around people and bumping into things. One time I went to a party, and I had been in the living room most of the night, and I got up to go to the bathroom. I had to walk through the kitchen where there was a group of people that I had not met. I thought I was doing okay, but I bumped a little bit here and there. On the way back, I brought my glass with me, and I asked somebody to fix me a vodka tonic. I heard this snickering and got handed a drink with no booze in it. I think they were taking responsibility for me because they thought I was drunk.

A new experience I had last year was being in a hot tub for the first time with three friends. I was really looking forward to this experience. I would have liked being able to see the other bodies, but I could not. I mentioned this to my boyfriend afterward. So the next time we did this, he described these people to me in graphic detail: "Her nipples point up; he's got a roll around his middle; he's got a large penis—Terri, it makes mine look like . . . ." His descriptions really made the experience fun for me.

Social skills

When I meet educators of the blind, I tell them that they should really help people to avoid using mannerisms common to blind people (blindisms). I think that the fact that I don't have these blindisms makes it easier for me to socialize with the sighted world. I walk upright. I point my face toward the person that I am speaking to or who is speaking to me. But a lot of people grow up with weird postures and habits. They may sit or walk differently. Many congenitally blind people turn their ear, rather than their face, toward the person to whom they are talking. This is a common problem of people with whom I do a lot of job counseling. I have to tell adult people who are blind that they look strange. They sit and fiddle with their clothes, or they rock. They need to do away with some of those mannerisms because they distract the people they are talking with. The persons they are talking to may not even hear what is being said because they are so uncomfortable with the mannerisms.

I think that educators do blind kids a favor if they help them not to do that. I understand why blind people have these mannerisms. They've developed them because it helps them be aware of their environment, their space, but this can be done without using such mannerisms.

I have trouble communicating with others in places like bars where there is often very little light (so I see absolutely nothing) and where the music is loud. In these situations, I don't always catch it when somebody starts talking, and I might not know when somebody else jumps into the conversation. So I always have to be careful not to jump in on top of somebody else's sentence. I have to concentrate a lot in order to be socially appropriate. Similarly, I am not always aware when people talk to me if I am in a group. They may ask me a question and if they don't mention my name, I'm not immediately aware that they are talking to me. I have to process all of this in my head. I have to ask, "Are you talking with me?" And I spend so much energy on things like this that sometimes I don't hear the content of what's being said. All of this takes a lot of concentration on my part.

I had an experience once that points out the difficulty of not having visual cues. I was in a bar with a date. He got up at one point and went to the jukebox. While he was gone, a man who was drunk came over to me and started talking. Because I don't have visual feedback available to me, I am usually friendly verbally so people stay there and talk with me so I can tell what they are like. Also, I do this so they won't be put off by the fact that I am not making eye contact with them.

But I find that this approach of mine is encouraging in a way that sometimes gets me into difficult situations. When my friend came back, he described this person to me and I realized that, if I had been able to see this guy when he came up to me, I would not have said a word to him. It is difficult for me to remove myself from situations like that because I can't spot a "safe" looking person across the room and interact with him to discourage the person I'm trying to avoid.

Finally, another problem in social skills with blind people is that we don't have current visual information from the world. Fashion is one example. I don't know what people wear these days unless somebody tells me. I always need someone to go shopping with me. Many blind women only shop with their mothers and end up wearing clothes that their mothers would wear themselves, or they dress like little kids. Being able to get advice on your appearance from someone you trust is very important.

♀ ABOUT THE AUTHOR ♀

Terrianne Straw, M.S., is director of the Employment Project of the Disabled and past coordinator of peer counseling for the Independent Living Project, United Cerebral Palsy Association of San Francisco. She received her M.S. in Rehabilitation Counseling from San Francisco State University. Her interests include working to increase public awareness of disability issues. Since birth, she has had retinitis pigmentosa, resulting in progressive visual disability.

7 Ostomy: the hidden disability

Joseph Handel

I grew up with many of the usual stereotypical concepts of what disability is. I assumed that everyone in a wheelchair had been injured in an accident and was paralyzed from the waist down, that "handicapped" people weren't sexual and didn't want to be, and that they were very different from me.

After high school, I went to work at a school for the mentally retarded. While working there as a counselor for 5 years, I was struck by the capability these people had to love, in spite of the wide range of intellectual abilities. I realized that, if I myself or a friend got a brain injury, we would still be able to love; that was the important thing. During those 5 years I became aware of the stifling atmosphere toward sexuality within this school for the retarded. The teachers, aides, and administrators alike all did what they could to minimize or disregard these people's sexuality.

The last year that I worked there, I became handicapped myself through disease. This experience made me really question my own sexuality and body. My nonvisible handicap is an ostomy. Because of disease, I had to have my colon removed; so now I wear a colostomy bag on my side. The main thing that carried me through the surgery and the recuperation was my lover's support (I am gay). It amazed me that somehow he could still love me and that he felt I was still the same person. In some ways it was almost too good to be true. I wondered if he were *really* only sticking with me because we had been together for so long and if he really would have wanted to be with a person who didn't have any body imperfection.

A turning point in my self-image happened about 6 months to a year after the surgery. I felt that I *had* to try out sex with another person. I was satisfied with the sexual aspect of my relationship with my lover, but had to find out if my body could also be acceptable to someone else. A comment that stands out most in my mind from that period of exploring being sexual with other people was when a lover said, "You know, you have one of the nicest bodies of any of the men I've been with." That one comment did wonders for my self-confidence—it was tremondous. At first I didn't want to believe it, but the sincerity of his statement made me think, "Yeah, well, I should like my body, too. Just because of this little imperfection, I don't have to chastise myself or put myself down about it."

In the past few years, we have come a long way with the legal recognition of disabled people's rights and with increased public awareness of accessibility issues and discrimination. But the now commonly seen wheelchair access sign itself can promote a stereotype that disabled people are easily recognizable. I'd like to remind people that, as in my case, not all disabilities are that noticeable. While in training at the Sex and Disability Unit at the University of California, San Francisco, I led a gay disabled group in which 90% of the men had nonvisible disabilities. As they began trusting the other group members and talking about their real feelings, I found that many were "closet disabled" people. In the eyes of the general public, they appeared to be able-bodied; and yet if they wanted to be physically intimate with someone, their handicaps would become apparent. This was a cause for much anxiety and concern. They did not want to "surprise" their sexual partners. In this way, a nonvisible disability can definitely be a handicap for people with an ostomy, arthritis, artificial limbs, hearing loss, brain damage, or mental retardation. Some mentally retarded people are not easily recognizable. I can think of five or so of the people I have worked with that if you met and talked with them on the street, you would quite likely not realize they were retarded.

In a similar sense, gay and lesbian people are nonvisible, too. It's a myth to think you can "spot them." It is important also for counselors and rehabilitation workers to keep in mind that people with nonvisible handicaps are often not considered "really" disabled among people in the disabled community themselves. The first time someone referred to my ostomy as a disability, I looked at him and laughed. It took awhile for me to see the common social stigma that many groups face who are disabled. I, however, prefer the term "inconvenienced." To me, sometimes my ostomy is just that and nothing more.

One last thing I'd like to mention to counselors and/or rehabilitation workers. If you are going to be talking about sexuality with your clients, or anyone for that matter, I hope you will have already examined your own personal sexual attitudes and values. Find out what is uncomfortable for you about other people's sexuality—it might be the sexuality of disabled people, homosexuality, bisexuality, or a variety of "nonstandard" practices. Even as sex counselors, we don't have to agree with every sexual life-style; but recognizing the limitations in our own ability to be accepting and, in some instances referring clients to other professionals, can be a very powerful way of helping.

♂ ABOUT THE AUTHOR ♂

Joseph Handel (pen name) is a sex educator in northern California.

8 Radical hysterectomy and vaginectomy for cancer

THE STORY OF A 22-YEAR-OLD WOMAN AND HER RECOVERY

Elizabeth Burger

At 22 years old, I was a "success" in the world. Having graduated with highest honors from nursing school and embarking on my career, I was flying. My colleagues were envious of my courage in taking a cross-country camping trip and moving east. The job I found at a hospital in Boston was fun and challenging; the city and the East Coast were exciting and full of history.

Being conscientious about my own health care, I went for a routine follow-up exam for dysplasia (abnormal cells) soon after my arrival in Boston. When the gynecologist asked me if my mother had taken any hormones during her pregnancy, I promptly wrote her a letter to inquire (as with many women, I didn't know my mother's gynecological history). She wrote back—yes, she had taken diethylstilbestrol (DES). At the time, I had no clues to the meaning of this drug or its impending impact on my life.

On return to the gynecologist 3 months later, I gave the doctor my mother's letter. This time the pelvic exam included a biopsy and a few words from the doctor that he saw something "unusual." My developmental years had been remarkably healthy and my experiences with doctors had always been positive. My denial system rose to defend against the thought of illness. Three days later, my doctor called me on the phone to tell me I had cancer in situ of the vagina. I wrote this down as if taking a report on another patient. He instructed me to return to the hospital for a more extensive biopsy of the vagina in 2 days. The reality of having cancer was shocking and unbelievable. I called my parents to inform them of the news.

The surgery was done under a spinal anesthetic in the knee-chest position. I remember that I awoke during the surgery and felt embarrassed at finding myself peering over my rear end (high in the air), and seeing my doctor's face. When it was over, I was told to return to the doctor's office in a week to discuss the findings. As the week wore on, I became anxious and fearful, terrified that the doctor had not called to allay my fears that the cancer had spread. Most of the night before the appointment was spent crying. My boyfriend at that time was an enormous comfort. He reassured me he would stick by and help me through the crisis. He would come to the appointment to discuss the biopsy results; being a medical student, he would know what questions to ask.

Upon arrival at the doctor's office, I was told that my condition was serious; unfortunately, I had malignant clear-cell adenocarcinoma of the vagina and needed radical surgery. The doctor, my boyfriend, and I discussed what the operation would entail: removal of the uterus, one ovary, the upper two thirds of the vagina, and bilateral pelvic lymph nodes; a biopsy of the bladder (my doctor wanted to remove my bladder due to its close proximity to the cancer in the vagina); and pelvic scraping. This illness and surgery led to my having to deal with many changes in my sexuality.

DES AND ITS EFFECTS

DES (and the other names under which it was sold), a synthetic hormone, was given to pregnant women in the United States from 1941 to 1971. Despite reports as early as 1953[3] that the drug was ineffective for its prescribed use in preventing miscarriage, it was given for such symptoms as bleeding during pregnancy, history of miscarriage or prematurity, or diabetes. It was billed as the wonder drug for bigger, healthier babies and given as a "vitamin" to some unsuspecting women. There are estimated to be 6 million DES mothers, 3 million DES daughters, and 3 million DES sons. In 1971, the Federal Drug Administration (FDA) withdrew its approval of DES for prevention of miscarriage. However, from 1971 to 1974, about 11,000 DES prescriptions were written for this purpose. DES is also used to suppress lactation in women who choose not to breastfeed, in estrogen replacement therapy for menopausal women, and until recently, in animal feed. It is also used as a postcoital contraceptive, the "morning after pill."

One out of every 1000 DES daughters will develop the same type of vaginal cancer as I before the age of 30. Most of the DES daughters have a benign condition of the vagina and cervix. Other studies show that some DES daughters have difficulty in becoming pregnant or in carrying a pregnancy to term.

DES sons show an increased risk of undescended testicles, underdeveloped genitalia, low sperm count or abnormal sperm, and reproductive tract abnormalities, such as epididymal cysts.[1] Studies examining possible relationships between DES exposure and testicular cancer are underway. DES mothers themselves may be at a higher risk for breast cancer.[2]

My mother, as did most who were given DES, took it during the first 3 months of her pregnancy with me. It is during this early stage of pregnancy that genital organs can be affected in such a way as to later lead to the development of cancer. The standard of medical care at that time supported prescribing DES.

THE SURGERY

The surgery I had was radical and was performed routinely to prevent this type of cancer from spreading to other parts of the body. (Some women have malignant metastasis from the vagina and must also have bowel and bladder urostomies.) The surgery was debilitating due to its 4-hour length, the loss of 5 pints of blood, and extensive removal of organs.

I remained in the hospital for 4 weeks and had much time to think about and try to understand what had happened to me. The days were long; sometimes the hours never seemed to pass. Minutes felt like an eternity. I began to experience depression over the losses of my body parts, of the "healthy" young woman I once was, and over the helplessness of my situation. I was overwhelmed by the nerve loss to my pelvis and was, to my surprise, totally incontinent of urine and bowel. Even though I was a nurse and "understood" I would have a pelvic scraping, I was unprepared for the loss of pelvic sensation. This led to my beginning distrust of my doctor. Disappointment that my body had let me down, as well as despair over its lack of functioning, weighed on me day after day, night after night. The initial euphoria over being alive and having been diagnosed early dissipated. I began to struggle with my loss of femininity and wondered whether anyone would ever physically want me with a missing vagina, a leaking bladder, and no control over my bowels. In my bedridden state, I couldn't run away from the horrors. I couldn't even get out of bed without help from someone.

A week after the radical surgery, my doctor made a new vagina for me out of skin from my buttocks. He sewed it on to the remaining one-third vagina and bowel. A glass test tube was inserted into this new vagina to keep it open. Other women who have vaginectomies don't necessarily have skin-graft replacement; some are able to have the remaining vaginal tissue dilated over time into a vaginal canal. The doctor explained that, over time, the skin would assume properties similar to vaginal tissue (except for lubrication) and that intercourse would be possible after healing.

SUPPORT PEOPLE

My family and friends were supportive during the surgery and aftermath. My boyfriend came to the hospital every day to visit, and also helped me change my dressings, etc. This was helpful to me, as I felt that it showed that he could accept me even though my body was scarred. I felt less freaky about my losses. My father and sister visited me in the hospital; my mother and brothers phoned.

A psychiatric nurse visited me before the surgery and every day thereafter while I was in the hospital. My initial response to her presurgery visits was, "Why do I need her? I don't have any problems." Little did I realize the depth of emotions I would face after surgery and the years following. The nursing staff was helpful, yet none of them had had much experience in treating a young woman whose vagina had been removed. Also, my age was close to that of many of the nurses who cared for me, and I sometimes felt their fear: "This could happen to me." There were also nurses who were supportive and lent a listening ear.

After the hospital

When the 24-hour support provided by the hospital was gone, I faced my greatest times of difficulty. I wanted to get better fast. Being helpless and dependent on others was hard for me, since I had never been ill and was used to being very active. My boyfriend was affectionate and compassionate, yet I felt disinterested in sex. It was a time of withdrawal for me, a time to take care of myself. I wanted most of all to go home to California to visit my family and talk things over with my mother.

California

A month after surgery, I flew home. My family was ecstatic to see me, even in my frail state (I had lost 20 lb), with a tube in my bladder and large pads that served as diapers for leaking urine. I showed my scars with no embarrasment. The talk was of how good it was that I was alive. A week after I arrived home, my mother died unexpectedly of a heart attack, a shock for everyone. For me, losing her was almost unbearable when placed on top of working through the grief I had already been feeling. Further, her death destroyed any opportunity for us to discuss together my feelings about the surgery and cancer and her feelings about having taken DES. I returned to Boston, wanting to get back to work as soon as possible, not wanting to think about my shattering losses.

THE FIRST 6 MONTHS

Returning to work made me feel valuable again. It gave me a sense of purpose and fulfillment. It also brought up the issue of how to tell others about my illness and surgery. It seemed that everyone at the relatively small hospital where I worked knew I had had the "big C," cancer. Bad news travels fast. Certainly I did not feel I could tell people I had cancer of the vagina and had it removed. The vagina was a "private part" and much harder to talk about than even a mastectomy. At this point I decided it best to say the minimum and try to understand what people were asking with their questions. A few intimate friends from work, and my boyfriend who was training at the same hospital, knew the whole story.

I experienced extreme loneliness about my feelings of disfigurement, my anxiety about bowel/bladder incontinence, and my cancer. I longed for someone to talk to who had been through a similar experience. The only other woman I knew was a 25-year-old who was in the bed next to mine when I was hospitalized. Tragically, her cancer had spread, and I knew she would die soon. In fact, she died 5 months after surgery. I wanted and needed to talk to someone who could help me sort out my feelings and understand. Family and friends were helpful to a point, but I needed someone to talk to who didn't need anything back from me. I went back time and again to see the psychiatric nurse at the hospital where my surgery was done. She provided a sense of continuity for me and could see my improvement.

About 3 months after surgery, I broke up with my boyfriend. I was still very focused on myself; I felt that a relationship was too taxing. After the support that he had given me through this difficult time, he was hurt and upset. I also wanted him to be free to date and see other women; it was important to me to know that he *chose* to be in a relationship with me, rather than feeling obligated due to the commitment to be supportive through the surgery and cancer. At that point I could not fathom being attractive to or desired by a man and still was not ready to resume sexual intimacy.

My bowel control returned within 5 months, but I leaked urine continuously and still wore a catheter. My pelvic area had no sensation but I felt encouraged that the return of my bowel control meant there was some nerve growth. I continued to use a hormonal cream and to wear the glass test tube in my vagina to keep it open and dilated. I used a hand mirror to look at my genitals and was continously reassured to see that I looked "about normal." Along with the mirror, I used a flashlight to look into the vagina; with the glass test tube in place, I could see the changes in the vaginal walls—ridges (as in a "normal" vagina) were developing. The ugliest part of the surgery was a red abdominal scar about 10 inches long. The incision was made below my bikini line in a horizontal fashion. This was good for my self-esteem because the scar was easily hidden.

Feelings that I was less than a whole woman were emerging. I again wondered whether anyone ever would or could be attracted to me once they knew about my surgery and my cancer. There seemed to be so many beautiful women (based on physical appearance) who were healthy and available; my friends additionally fit into that category. I felt jealous of women who seemed perfect, and angry that I had to go through this experience. These feelings alternated with the joy of being alive. Mixed feelings in hand, I went to my first party 4 months after surgery. My expectations were to go, socialize, and have a good time. I was well received by the people I knew, and they were delighted that I looked so well and was getting about. The evening was fun. I danced and laughed. I looked lovely with new clothes; I wore pants to hide my catheter and bag. I remembered how good it was to be held and touched, and a reawakening of my sexual self was beginning. I was starting to like myself again and began to feel better.

Six months after surgery, my remaining ovary was greatly enlarged. I thought for sure my cancer had spread. Once again, I retreated into myself. Reliving the surgery and watching in my mind the 25-year-old woman die of clear cell adeno-carcinoma were pervading my thoughts. Luckily, the enlarged ovary was due to a cyst. Later I learned that cystic breasts and ovaries are common in DES daughters. Relief and a chance to begin again—these crisis states were stressful and tiring. Facing the threat of death, mortality, and vulnerability is a heavy weight, and the need to be with people and be accepted became greater.

THE SECOND 6 MONTHS—SEXUALITY

Return into the social world was my goal. I renewed my relationship with my boyfriend. We started going out and talking, spending time together, doing the romantic things we used to do: ice skating, drinking hot chocolate in cozy places. I wondered about having sexual intercourse; my new vagina was ready for use. On going to bed, he was unbothered by my scar, which he had seen, the catheter to my bladder, or any other of my urinary incontinence paraphernalia. Since this new vagina did not lubricate itself (which my doctor had informed me), I was all set with my Vaseline Intensive Care Lotion (water base). The first attempt at intercourse was a mess. My bladder leaked all the more. My innervation to my genitals was still not present. Orgasm was nowhere for me. Tears and tears could not express my feelings of this added loss. It seemed the unexpected things would never stop. I began to question why he stayed with me. What was in it for him to have a girlfriend who was mutilated and disfigured? Much of that was how I perceived myself.

What next?

I returned to the surgeon to ask about my pelvic nerves. I told him I had not been able to have sensation and asked, "What about orgasm?" My despair and anger were apparent. He defensively told me he hadn't cut any of those nerves and any such problems were "all in my head." I was enraged at his attitude and realized that he just didn't know how to address sexuality with his patients. The psychiatric nurse from the hospital was my next resource. Certainly I felt I couldn't ask my family about these issues, and my girlfriends wouldn't understand what to do or say. I still had not found any other women who had had similar surgery with whom I could talk and share experiences. The psychiatric nurse was great, both because she listened as I ventilated and because she said she didn't know how to answer my questions—she admitted to her limitations openly and freely. She did not feel she had to know it all and helpfully referred me to a psychiatrist.

The psychiatrist

This man had had experience treating men who wanted to become women (transsexuals) and who had surgically created vaginas like mine. He was just what I needed because he had the medical knowledge and the understanding to deal with my problems. I clearly remember my first session in which I outlined the problems. He said, "I don't know whether you can have clitoral orgasms anymore, but there are other ways to be sexual." Again, the tears flowed. What does he mean "other ways to be sexual?" I thought, on top of all this, if I can't have orgasms, my vagina is missing (and I ran through the rest of my losses mentally), I may as well be dead.

Over time and many sessions, he discussed with me other ways to have orgasms. I had very good and varied sexual experiences before my surgery, and my brain knew how to have orgasms. All that was necessary was for me to relearn how to have good sensations. This process of learning went against my upbringing, however; the idea of touching my genitals (i.e., what was left of them) and of stroking my thighs and genitals to stimulate the nerves was something no one I knew did to themselves. I needed permission. He gave me exercises to do with a periometer, a device which gave me the feeling of being able to squeeze with this new vagina. New doors opened and rays of hope began to filter in slowly.

I had broken up with my boyfriend again, and the psychiatrist encouraged me to go out and date. I needed support to reenter the world of dating men. I went to parties and dinners but I thought, what will I say if a man starts to get into heavy petting and asks me why I have a catheter and urine bag? I was afraid of being rejected, but I also had the hope that things would get better. I thought, "I'm 23 years old and I want to be able to date and have relationships and orgasms." I was ready.

Dating

Before the surgery, I had dated a lot. I had had my pick of men and had been in some good relationships. Now I felt vulnerable and unsure. I thought the scar on my abdomen was ugly. I dated a variety of men just for the experience. I didn't want a serious relationship. I didn't want to get too involved. I wanted to experiment but also to protect myself from getting rejected. With the encouragement and support from the psychiatrist and friends, together with the return of my sense of humor, I was willing to try. Some men dated me out of curiosity because I had cancer; I had been through something unusual. I had to decide who to tell and who not to tell, what to say and what not to say. Some men took me out once and never called back. I dated a salesman and when he didn't call me back for days or weeks, it was easier to take; he could say he was on trips. A psychology student and I dated for several months. He was extremely ambivalent but tried to hide his negative feelings. He could talk with me and be understanding, but he was completely turned off to me physically. After a time, he stopped calling. This process was very important. I learned that I could tolerate rejection and that some men were interested in me despite my illness or surgery. As I started feeling more comfortable about myself, I could relate better to men.

Incontinence

My bladder, meanwhile, was still in the same leaky state and had not improved. I returned to the surgeon and asked for a urological consultation. He had been resistant to this idea. This was unhelpful. He could not and would not recognize his limitations. Finally he referred me to a friend of his who was a urologist and who I found I also did not trust. I gave him 2 months to figure out the problem and still did not trust him. The incontinence made my life complicated by having to have extra paraphernalia: a catheter, urinary bag on the leg during the day, a larger collecting bag for the night, pads, plastic pants, plastic sheets for the bed, an extra set of clothes in case the urine leaked through to my clothing. It was unappealing in every way and unacceptable to my sexual image. Once while at work, when my urine leg bag was nearly full and the urine was sloshing about, a man said, "Hey, you should take your shoes to be fixed, they really squeak." At another time in the cafeteria line, a woman asked me, "Why do you always wear long skirts?" I was speechless. She wanted to know if it was because of my religion. (In a way, she was right—I religiously wanted to keep my urinary leg bag hidden!) Comments like these were hard to field at first, but as my self-esteem got stronger, I could laugh them off. I had to learn to be creative with my answers.

Consultation

My friends and my psychiatrist supported my strong desire for another urology consultation. My surgeon was against the idea; his resistance was intolerable. Simultaneously, I started talking to a nurse about urinary ostomies and proceeded to talk with eight different doctors. Taking an active role in making the appointments was extremely helpful. I felt like I was really doing something for myself. I couldn't face a urinary ostomy, losing another body part. Despite this, five of the doctors told me that was the only solution to my nonfeeling bladder. I picked a distinguished urologist/plastic surgeon in California who I found to be knowledgeable. He also had a warm and open bedside manner. After extensive testing, he offered me a series of three surgical repairs with a 40% chance my bladder would work better. What was helpful about his approach was his (1) taking time to explain the pros and cons and the risks and benefits, (2) drawing pictures, (3) giving me the choices of what I wanted to have done, (4) instilling realistic hope, (5) his feeling okay about my checking for further consultation, (6) including me in the plans for treatment, and (7) referring me to another gynecologist for opinion on my grafted vagina (it had developed a sinus connection to my bladder, and urine leaked through that opening constantly). I had been afraid to give up my original gynecologist-surgeon despite my mixed feelings about him postoperatively. I thought no one else would know about this rare cancer or what I personally had left after surgery; this was an erroneous myth.

Back to California—new growth

I chose to move back to California to try this surgery to repair my bladder. If it turned out to be unsuccessful, I would have a urostomy. The urologist recommended I not wear my catheter or urine bag any more so my bladder could develop whatever muscle tone possible before the surgery in the fall.

While in California, I saw a gynecologist-hypnotherapist on recommendation from my father. This physician started me on self-hypnosis. I worked on visualization of nerve growth to my pelvis and bladder. In my mind I played "memory tapes" of good times, times when I was feeling well, times of relaxation, and what it was like to have orgasms in a healthy, loving relationship. Once again, I was taking an active role in my care, and I felt good. I could tolerate the uncertainty of the unknown outcome of the urology surgery; I had faced the unexpected before and felt my situation could only improve. My vanity prevented me from accepting the catheter; I wanted to feel intact and whole. I was definitely interested in sex and wanted to have the best chance I could of feeling attractive.

Back to Boston

Once again I dated my boyfriend with whom I wanted to have a relationship. This time I felt optimistic about myself and my future options. My catheter was out; I felt attractive in spite of my cancer and my surgery. "Little by little, the painful memories of suffering and illness become less poignant and it's easier to renew and enjoy thoughts of earlier happier times."*

The feeling of closeness, of being accepted and wanting sexual intimacy—the time had finally come. My pelvic innervation was scanty but improving. My urinary leakage was the same. However, my relationship with my boyfriend was strong, sincere, and genuine. After an evening of good times, we went to bed. Touching, caressing, and experimenting—I was able to be orgasmic. Once again a flood of tears came, but for joy! My relief at this enjoyment created another new hope.

THE SECOND YEAR

My bladder reconstruction was to start in October, the second surgery would be to reconstruct the vagina and sew up the hole where the urine leaked; the third and final stage would be an abdominal approach to further repair the bladder. I was unable to work at my usual job between these operations because no exact dates could be given; the dates had to be set according to the clinical progress of the healing and to an increased bladder capacity for urine. I put this time to use by working temporary jobs, a new experience for me. I was back in California and visited my friends up and down the West Coast. It was a time to try out new

---

*Zalon, J.: I am whole again, New York, 1976, Random House, Inc., p. 37.

things. These surgeries were not debilitating, as the radical procedure had been, and I was looking forward to being put back together again.

I took nonnursing related evening classes. My schooling hadn't allowed time for some of my interests, and this was the perfect time to pick them up.

A new relationship

I took an evening class from a handsome, attractive man. At the time I was not looking for a relationship. Most of my energy was being spent in gearing up for phases 2 and 3 of the bladder surgery. The first evening of class, he asked me out to coffee. This was the beginning of many long enjoyable hours of drinking coffee and talking. Over time, I told him about myself, my surgery, and cancer. We talked about everything. I now really felt and believed I could have a relationship with a man. My personality, intelligence, and creativity far outweighed my physical limitations. The feelings of being overwhelmed by my surgery, of feeling ugly, undesirable, ashamed, disgusting because of my urinary leakage, inadequate because of the nerve losses, and ostracized and lonely because of my cancer had dissipated. The fears of rejection were gone.

He shared his life's hopes and dreams, joys and sorrows, the painful and vulnerable aspects as well as the joyful ones. A bond developed between us that was strong and we mutually accepted each other. Our physical relationship was satisfying, and we developed a close, stable relationship.

He was not bothered by my urinary leakage and was able to adapt to new positions for intercourse. Once lubricated with water base cream, my vagina could accommodate his penis. He would put the cream over my labia and clitoris, my anus and nipples. I found I needed to give directions to what areas were sensitive and arousable. My nerve sensation around my labia and clitoris was less than 50% of what it had been prior to my radical surgery. However, other parts of my body seemed to develop increasing sensitivity. I was orgasmic in new ways, such as through breast and neck stimulation and fantasy. Yes, these orgasms were different, but sexually satisfying. There was openness to try new techniques.

THE THIRD YEAR: A SECOND VAGINAL RECONSTRUCTION

Exactly 2 years after the extensive biopsy that showed I had cancer of the vagina, I had my vaginal reconstruction. The reconstruction consisted of opening a narrowed band of vagina that had constricted and closing the hole at the distal apex of the vagina. This hole was one of the places from which my bladder was leaking urine. One month prior to surgery, I started seeing a female social worker once a week to talk about my feelings about the upcoming surgery. It helped me to speak candidly about my worries and anxieties, since the memories of the radical surgery were resurfacing. The unexpected losses that had occurred 2 years before were now giving me nightmares. I talked more about the loss of my vagina; by now I was over feeling that I had lost part of my femininity. My female identity was well established and I had a successful relationship and sexual experience. My new grafted vagina served a utilitarian purpose, since there was no feeling or sensation except that of fullness or penetration. The grafted vagina was more rigid, less stretchable. That also meant that anal intercourse would be affected since the bowel had been sewn to the vagina. I didn't have enough stretch in my vagina to allow for penile-anal intercourse, but that may not be true for others who have had vaginal grafts.

After the reconstruction, I again wore a mold. This time it was of Styrofoam, cut to the shape of the vagina and covered with a condom. This was much more comfortable than the glass test tube I used after the first vaginal construction. My boyfriend made me a new foam piece several times and enjoyed being able to participate in my recovery. I was embarrassed to buy condoms for the covering of the foam, so the nurses in the hospital ordered a case for me to take home on discharge.

This new vagina no longer leaked urine! What a relief. I felt more like my old self, another step toward getting what I wanted out of the reconstruction. I wore the mold every day and night until we could assume regular penile-vaginal intercourse. Intercourse also served the medical purpose of helping the vaginal graft stay open, keeping it from restricting.

I remembered from my hypnosis treatment that orgasm was very healthy. In addition to pleasure from the sensations, blood would flow to the area of my genitals and promote healing. This was a good incentive for practicing orgasms.

The final stage of the bladder reconstruction occurred just after the third year anniversary of the radical surgery. The results would not be known for at least 6 months. The bladder fistulas were repaired, the bladder had to be made smaller to sew up the holes, and the bladder neck was lifted up to prevent the bladder from continuously draining. No further nerve innervation had developed to the bladder, but over the next year time would tell.

Return to work. I was able to go to work in the fall, my first nursing job in over a year. While at the job, I was able to serve on a committee to develop direct service programs for cancer patients.

Workshops. I met a social worker who invited me to give talks on my personal surgery and recovery to demystify the cancer experience. This was a boost to my self-esteem, and I realized I could teach others about my cancer and what to expect from the surgery. I began to get referrals from her and from the hospital where I had had my surgery to talk to other women who had had radical genital surgery.

Cancer group. I learned about a group of men and women who met together once a week; all of them had cancer and were around my age. This group provided me with the opportunity to ventilate my feelings about my cancer, to feel accepted and less isolated. I no longer felt alone in my fears, fantasies, or experiences. No one in the group had my type of cancer, yet all of them had faced similar challenges: fears of starting new relationships and worries about attractiveness, among others. The support from those who have suffered similarly was valuable and helpful, a good learning experience for me about myself. They were also the first people I had talked with in depth about the radical surgery other than close friends, relatives, or therapists. Telling about the removal of my vagina was less difficult because each of them also had areas of vulnerability and shared them equally. I was able to talk about the other losses I had experienced—physical losses as well as the death of my mother—and felt listened to. I learned that old memories were very much alive, but I was creating new memories. Time also served as a healer; the 3 years since the radical surgery made it less traumatic to discuss.

DES action. Three years after surgery, I went to a training workshop for health professionals on diethylstilbestrol. My sister-in-law had given me the brochure. It was the first time I found a group that understood my illness. Since then I have served as the nurse-trainer for many workshops on DES. It was through this group that I was finally able, 7 years after surgery, to meet a woman who had also had clear cell adenocarcinoma. Her surgery was similar to mine except that she had not needed a vaginal graft; her vagina was able to be stretched from the remaining one third to an adequate size. She and I talked and shared and understood. I highly recommend sharing in this way with someone who is adjusting in a positive fashion.

Human sexuality workshop. Five years after surgery, I went to a 3-day weekend workshop on human sexuality. It was an eye opener for me and I learned a great deal; it also served to validate what I had learned about my sexuality and orgasms. Several men and women spoke of their illnesses and disabilities and how it affected their sexuality. In fact, I was moved to tears often during the presentations; their stories struck painful as well as joyful memories of success over mastering the difficult times.

I had never thought of myself as "sexually disabled" but the experiences discussed by others fit many of the traumas I had incurred. It was comforting and hopeful to see that others can be supported in discussing their thoughts and feelings on sexuality. An additional area I learned about was masturbation. Masturbation had been a taboo that I learned from my family. I don't remember ever discussing it at home. I do remember funny cracks about developing warts on your hands or going crazy. I knew these things weren't true, but masturbation was for other people. My myths about masturbation stretched a mile long.

I had been married 2 years by then and, although my husband had not wanted to go to the workshop, he was happy to discuss what I had learned. About 2 months after the conference, I bought an electric vibrator and began to use it tentatively; it seemed overstimulating. My husband and I talked about it and about his concerns: Why did I need it when I had him to stimulate me any way I wanted? This helped us discuss his myths, too. I wanted to learn for myself what areas of my genitals had feeling and what additional sensation I could develop with practice. In time, my husband used the vibrator to stimulate me and I tried using it on him. This practice was at times awkward and funny but eventually paid off. I was able to masturbate with my hands 4 months later. The first time was in the bathtub where there was peace and quiet. Approximately a year later, my husband and I were talking and he said he thought it would be exciting if I masturbated and brought myself to orgasm while we were lying together in bed. After that, we were able to be much more comfortable about the whole topic. Learning that it was okay to masturbate was a slow but very helpful process for being able to know myself, what turns me on, and being able to give my husband cues. It has provided an enriching experience for our sexual relationship.

CONCLUSION

The years have brought me an acceptance of the cancer and my surgery. The growth in my ideas and experiments with sexuality have increased greatly since my surgery. What was most helpful was being able to share my experiences with people who could understand and be accepting and finding people who were trained and had accurate information on how I could help myself. We, as health professionals, don't have to have all the answers; what is crucial is to have enough sense of our limitations to be able to refer to an expert when necessary. I firmly believe it takes a team of people to support someone going through radical cancer surgery and recovery, or any major disability, for that matter. Most of all, the support of family, friends, and partners is needed; the strength of those relationships made the hard times bearable.

I am pleased to be able to share this process of my recovery with you.

REFERENCES

1. Bibbo, M., Gill, W.B., Azizi, F., et al.: Follow-up study of male and female offspring of DES-exposed mothers, Obstet. Gynecol. **49**:1-8, 1977.
2. Bibbo, M., Haenszel, W.M., Wied, G.L., Hubby, M., and Herbst, A.L.: A twenty-five year follow-up study of women exposed to diethylstilbestrol during pregnancy, N. Engl. J. Med. **298**:763-767, 1978.
3. Dieckman, W.J., Davis, M.E., Rijnkiewica, L.M., and Pottinger, R.E.: Does the administration of diethylstilbestrol during pregnancy have therapeutic value? Am. J. Obstet. Gynecol. **66**:1062-1081, 1953.

SUGGESTED READINGS

Adam, E., Decker, D.G., Herbst, A.L., et al.: Vaginal and cervical cancers and other abnormalities associated with exposure in utero to diethylstilbestrol and related synthetic hormones, Cancer Res. **37**:1249-1251, 1977.

Aldrich, J.O., Henderson, B.E., and Townsend, D.E.: Diagnostic procedures for the stilbestrol-adenosis-carcinoma syndrome, N. Engl. J. Med. **287**:934, 1972.

Anderson, B., Watring, W.G., Edinger, D.D., Jr., Small, E.C., et al.: Development of DES-associated clear-cell carcinoma: the importance of regular screening, Obstet. Gynecol. **53**:293-299, 1979.

Barbach, L.G.: For yourself: the fulfillment of female sexuality, New York, 1975, Doubleday Publishing Co.

Barnes A.B., Colton, T., Gunderson, J., Noller, K.L., et al.: Fertility and outcome of pregnancy in women exposed in utero to diethylstilbestrol, N. Engl. J. Med. **302**:609-613, 1980.

Benton, B.: Stilbestrol and vaginal cancer, Am. J. Nurs. **74**:900, 1974.

Bernstein, L.: The DES mystery: one million men are silent, Long Island Magazine, March, 1980, pp. 60-63.

Burke, L., Apfel, R.J., Fisher, S., and Shaw, J.: Observations on the psychological impact of diethylstilbestrol exposure and suggestions on management, J. Reprod. Med. **24**:99-102, 1980.

Cheek, D.B.: Clinical hypnotherapy, New York, 1968, Grune & Stratton, Inc.

Epstein, S.S.: The politics of cancer, San Francisco, 1978, Sierra Club Books.

Featherston, W.C.: Squamous neoplasia of vagina related to DES syndrome, Am. J. Obstet. Gynecol. **122**:176-180, 1975.

Forsberg, J.G.: Estrogen, vaginal cancer and vaginal development, Am. J. Obstet. Gynecol. **113**:83, 1972.

Forsberg, J.G.: Cervicovaginal epithelium—its origin and development, Am. J. Obstet. Gynecol. **115**:1025-1043, 1973.

Goldstein, D.P.: Incompetent cervix in offspring exposed to diethylstilbestrol in utero, Obstet. Gynecol. **52**(Suppl.):735, 1978.

Goldzieher, J.W., and Benigno, B.B.: The treatment of threatened and recurrent abortion: a critical review, Am. J. Obstet. Gynecol. **75**:1207-1214, 1958.

Heinonen, O.P.: Diethylstilbestrol in pregnancy: frequency of exposure and usage patterns, Cancer **31**:573, 1973.

Herbst, A.L., Hubby, M.M., Blough, R.R., and Azizi, F.: A comparison of pregnancy experience in DES-exposed and DES-unexposed daughters, J. Reprod. Med. **24**(2):62-69, 1980.

Herbst, A.L., Norusis, M.J., Rosenow, P.J., Welch, W.R., and Scully, R.E.: An analysis of 346 cases of clear-cell adenocarcinoma of the vagina and cervix with emphasis on recurrence and survival, Gynecol. Oncol. **7**:111-122, 1979.

Herbst, A.L., Poskanzer, D.C., Robboy, S.J., et al.: Prenatal exposure to stilbestrol: a prospective comparison of exposed female offspring with unexposed controls, N. Engl. J. Med. **292**:334-339, 1975.

Herbst, A.L., and Scully, R.E.: Adenocarcinoma of the vagina in adolescence, Cancer, **25**:745, 1970.

Herbst, A.L., Ulfelder, H., and Poskanzer, D.C.: Adenocarcinoma of the vagina: association of maternal stilbestrol therapy with tumor appearance in young women, N. Engl. J. Med. **284**:878, 1971.

"J": The sensuous woman, New York, 1969, Dell Publishing Co.

Kaufman, R.H., Binder, G.L., Gray, P.M., Jr., et al.: Upper genital tract changes associated with exposure in utero to diethylstilbestrol, Am. J. Obstet. Gynecol. **128**:51-56, 1977.

Lanier, A.P., Noller, K.L., Decker, D.G., et al.: Cancer and stilbestrol, a follow-up of 1,719 persons exposed to estrogens in utero and born 1943-1959, Mayo Clinic. Proc. **48**:793, 1973.

Lebherz, T.: Diethylstilbestrol—screening DES daughters for vaginal cancer, Nurs. Update **7**:15-16, 1976.

Mann, J.: Common sexual dynamics of the family, Primary Care **2**:501-512, 1975.

Mann, J.: The dynamics and problems of sexual relationships, Postgrad. Med. **58**:1975.

Mattingly R.F., and Stafl, A.: Cancer risk in diethylstilbestrol-exposed offspring, Am. J. Obstet. Gynecol. **126**:543, 1976.

Ng, A., Reagan, J.W., James, W., Nadji, M., et al.: Natural history of vaginal adenosis in women exposed to diethylstilbestrol in utero, J. Repro. Med. **18**:1, 1977.

O'Brien, P.C., Noller, K.L., Robboy, S.J., Barnes, A.B., et al.: Vaginal epithelial changes in young women enrolled in the national cooperative diethylstilbestrol adenosis (DESAD) project, Obstet. Gynecol. **53**:300-308, 1979.

Registry for clear-cell adenocarcinoma of the genital tract in young women, Boston, Mass., 1978 Report.

Robboy, S.J., Kaufman, R.H., Prat, J., Welch, W.R., et al.: Pathologic findings in young women enrolled in the national cooperative diethylstilbestrol adenosis (DESAD) project, Obstet. Gynecol. **53**:309-317, 1979.

Rosenfeld, D.L., and Bronson, R.A.: Reproductive problems in the DES-exposed female, Obstet. Gynecol. **55**:453-456, 1980.

Sandberg, E.C.: The incidence and distribution of occult vaginal adenosis, Am. J. Obstet. Gynecol. **101**:322, 1968.

Sandberg, E.C.: Benign cervical and vaginal changes associated with exposure to stilbestrol in utero. Am. J. Obstet. Gynecol. **125**:777, 1976.

Schmidt G., Fowler, W.C., Talbert, L.M., and Edelman, D.A.: Reproductive history of women exposed to diethylstilbestrol in utero, Fertil. Steril. **33**(1)21-24, 1980

Schwartz, R.: Psychological effects of diethylstilbestrol exposure, J.A.M.A. **237**:252-254, 1977.

Seaman, B., and Seaman, G.: Women and the crisis in sex hormones, Brattleboro, Vt., 1977, The Book Press.

Servatius, D.: Easing the shock of radical vulvectomy, Nursing **75**:24-31, 1975.

Sherman, A.I., Goldbrath, M., Berlini, A., et al.: Cervical-vaginal adenosis after in utero exposure to synthetic estrogens, Am. J. Obstet. Gynecol. **44**:531-545, 1974.

Smith, O.W.: DES in the prevention and treatment of complications of pregnancy, Am. J. Obstet. Gynecol. **56**:821-834, 1948.

Stafl, A., Mattingly, R.F., Foley, D.V., and Featherston, W.C.: Clinical diagnosis of vaginal adenosis, J. Obstet. Gynecol. **43**:118-124, 1974.

Veridiano, N.P., Tancer, M.L., and Weiner, E.A.: Squamous cell carminoma *in situ* of the vagina and cervix after intrauterine DES exposure, Obstet. Gynecol. **52**(Suppl. 1):305-345, 1978.

Washington correspondent, Nature **238**:67-68, 1972.

Wiley, L.: Emphasizing the positive, Nursing **77**:30-34, 1977.

Yalom, I.D.: The theory and practice of group therapy, New York, 1970, Basic Books, Inc.

♀ **ABOUT THE AUTHOR** ♀

Elizabeth Burger (pen name) is a head nurse on a child and adolescent inpatient unit in a California hospital. She is a volunteer for a DES action group and serves as nurse-trainer for teaching health professionals about the effects of DES. This is an autobiographical account of her clear-cell adenocarcinoma discovery, surgery, and recovery. It has been 8 years since her radical surgery.

9 Choosing the penile prosthesis

Reese N. Epstein

In December, 1968, I retired from a career of active military service for reasons of physical disability. This was a shock after 27½ years of active combative service. I had participated in three wars, incurred injuries in two of them, and had developed diabetes mellitus and heart disease. None of these affected my performance in the field of war or in the bedroom, but according to the military, I was no longer fit for duty.

I returned to the process of finding a job, which was not so easy with a diseased body. All kinds of rhetoric was used to justify not hiring me: I was seen as "too old," in too "poor" health, or the interviewer was antimilitary. This job search and rejection affected me and may have had an effect on my deteriorating sexual performance. I felt a little burned out but was motivated to work and live fully despite my medical problems.

In 1972, my first round of sexual dysfunction occurred. I spoke to a physician about it, and she told me it was all in my mind. Angry at such a simple assessment, I asked her if she wanted to do some field work with me, but she declined this offer of proof on my part. In time, though slow to erect, I was again sexually active. The physician felt that my job search and working on my first graduate degree at night, together with antiwar sentiments directed at retired military personnel like myself, all had contributed originally to my problem. At the doctor's recommendation, I undertook a behavior modification program to deal with my "type A" behavior, which was dangerously stressing my heart. This led to my exploring self-hypnosis and taking a complete program of biofeedback. Meanwhile, my diabetes continued to increase in severity, so much so that I began taking an oral medication to help control it. My heart problems also increased. Over this period of time, my sexual performance wasn't to my satisfaction. Although my wife didn't complain, at times her remarks hinted that I was slowing down, that I shouldn't try so often, etc. "Stop lighting a fire that you can't put out" describes what I thought she felt.

By 1973, I had had three open heart bypass surgeries. I developed diabetic neuropathy; my lower legs and feet were uncomfortable. Then I began not to be able to get an erection in the morning. Vitamin treatment and hormone shots didn't help. I tried a session or two of self-hypnosis again but to no avail. My wife, a patient person, had a philosophy which precluded her from doing anything but accept what was. However, I was bothered by the absence of sexual activity. At 56 years of age, I was too young to give up and live a monastic life in the bed of my wife who still excited me and made me quiver within when I saw her clothed or unclothed.

The impotence definitely affected me emotionally. I couldn't reconcile myself to the loss of our sexual intimacy. I still tried to have sex with my wife; closeness and touching were not enough. I knew there were other ways to sexually please both of us, but we missed intercourse. I even suggested to my wife that she find satisfaction elsewhere, but she responded with tears. I hadn't considered the philosophy that her mother had instilled in her, which was that a marriage is a marriage and that nothing interferes. She told me not to worry, that she didn't mind and could live without sex. We were together and that was all that mattered to her. She also thought that men in their fifties naturally went downhill anyway when it came to sex.

So it went—no sex. I stared at some women with desire, almost tearful at the prospect of no longer being able to make love. I continued to attempt to have intercourse with my wife, but my vigor was all gone. I told her I no longer felt like a man. The thoughts going through my mind were dismal. I also felt the pressure from working on my second graduate degree, and this may have added to the problem as I experienced it.

I knew of one VA medical center that specialized in helping persons with spinal cord injuries develop an enjoyable sex life, but I couldn't bring myself to go there; those veterans had been in the thick of combat and had given up more than I had. My conscience wouldn't allow me to visit there. Some of those veterans could no longer walk without help, and I would be walking in complaining that I couldn't function sexually. My hearing had been blasted during the war, I had been burned from head to waist (with no residual scars), and the scars from my circulatory problem and my diabetes didn't show; I could walk, drive, and do many things they could not.

When my diabetes physician suggested I see some sex counselors at another VA medical center, I pooh-poohed her. I just didn't believe that it could help. However, I made an appointment. Eventually, through the efforts of the sex counselors, I was evaluated and had surgery by a urologist who had trained with Dr. Small, one of the developers of the prosthesis that I had inserted. As a diabetic, I was at risk for any kind of surgery, but I had surgery with a spinal anesthesia while talking with the two doctors performing the operation. They described how the implant goes deep into the sphincter muscles and that a pocket is carved in the cavernous area of the penis. A catheter was inserted in my bladder while I recovered from the operation. The doctors then released me from the hospital, admonishing me to wait at least a week before using the prosthesis.

In the past, attempting to have sex with my wife was like trying to squeeze the toothpaste back into the tube. Now at home the first day, I told her I had to try it out. I knew my erection would never be like it used to be; it had lost circumference and length, one of the drawbacks of the penile prosthesis. It was only semirigid, unlike the hydraulic model (the Scott prosthesis) that resembles a more natural erection. Mine required assistance for penetration, but on the first night I was like a cat scratching raw silk; there was laughter from my bride and purrs of pleasure from me.

Since my surgery, I have always wanted to get the hydraulic implant, but was told that diabetics often have problems with them. My implant leaves a bulge in my pants, and my wife sometimes complains about people seeing it. It doesn't bother me, and since wearing a jock strap all the time is too tight and jockey-style underwear isn't helpful, I just let the implant hang. I get stares in public sometimes, but I don't care; what is important to me is that it works and has helped restore a wonderful part of my relationship with my wife.

I feel that the implant has given me a new lease on life and has improved my morale. I now have intercourse with my wife three to four times a week, compared to twice a week before all the problems began several years ago. We've maintained this level of activity despite going through two bouts of heart failure, five heart attacks, and assorted other cardiac worries.

My sex life is more active, my wife is more willing, and I find that my sexual aggressiveness has returned. This is only limited by the need to not overexert because of my heart. I am on insulin now, and I think it adds to changes in my sexual performance, since it controls the neuropathy that interfered with functioning in the past.

Earlier this year, a middle-aged woman made some seductive overtures to me. This caused me some moments of unrest. I knew her only casually, but she persisted in her advances. I felt I couldn't reconcile an affair with my conscience; I had never had an affair since my marriage and didn't want to jeopardize my relationship with my wife. But the feeling from knowing that I *could* flirt if I wanted or even *could* respond if given the opportunity was wonderful.

There is one drawback to this type of rigid penile implant. I have been advised that I have an enlarged prostate. To scrape this in a normal male involves entering the urethral channel, reaching the prostate and scraping around it, and removing the fibrous tissue causing the problem. However, for such treatment, my rigid implant must be removed. I don't like this idea, but if it is removed, I may be able to get the hydraulic implant later.

In trying to get information about the implant, I have learned that there is little available; few qualified sex counselors and few physicians know about the prosthesis or understand the destructive emotional process a man goes through when his erection fails. Dealing with erection failure should be a part of medical education. At first I thought the implant surgery was done by plastic surgeons and was a cosmetic prop. Recently, I spoke with a nephrologist who knew very little about the implants, although he worked closely with a urologist. The general public needs more information, although a little more may be beginning to be presented. A recent national television talk show featured a urologist who had done over 400 implants and there was a discussion by a psychiatrist who advises about the implant. This was the first public view I've seen of the inflatable pump and the first serious public discussion of prosthesis surgery complete with questions from the audience and from telephone callers. There are also beginning to be newspaper and magazine articles about this subject.

Another problem with sexual functioning that was not addressed until my sexual counseling was the possible side effects of medications. The drug manual that I have lists many of the side effects of medications I take but doesn't say anything about sexual dysfunctions the medications may cause. Maybe the drug companies would rather skip this information, but I think there is an obligation to inform patients if such a possibility exists with the medications they are taking.

In summary, I had been a sexually aggressive individual until about age 28. Then I continued to function sexually but with more pleasure for both me and my partner and with a more leisurely, caring approach. In my middle fifties I began to slow down. At 56, my sexual function ceased, I was usually unable to obtain satisfactory erections, and I went through all kinds of mental hell as I thought I had to learn how to survive without this important activity—I thought sex was over for good. I didn't really think at the onset about my wife's feelings, only mine. I am now able to function sexually without problems, except that at times I get mild angina. I take nitroglycerin before intercourse as a prophylaxis and am able to have intercourse morning, noon, or night—sometimes twice a day—despite several medications and a fragile left ventricle. I read with interest any information I can find about the penile implant and am dismayed that much of what is available isn't in layman's language. My feeling is that with more public information, many people will live better lives with the extra assistance these implants can give.

♂ ABOUT THE AUTHOR ♂

Reese N. Epstein, M.S., M.P.H., is a retired U.S. Air Force Senior Master Sergeant and a retired college director. His degrees are from San Francisco State University and Golden Gate University. Currently residing with his wife in northern California, he is involved in poetry and creative writing.

10 Becoming active partners

A COUPLE'S PERSPECTIVE*

Robert Lenz and Bernadette Chaves

Bob: I broke my neck in an auto accident when I was 16. I'd been sexually active before I broke my neck, but suddenly everything was different. Nothing worked like it used to, and I didn't know if it ever would again. I spent a lot of time wondering what my life was going to be like; not just my sexual life, but my entire life!

"Accept" is one of those words I have a really hard time knowing what to do with. I feel like I've accepted the physical side, the limitations side . . . but there are days when I feel frustrated, there are days when I feel angry. I don't know if I'll ever "accept" that, but I know that even when I feel down, depressed, and angry I'm much better at dealing with those feelings. It's taken awhile, and I can't give anyone a timeline on this.

In the rehabilitation center I learned a lot about maneuvering a wheelchair, bowel programs, catheter care, fluid intake, diet, pressure points, and decubiti (pressure sores). All these were things I needed to know to survive, but I wasn't told much about living or anything about sex. When I left there and went home to my parents' house, the only thing I knew about my sexuality was that I could still get erections, although with an indwelling urethral catheter and no genital sensation, I didn't know what good they were. Another patient in the rehabilitation center had said, "As long as I've got a tongue that works, I've got it made." It took me a few days to figure out what he meant, but it finally clicked.

At home I felt like the town eunuch for a few years. I saw a lot of the women I had been dating before I broke my neck, but now there was nothing sexual going on between us. I kept secretly blaming them for not giving me a chance, not treating me as needing or wanting or even being capable of having a sexual relationship. Now I realize that I wasn't *acting* like I needed or wanted or was capable of having

---

*This chapter adapted with permission from the film "Active Partners," Robert Lenz and Marvin Silverman, producers, 1979, distributed by Multi-Media Resource Center, 1525 Franklin St., San Francisco, Calif., 94118.

a sexual relationship. The simple truth was that I was just plain scared. I didn't know what I could do, how I could pleasure or be pleasured, and I sure didn't want to look like a jerk while trying to find out, or worse yet, find out I was a failure and face the eventual rejection.

My eunuch years also included a lot of martyrdom. I remember deciding that if I ever really fell in love with someone, I would end the relationship because I thought, being in a wheelchair, I could never really make anyone happy.

Bernie: When I first met Bob, I really felt sorry for him. I wouldn't ever say no when he asked me to do something that I didn't want to do or let him know when I was angry with him. After all, he is handicapped! Boy, has that changed and I sure like it! I don't feel like a maid anymore. I guess we're both lucky we don't stay mad long.

Bob: I feel much better about our ability to fight and argue now. I remember . . . 2, 3 years ago, I was so scared of fighting with Bernie because I felt that if I fought with her, she wouldn't like me. And God knows, I really wanted to be liked, particularly by her. That was really important to me.

Bernie: One of the advantages for me, of Bob not being able to physically do some things, is that he's gotten into the habit of asking for what he wants. It's great when he says, "I'd really like to make love" or "I'd like to hug you" because I know that's what he wants, and I can decide whether that's what I want or not; all of the physical game playing that happens in other sexual relationships isn't there.

Bob: It's not that we don't physically play with each other. We do that a lot, but I can't do all the subtle physical maneuvering I used to go through so my date would suddenly find herself in bed. It's hard to be subtle when your partner has to throw you in bed and undress you.

Simply letting your date or partner know that you'd like to make love sure sounds easy now, but it was really scary for quite awhile. What if she said no? Some did. Then how would she feel about all the work of putting me in bed, undressing me, and dealing with my catheter and my spasms and on and on and on.

Bernie: Getting Bob into bed and undressed is work, but it's not all work. We play a lot. I know sometimes people think I'm too rough with him, but I learned really fast that he's not fragile. If I'm being too rough he'll let me know.

Bob: That's true. I learned very shortly after getting out of the rehabilitation center the difference between the proper, medical way of doing things and the practical, easy way of doing things. I've gotten very pragmatic—you might say that she drops me into bed. Now that's what I call pragmatic! Getting up is a little different though. That usually requires two people or my Hoyer lift.

Before I broke my neck, orgasm *was* ejaculation. I took a long time to emotionally unlearn that, even after I intellectually knew the difference between the two. Now orgasm is more emotional than physical for me. Who I'm with is much more important than exactly what I'm doing.

Bernie: Bob's great to cuddle with. His body is almost always really warm and I'm usually cool, so I love to wrap myself around him or scoot up behind him and sleep spoon style. Besides, I love feeling his skin against mine.

Bob: One thing I do know is that I'm a much better lover now than I ever was before. There are a lot of reasons for that, but one of the biggest is that I'm more relaxed. I don't have a list of do's and dont's, a timetable or a proper sequence of moves to follow, or the need to "give" my partner an orgasm every time we make love. Sex isn't just orgasm for me; it's pleasuring, playing, laughing, and sharing.

♂ ABOUT THE AUTHORS ♀

Robert Lenz, M.A., is a private consultant in the area of sexuality and disability. He received training at the Sex and Disability Unit of the Human Sexuality Program, Department of Psychiatry, University of California, San Francisco, and later wrote and coproduced "Active Partners," an award-winning film about a spinal cord–injured quadriplegic and his able-bodied female partner. He is currently a counselor with the Disabled Student Services at Merced College in Merced, California, and is collaborating on additional films dealing with sexuality and disability issues. He received a quadriplegic spinal cord injury 15 years ago.

Bernadette Chaves was in the film, "Active Partners." She is a reading specialist for adults and is also involved in preschool education. She has worked as a counselor in a summer camp for disabled children and adults.

FAMILY PERSPECTIVES

11 Being a disabled mother

Loretta J. Ferris

I am going to discuss some of my experiences as a disabled parent, as a single parent, and as a parent who has also relinquished primary custody of her children. I am going to focus on two aspects: my experience of being a disabled parent and some of the challenges my children have faced, and how I help other women deal with these issues on a professional basis in my role as a counselor.

First of all, the myth that a disabled woman can't have children is very prevalent. I often find that people assume my children are adopted rather than that I have given birth to them. People also make the assumption that, if you have a physical disability, you cannot go through natural childbirth. My disability is polio. I have had polio since I was 4 years old. In most cases polio does not interrupt any sexual functioning or restrict a woman from being able to have children through natural childbirth. My last child was born at home, a very exciting experience (perhaps *especially* so because our "plans" had been otherwise).

Another issue which I faced and experienced was the issue of abortion. When I was first pregnant, it was suggested to me that it would perhaps be better if my husband and I would consider abortion, because how would I take care of the children? How would I teach them to walk? How would they learn to run? How would I take care of their physical needs? How would I be able to raise them? Some members of my family were very frightened of the fact that I was going to have a child. I am sure that these concerns stemmed from their own fears that they would have to assume parental responsibilities if I couldn't handle it myself or if my husband left me.

After my first son was born, it was suggested that my husband should have a vasectomy because, after all, wasn't *one* child enough in this situation? To me, that also implied that I could not handle my own birth control, that I could not be a responsible woman, and that all the responsibility lay with my husband, who was able-bodied. We didn't choose to have a vasectomy and later had our second son.

I was very conscious of the issue of discipline in raising my children when they were young. Because of the fact that I was unable to run after the children if they ran off, I felt that I had to be a little more assertive and a little stronger in getting my point across and using my voice to command "come here, come back," as well as in letting my family and friends know that I was in charge when they were well-meaning in trying to help. If one of the boys did something wrong or ran away from me, I might or might not allow others to take the responsibility of going and getting my son and bringing him back to me or doing the disciplining. I let my children know that whatever the situation was, I was the one in control, and I was their mother. If they would fall down, people would want to go get them for me, and I had to let friends and family know that it was my job. It might have taken me a little longer to get off my crutches and get on the floor with them, or whatever had to be done, but it was my responsibility.

I was divorced after 6 years of marriage and continued to keep the boys with me for another 3 years. My ex-husband and I then made a joint decision that it was time for the kids to live with him, so I became the single mother who did not have custody of her kids. This brought me face-to-face with the stereotype that you are a "bad or unfit mother" if you don't have custody. Although my boys live with me on the weekends, people ask, "How could you love your children? You went off into the world to be a women's libber or a feminist or whatever." That battle in itself is hard enough, but when you are a mother with a physical disability who doesn't have custody of her children, the additional assumption is always made that they were awarded custody to their father because of physical limitations. Although it was hard to admit for a long time, that kind of assumption was hurtful to me. It doesn't hurt so much any more because I think there is more awareness now about the reasons why women in general may relinquish custody to the father.

Having a disabled parent, in my opinion, has been a very healthy experience for my boys and certainly for me; a little hard to get used to, perhaps, but good for all of us. Some of the challenges they have faced in having a parent who is disabled came about when they started school. Until that time there was never really any talk in our home about disability or disability issues. We lived in a small town when my son was in first grade, and I worked as a teacher's aide in his classroom. One night after he had gone to bed, I heard him crying. I went in and asked, "Rick, what's wrong?" He said, "Mom, I don't want to tell you." I tried to gently coax him in the way you do to try and help a child in a stressful situation. He then said that he didn't want to tell me for fear that it would hurt my feelings. When I assured him that I would try not to let it hurt my feelings, he said, "I don't want you to go to my school anymore." Further questioning led to the reason: "I'm the only kid that has a crippled mom." I can tell you that that was the most hurtful thing that I have ever experienced for my children and also for myself. It was also frustrating because I realized then that, no matter what values you attempt to teach in your own home and what you think about yourself, we are all tremendously influenced by stereotypes and values of society. As we continued to talk, he said, "Mom, sometimes the kids make fun of you and imitate the way you walk, and they laughed when you fell in the classroom." When I asked if this embarrassed him, he threw his arms around me and said, "Yeah, Mom, sometimes I get embarrassed." I told him that it was okay for him to be embarrassed at those times, that we all go through embarrassing situations and that there were times when I was embarrassed myself. Sometimes being clumsy *is* embarrassing, as anyone knows who has ever fallen or dropped something or lost a train of thought in giving a speech. We all have to learn to cope; perhaps my boys had the advantage of learning how to cope with those embarrassing moments of everyday life at an early age. It was at that time in raising my children that I realized the importance of communication and being honest and open with your children.

Another major issue was the fact that we moved a lot as a family. My husband was a teacher, and as his career developed, we moved to different places and had to get used to new environments fast. Our sons had a lot of practice in bringing their new friends to our home, introducing them to me, and answering their questions. If the children were having problems in school, sometimes their teacher would assume it was because they had a disabled parent—that I couldn't parent well enough or couldn't help them educationally. It is stigmatizing for a child to hear, "Well, you know, Randy's mother has a physical handicap; that's why he failed ball throwing in kindergarten."

But, again, there are positive things that come out when children have a parent who has a disability. For one thing, they learn early that there are all types of people. My children are very accepting of other people. They are even more patient with persons who have a speech impediment than I am. They know a little sign language, they know about wheelchair basketball, and both of my boys are very athletic. I'm very proud of them. They recently went to Germany on an all-star soccer team. They are also interested in wheelchair sports, and we have many other interests in common.

I think they're comfortable with their self-image; they're accepting of their limits; they're creative and independent. I didn't carry them around a lot. They learned to walk at an early age, and that all may have contributed to their healthy attitude toward their own sexuality and their acceptance of other people. They look at themselves as total persons. My youngest son had a girlfriend last year and he related to me that some of the guys in school laughed and teased him about her. When I asked why they were teasing, he said, "Well, Mom, it's because she's kind of fat. But I don't care, she's a nice person." I was really proud of that.

Professionally, when I am doing counseling with young women who are disabled and thinking of getting married, they ask questions such as: Could I be a mother? Would I be able to take care of children? I try to share some of these things that I have gone through in raising my children to let them know that, yes, they do have options; they're capable. If they are severely physically limited, they can use adaptive homemaking techniques. I think all those things are really important for a counselor to relate.

Several months ago, one young woman who was pregnant came to talk with me. She was also single and was being pressured into having an abortion, not because she was single, but because of her disability. So, we discussed her options and her choices. I don't know the decision that she made, but I believe that it will have been based on her capabilities and what *she* really wanted rather than on what other people thought she should do.

An incident that I had with my youngest son tells a little bit about some of the stereotypes we have. He had been surfing one summer and had an accident. He hurt his knee and had to temporarily use a brace and crutches. When we left the hospital and were driving down the street, he said, "Oh, no! Mom, we better not go anywhere together; people are going to believe the myth is true." I said, "What's that?" He said, "That disabled parents have disabled kids."

♀ ABOUT THE AUTHOR ♀

Loretta J. Ferris was trained at the Sex and Disability Unit of the Human Sexuality Program, Department of Psychiatry, University of California, San Francisco. She is currently a member of Women in Transition, Inc., Santa Cruz, California, a private, nonprofit counseling group. Her particular interest is helping disabled women build self-esteem, develop a positive self-image, and deal constructively with attitudinal barriers they often face in relation to sexuality, marriage, divorce, parenting, employment, and education. She is the mother of two teenage sons.

12 Being a disabled father

George W. Hohmann

I will discuss some issues in regard to parenting from the perspective of having been married for 32 years, having been a disabled parent for 26 years, and, as a psychologist, having investigated some questions about the effects of parental disability on child development.

After my wife and I were sure that our marriage had stabilized and that it seemed to be a good continuing relationship, we began to consider the possibility of becoming parents. Since I had been a paraplegic for a number of years, the question of my fertility immediately arose. Tests indicated that I had a few motile sperm, about 4 million per milliliter in contrast to the 20 million often cited as the minimum necessary for conception. Nonetheless, we went through a period of attempting to induce pregnancy with specimens from me used for insemination. After several months without success in producing pregnancy, we decided to try adoption. We decided against accepting donor sperm. After calling and visiting several adoption agencies, we collected several rationales for being rejected as adoptive parents: I could not be a satisfactory father because I could not play ball with the child; a male child could not adequately identify with me as a father because, since I was disabled, I would play a passive role and therefore cause the child to have an inadequate sex role identity; the child would probably grow up to be hypochondriacal by identifying with a sick (disabled) father. Some of these opinions were to be found in the professional literature in the early 1950s and maintained that children with a disabled parent would probably become neurotic. It was also thought that any child who grew up with a disabled parent would be neglected because the able-bodied parent's attentions would all be focused on the disabled partner. Lack of financial security would likely have been raised as a further objection had I not been injured in military service and in receipt of substantial compensation from the Veterans Administration (VA).

At any rate, after several years we prevailed through these objections, arguments, and resistances and our son John was placed with us. Our postplacement follow-up studies, probationary period, and final legal adoption proceeded uneventfully. About 2 years later it was much easier to adopt our daughter Ann. It was then the policy of the agency who handled our adoptions, Children's Home Society of California, that if the first adoption went well, request for a second child was usually approved. Subsequently, that agency placed children with a number of other paraplegics and quadriplegics. Our children have turned out well, and our family has not encountered any serious problems related to the effects of my disability on my parenting ability.

Several years later I made a career change away from working with physically disabled people and worked in a psychiatric setting for about 10 years. In 1968 I became reinvolved with rehabilitation programs for the spinal cord injured. In this capacity I talked to many Vietnam veterans and other spinal cord–injured men all over the country who wanted to establish families and have children. Although it had been nearly a generation since we started our family and many young adults had been successfully raised by disabled parents, these people were given the same reasons for not allowing disabled people to adopt children that we had heard in the late 1940s and early 1950s. In the late 1960s and early 1970s things were just as bad as ever, and little seems to have been learned from the experiences of our group. Children's Home Society, I understand, had stopped placing children with anyone with a disability after having made, to my knowledge, at least 8 or 10 successful placements in the early to middle 1950s.

After discussing this problem in a seminar at the University of Arizona, one of my students, Frances M. Buck, wanted to find out how those young adults who had been raised by disabled fathers had turned out. We knew that finding these people would be difficult but felt that through the VA system we could locate young adults who had been raised by at least one disabled parent and thus complete an outcome study on the effects on children of being raised by a paraplegic or quadriplegic father. A review of the literature, except for one study of the effects of multiple sclerosis in parents on children's body image which used drawings of the human figure as a methodology, revealed articles based on opinion rather than data. They uniformly concluded, with one or two exceptions, that it is a terrible thing for a child to have a disabled parent. Even in *Not Made of Stone*,[1] an excellent book on sexuality and disability, a hierarchy of deleterious effects of parental disability on child development is established ranging from least problematic (disabled father) to most (both parents disabled). They discuss whether prophylactic sterilization should be done to disabled people who get married or develop a sexual relationship.

The lack of scientific basis for such speculations spurred us on. We were able to locate through the VA system 45 young adults between the ages of 18 and 30 who had been raised from before the age of 2 through the age of 15 in an intact family with either a paraplegic or quadriplegic father; we termed this our disabled parent (DP) group. A comparison group of young adults with nondisabled fathers was matched with the DP group for economic status, educational level of the father, age of the father, and area of residence. From each person in each group, we obtained measures of personality *(MMPI, 16 PF)*, sexual identity *(Bem Sex Role Inventory)*, personal values *(Rokeach Value Survey)*, parent-child relations *(Siegelman-Roe PCR II)*, body image *(Body Cathexis Scale)*, and a questionnaire *(Buck-Hohmann)* developed on the basis of interviews with children of disabled parents exploring such factors as health patterns, athletic interests, interpersonal relations, social skills, friendship and dating patterns, and relationships between subjects and friends and parents.

A detailed report of the results of the analysis of the massive data base generated by this study can be found elsewhere.[2] In summary, it may be said that there were few significant differences between the two groups, and little or no support for the presumed deleterious effects of parental disability on children. Indeed, of those differences which did emerge, most suggested superior parenting skills, better parent-child relations, and greater family solidarity in the DP group.

We also examined the data of the DP group on three disability-related characteristics: severity of disability (quadriplegic versus paraplegic fathers), father's employment status (employed versus unemployed), and family economic security (service-connected versus non–service connected). These comparisons showed that only economic security produced a few significant differences in the child development variables measured, and I suspect that is probably true of all families. We concluded that, at least for the group studied, the children of disabled fathers were healthy, well-adjusted young adults and that there was little or no support for the speculations about the negative effects of parental disability on children, nor justification for courts or adoption agencies to deny the parental role to disabled people.

REFERENCES

1. Heslinga, K., Schellen, A.M., and Verkuyl, A.: Not made of stone, Springfield, Ill., 1974, Charles C Thomas, Publisher.
2. Hohmann, G.W., and Buck, F.M.: Influence of parental disability characteristics on children's personality and behavior. Presented at the Eighty-seventh Annual Meeting of the American Psychological Association, New York, Sept., 1979. Available from the first author c/o Department of Psychology, University of Arizona, Tucson, Ariz. 85721.

♂ ABOUT THE AUTHOR ♂

George W. Hohmann, Ph.D., is professor of psychology and adjunct professor of psychiatry (psychology) at the University of Arizona and was formerly chief of the psychology service at the Tucson Veterans Administration Medical Center and a national consultant to the VA's Spinal Cord Injury Services. He received the Ph.D. in psychology from the University of California, Los Angeles, in 1955 and has written and lectured extensively in the areas of rehabilitation and medical psychology. Dr. Hohmann is a fellow of the American Psychological Association and past president of the Arizona State Psychological Association (1969), which awarded him its first "Psychologist of the Year" award in 1975. He is a trustee of the Technology and Research Foundation of the Paralyzed Veterans of America and provides consultation and advisory services to several rehabilitation projects. Dr. Hohmann has had a spinal cord injury (paraplegia) for the past 36 years.

13 Being parents of children who are disabled

Barbara Capell and Joseph Capell

JOSEPH CAPELL

My wife Barbara and I have a disabled youngster who is a little over 4 years old. Since I am a specialist in children's rehabilitation (as a pediatrician and a physiatrist), I will address some issues in raising disabled children from the professional's point of view, and Barbara will present our own family's personal experience.

For the last 6 years, I have worked at the University of Minnesota and taught children's rehabilitation at the Medical School Hospital. Of all the things I learned, one really startled me: In the whole process of rehabilitation, including rehabilitation from traumatic injuries, but also for birth injuries, birth defects, and injuries in early childhood as well as adult life, there is an incredibly vast difference between people who became injured as youngsters and those who became disabled after early adolescence. There is a world of difference between people who were injured at age 6 versus 12.

One experience that really brought this point home to me occurred when I first started in rehabilitation and worked with a 30-year-old man who was raised on a farm. One of eight children, he was born with spina bifida, an incompleteness in his spinal cord, which resulted in paraplegia from the waist down. He used braces and canes to walk, lacked bowel and bladder control, and had little or no sensation in some parts of his legs. At the University of Minnesota, we were all taught to discuss sexuality with patients and to provide sexual information and counseling when appropriate. In fact, some of the patients felt, "If one more person asks me if I masturbate or not, I'm going to scream." All the rehabilitation physicians, orderlies, nurses, speech pathologists, and social workers were trained in human sexuality. I got a pretty thorough sexual history from this young man while he was in the hospital because of a bladder problem. I found that the knowledge he had about his own sexuality and his own sexual experiences was extremely limited. He knew very little about what really happens in sex. He hardly knew anything about where babies came from. He had only vague ideas about why boys and girls and men and women dated, or what people like to do in the way of kissing, petting, or other sexual activities. Somewhat, he developed his own private mythology to explain how babies were born and why men and women marry. I wondered to myself, how could someone growing up on a farm *not* see the facts of life? With farm animals around, doing what farm animals do, and with brothers and sisters around, developing acne and breasts, dating and kissing, getting married and pregnant, and all those things that brothers and sisters do, how was it possible that at least some of the facts of life didn't sink in?

I talked more with him and then eventually with his parents; they indicated that when he was 1 or 2 years old they realized that he just wasn't going to be competitive sexually. They felt he wasn't going to date a cheerleader and wasn't going to be a king of the Mardi Gras or captain of the football team. So rather than have him hurt because he would be excluded from those things, I think they made the decision, "Let's not enter him in the contest in the first place. Let's save him from being hurt by not letting him know about sex." Well, that plan didn't work because he was a sexual person anyway. The really amazing fact to me was the collusion—and I don't mean that in a bad way—of the rest of the family. The parents must have made this decision, and somehow the brothers and sisters were involved—they didn't supply sexual information either. How the farm animals were involved in the conspiracy, I don't know. Possibly, too, he may have absorbed some of the collusion and concluded that sexuality was something he could never be part of, *shouldn't* know about, observe, or understand. Somehow, sexual information from brothers, sisters, and the other kids at school, and from books, magazines, and newspapers, is often not part of the experience of the disabled child.

We don't really know for sure how a person becomes whole, competitive, adequate, and able to receive and give love, pleasure, and intimacy as an adult. If we did, it would make everything so much simpler. It does seem reasonable to assume that probably normalizing the experiences of the disabled child as much as possible is going to go a long way in that direction.

The effects of overprotection are strong. They are basic and almost at a reflex level. It is often hard for parents to allow their disabled children to take natural risks. We often hear arguments such as the following:

"Let him climb to the top of the ladder, even if it's only hand-over-hand."
"Well, but he might fall!"
"Yes, anybody might fall."

Or, "*Let* him play with the kids on the block."
"Well, he might get pushed over."
"Yeah, he might, anyone might."
"He might get a broken finger, he might trip . . ."

All of those adventures of childhood—the fracases, the scrapes, the bloody nose, and all that—I think are the right of every child, and the disabled child shouldn't necessarily be excluded from them. This overprotection, I am sure, is a decision made in love. It's built in, not only in parents, but in society, families, and everyone.

It has perpetrated another problem. We health professionals have a basic difficulty with this "normalizing" process in that we never see the results of what we have done. Pediatricians don't take care of 50-year-old people with spina bifida; they don't have the faintest idea what happens beyond 18 years of age. They don't see cerebral palsied adults unless they watch telethons. They never see kids who were born with phocomelias—limb discrepancies and limb anomalies. Also, pediatricians are often absolutely delighted if a child *doesn't* have a sexual problem, which to a pediatrician may mean something like "excessive masturbation." They will deal with sexuality only if it is presented as a problem that they can solve. There are fortunately exceptions to this. There are pediatricians who seem to have a nurturing, commonsense attitude that encourages exploration and development in the able-bodied as well as the disabled child.

I have done many consultations for youngsters with disabilities for private physicians, and I have never had one say, "You know, the problem with this youngster and his family is that he never asks anything about sex." That has never been a concern. In fact, this "ask nothing" situation is *not* a concern, it is seen as an absolute delight. It is not thought of as a problem to deal with.

In looking to the future, it may be useful to realize that it has only been in the last 4 to 6 years that pediatricians have become interested in "adult" problems such as obesity, arteriosclerosis, and heart disease. They don't see those problems in their own practice, although pediatricians know an awful lot about nutrition in infancy and childhood. Research from The National Institutes of Health and other organizations has shown us that we have to pay more attention to these problems, which we now know begin in infancy and early childhood. We know that they are tremendously affected by nutrition, weight, and exercise during the first few years of life. Pediatricians are becoming involved in these issues, and I hope the same thing will happen with sexuality.

The sexuality of adults has finally gotten official sanction. Clients have been saying they are entitled to information about this important part of their lives. I think we will be successful, though, when we see that professional organizations providing services for children, such as the American Academy of Pediatrics and the American Academy of Cerebral Palsy and Developmental Medicine become more active in their support of sexual health care issues.

BARBARA CAPELL

I was a professional in the field of handicapped children before I had children, so I *knew* how to raise them. I had read a lot and was going to be one of those really wonderful parents. Before our son Romeo, who had an observable, physical disability, joined our family, I instructed parents on how to raise handicapped children. I sometimes feel I would like to take back those pearls of wisdom I gave as a counselor and apologize. There is a lot Romeo has taught me about children in general and about those with a disability in particular.

I would like to discuss personal feelings. Rather than engaging in a professionally oriented treatise, I'm going to try to describe how it feels to be a parent and to have a child with a disability.

We have 4 children, having adopted our first who is now 8 years old; she came to us at 6 months of age. She has, it turns out, a mild learning disability. She is able to learn in a regular school class but requires additional tutoring. The second child, a son, was born to us 15 months later. The adage that you adopt and then get pregnant was certainly true in our case. It has been difficult for me to accept that our son is going to be in special education classes. He has dyslexia and has a very difficult time learning to read, despite really putting in a lot of time and effort and being a bright child. Then our third child came along, and he is now 5 (we had 3 kids in 2½ years). He has a disability that we don't usually categorize as such: he is a mentally gifted child. He is in kindergarten and reads at the 5th-grade level, takes Spanish, knows sign language, plays the violin, and drives everybody just a little bit crazy. Our fourth child was also adopted and was from South America. He has a physical disability called arthrogryposis that affects the lower extermities. He is like a paraplegic but has total sensation and can walk with crutches.

One of the questions we have been asked is, "Why would you want to adopt a child with a disability when you have three beautiful, healthy, *normal* children?" Our reply is that we didn't adopt a child with a disability; we adopted a child who also happened to have a disability. Other people were looking at him from the waist down, while we were looking at the whole child. Two of the most beautiful things about this child that we recognized when we first met were his eyes and his ability to relate; he's a neat kid. We had always wanted four or five children, so with the last addition, we came to be a family. How we meld together and grow is a different topic.

A common experience of parents with disabled children is judgment by professionals. Someone once said at a conference that parents often don't know how to relate to "these" children, and that even when professionals describe and prescribe what these parents should do, they don't do it. Let me try to describe why these "recommended ways" of raising a disabled child are not all that easy to do.

People involved with my physically handicapped child's life include his physical therapist, occupational therapist, speech therapist, pediatrician, pediatric physiatrist, teacher, grandmother, grandfather, social worker, and orthopedist. They *all* tell me what I *must* do for this child—10 people. Now it would be really nice if these 10 people all gave me the same information, but you know what? To the orthopedist, the most important thing is that Romeo get the surgery done tomorrow. To the physical therapist, the most important thing is for me to spend 20 minutes twice a day doing his stretching. To the social worker, the most important thing is that I socialize him. To his grandparents, the most important thing is that I love him, give him a little more attention, and spend some more time with him. The pediatrician wants me to feed him correctly (he also happens to be allergic to some foods), and the teacher wants me to teach him. My whole day would be taken up with things I *should* do.

But I'm sorry, I can't do that. Not only can't I personally do that, but I have other children who have needs. As a parent, I have to set priorities. I do the 20-minute stretch once a day. As a matter of fact, I talked to the orthopedist, who said, "Maybe we could get a brace that would do the same thing." Fine; I put the brace on at night. I feed him three meals a day, with two snacks, the same food as and at the same time as everybody else in our family. I try to treat him as well as I do the other children, read him as many stories at night, and love him as much as I do the other kids. We try to fit in all the "prescriptions."

I think parents are judged not only by professionals, but also by society. Somehow, if you have a visibly handicapped person in your family, when you walk down the street you become public property. People may have donated to a telethon and may also feel that they have a right to tell you what you should do. As an example, try to visualize how we walk down the street. One child is holding on to my leg, one child is holding my arm, one usually runs somewhere up ahead, and the one on crutches is behind me saying, "I don't walk, I can't walk." That is how we look when we are going down the street to the mailbox. I have been told that it is important that the littlest learn to walk and that, whatever I do, "Let him walk; don't pick him up; he has to learn to be independent." However, at the mailbox, a kind, loving neighbor will come up and say, "Let me carry him for you. You are walking too fast." How could anybody walk too fast in a procession like this?

When the 2-year-old throws a tantrum, we let him throw it. When I have gone somewhere out of sight, he will come running around that corner, faster than anything, hunting for his mother. But when the child is disabled, somebody will come along and say, "Oh, did she leave you? Did she walk faster than you? Oh, you poor thing," and bring him to me. It hurts sometimes to be judged as not loving him, not meeting his needs, or not caring for him. Sometimes love makes it hard to stick to your decisions for your children to be independent, to walk away, to not turn back when they are crying, and to wait for them to discover the joy of being independent. Sometimes that doesn't happen overnight. There is a fine line to be observed in deciding when to walk away and when to go back. Society acts as if decisions should be totally different for the child with a handicap.

Another thing that we often hear is, "The child needs more attention." If you ask any of my kids, they will tell you that they are the one who needs more attention. My oldest child needs more attention because being the oldest is a real rough spot; my middle child needs more attention because he *can't* read; my kindergartener needs more attention because he *can* read, and he needs to be taken to violin lessons, etc. Their father, my husband, needs more attention.

Somehow, as a parent, I have to decide how to meet everybody's needs. I remember one day that I came home and cried. I put my head under a blanket and said, "I quit." Joe said something like, "Well, you can't quit; you can maybe take a vacation for a day, but you can't quit." It was nice for me to say it though.

Once our boy with arthrogryposis acted as if he were in great pain every time he walked, so I cancelled a speech I was to give to rush him over to the orthopedist who said, "Nothing is wrong. If he wants to be carried, carry him." Well, 2 days later we went to a television station where Joe was going to talk about cerebral palsy. Our boy was with us and saw a camera; we had never allowed him to be filmed, that is one of our rules. But he saw the camera, and being such a ham, he was up and about quite nicely with no expression of pain. Joe said, "Just buy a camera and carry it down the street, he will walk fine for the rest of his life."

The same day that I got the information from the orthopedist to carry him, I had school conferences. My daughter's teacher said, "Mrs. Capell, she needs you to spend more time doing arithmetic and reading with her. She is going to need special attention, and we want to keep her back a year." "Well, that is fine, teacher," I replied, "but we have another child right behind her. You have only one class, so we will have to find another school for her if you keep her back. She is the oldest kid in the class as it is. Let's discuss this a little further next week."

I then went to the meeting with our oldest son's teacher. She said, "Mrs. Capell, we feel that if you had spent more time playing Pla-Doh, developing your child's hand-eye coordination, he would be doing much better now." I *hate* Pla-Doh. You know what Pla-Doh is good for?—getting caught in a rug and hardening. Offer finger paints, I might do that; offer making bread, I might do that; but Pla-Doh does not belong in my house. So, I said, "Okay, I will think of some hand-eye coordination type activities for my child." Then I went to kindergarten. "Mrs. Capell, I understand you are a busy woman, but your child is going to need more of your time." Yes, he is in Spanish, I take him to violin lessons, and he knows sign language. "Well, Mrs. Capell, maybe we ought to put him ahead into the first grade." "No, teacher, I *have* a child in first grade; besides, he can't ride a tricycle in kindergarten, he's the youngest child in kindergarten. He needs to be with his peer group." "Well, Mrs. Capell, you had better figure out how you can spend more time with him." "Yes, I will." Now I have all these orders, and Joe says I can't quit.

So it's difficult. As I say, don't judge parents, don't put us in categories by thinking that we don't care, we don't know what we are doing, we are still in the "anger" or "denial" stage, or we all need counseling. I remember hearing that if parents have more than one child, they need counseling. Now, I don't happen to agree with that statement, but I suspect that all parents feel overwhelmed at some times, whether they have disabled or able-bodied children.

For a professional, knowing *how* to help is really important. Sit a minute, listen, and find something positive to say. There may be all kinds of bad things happening in that family, but the professional should find something positive and tell the parent that.

Finally, I am often asked how I want others to see my son. In this discussion I have been dwelling on how I don't want you to see him. When you see my son, you should see him as a person, one who may work alongside you some day. If you think of him working with you, you are going to treat him with respect and are going to expect him to do and to accomplish. Notice his lovability, and see him as somebody who might marry your daughter. (Disabled children are often taught only how to receive love, not how to be responsible givers.) If he is going to marry your daughter, you are going to want him to be able to love her the way you love her, the way you care about her. So, if you think about my son marrying your daughter, you will want him to be as capable as can be.

♀ ABOUT THE AUTHORS ♂

Barbara Capell has been a private lecturer and consultant in disability and sexuality for the past 6 years. She was trained at the University of Minnesota's Program in Human Sexuality with particular emphasis on "sexual attitude reassessment" workshops. She is the mother of four children, one of whom has a physical disability. She is a student in psychology and a member of the board of directors for Central California United Cerebral Palsy.

Joseph Capell, M.D., is a specialist in children's rehabilitation at the Leon S. Peters Rehabilitation Center, Fresno, California. He was coordinator for the Sexuality and Disability Advisory Committee of the University of Minnesota School of Medicine, and past chairman of the Sexuality and Disability Task Force of the American Congress of Rehabilitation Medicine.

UNIT THREE

WOMEN'S ISSUES

14 Body image and the woman with a disability

Jane Elder Bogle and Susan L. Shaul

In the process of gathering information on family planning and disability, we interviewed a woman who was of small stature (defined as anyone under 4 feet 11 inches) who had a severe scoliosis. She presented her concern to us in this way:

This guy I'm involved with now realized just a week ago that we'd been having some really neat experiences together and that it was time to discuss our future. He told me that he'd met a new girl. He said, "You realize, there could never be anything between us, except that we could go on being good friends."

I listened, but it just didn't sound right to me. What I thought he was saying was that we could never have any physical intimacy and that I certainly must understand that, that it just wouldn't work out because he was such a great big guy and I was such a very small woman. But then I realized that wasn't what he was saying.

I'm having a hard time now even considering him as a friend. I just hurt so bad, because after awhile, I thought, "How in the hell can you think about me as a person and yet ignore the fact that I'm a woman and I'm not just a sexless thing?" I really am a woman and I'm proud of that, and I think that being a woman is an important part of my whole personality. How can anyone separate it?

I'm just trying to get it straight in my head right now. I'm even thinking about getting into counseling about that. It just really threw me. I wonder if that is the kind of thing I'm going to keep running into? I've actually had people say to me that I should at least try to accept the fact that maybe I will be single all of my life. I want to be considered a whole person. It used to be enough for me to say, when I was getting to know a guy, "Gee, I hope you think I'm really nice and sweet and good." Now I want to be sure that he knows I'm a woman, I'm a good woman, a nice woman, and a sexy woman, and I'm not just a person.

Suddenly, it's not enough to be just a person. Disabled women have special sexual concerns that are distinct from the sexual concerns of disabled men. These concerns have been too long neglected and denied by the professional community. It is true that the majority of spinal cord–injured persons are men. But it is also true that the percentage of spinal cord–injured people who are woman is increasing and that significantly more women have diseases such as multiple sclerosis and rheumatoid arthritis.

A positive body image is critical to the sexual well-being of women with disabilities. In the work that we've done with disabled women, body image has been the hub around which sexuality revolves. Being comfortable with and learning to live with one's own body prepares the way for sexual acceptance and growth.

We will first present some basic issues in regard to body image and then address what the health professional can do. These suggestions are not all-inclusive and are not for everybody and every situation but might be helpful in some particular instances.

ISSUES IN BODY IMAGE

Body image includes how our bodies look and how our bodies function. Disability has a tremendous impact on both function and appearance. As disabled people, we live in bodies that don't always function correctly, whose appearance is usually not "normal." Our society still tends to judge female worth in terms of physical appearance and in terms of sexual marketability.

For disabled women, the body image dilemma is etched in even bolder relief than for the able-bodied. The media sex symbol of the day is an impossible standard for any woman to live up to, but disability places you at an even greater disadvantage. If you spend most of your time in a wheelchair, and if you wear braces, and if you have a scoliosis, no matter what you do, you're not going to look like Cheryl Tiegs or Marilyn Monroe.

There's a very common idea that disability precludes beauty and that disability eradicates sexual attractiveness. Several women talked with us about reactions they got from others following their disability. It was not uncommon to hear comments like this one: "What a pity it happened to you. You were so pretty before your accident." This is outrageous and illogical, to say nothing of being destructive to one's sense of self-esteem and sexual desirability.

There are four major issues that contribute to our sense of negative body image or our feelings of not liking our bodies as disabled women. The first is that we get many reactions from the world that our bodies are negative and that our bodies are unacceptable. One of the hardest things about being disabled is getting that kind of negative attention, and we're always getting it as disabled people, particularly as disabled women. There's no positive value, in the outside world, on having a disabled body, no matter how well it's functioning, or how unique or how beautiful it might be. It's very easy to consider one's body as the enemy when you're getting all negative input from the outside world. Your body can be the source of a lot of pain, embarrassment, trouble, guilt, expense, and, for some people, isolation with long periods of hospitalization and separation from the people that they love.

Lack of control is another major concern for us as adults because it is sometimes difficult to incorporate bowel and bladder incontinence, physical dependency, and involuntary movement into our concept of adulthood. We usually think about those things as being infantile kinds of behavior. One of the results of considering your body to be the enemy is a sort of disassociation. This disassociation manifests itself in a feeling of not owning one's body because it is causing so much trouble. It may happen that someone else is spending a lot of time taking care of it, so it is really easy to just hand it over to that other person. Consequently, we see a mind-body split, which has a lot of implications when we're thinking about sexuality.

For people who have grown up with disabilities, "the body is the enemy" becomes even more complicated because of some of the parental dynamics. We are aware of how much trouble our body has caused our parents. There is a great deal to be said about those implications, particularly as we grow up and go through adolescence. We talked with one disabled woman who said that her parents would never display pictures of her that showed her disability. We also talked with another woman who said her mother went to incredible expense, time, and trouble to find clothes that would hide the fact that she had a disabled body.

There is also the issue of appliances. Most of us need to rely on some hardware to get around, such as braces, crutches, wheelchairs, and catheters. They can be very difficult to incorporate into our concept of being sexually desirable people. Generally, they are metal; they're hard, cold, angular, and usually ugly. It's difficult to integrate that into the sense of being warm, squeezable, and lovable. The whole idea of learning how to accept, appreciate, and develop affection for one's appliances is a major challenge for us as disabled people and particularly as disabled women.

Partner reaction is another whole issue. We all fear that our bodies will become the reason for sexual and/or social rejection. This fear can be the reason that we as disabled women may choose to isolate ourselves and not take the risks necessary to develop intimate relationships.

THE ROLE OF THE HEALTH PROFESSIONAL

It is essential to encourage the individual woman to develop an attitude about her body that is realistic to her experience. This means that it is inappropriate to launch immediately into, "Let's all learn to love our bodies," avoiding her realistic feelings about her body. Body image and acceptance of one's body change over time. Thus it is possible that a person can go through one phase of body acceptance, or learning to live in conjunction with the body, and then 10 years later have the issues come up again. I think it is possible to prepare people for that and say, "Sure, this is an issue that you might deal with for many years to come, but that does not negate the work that you have done already."

It is important to develop an internally based body image or sense of body, rather than something that is determined by the way society reacts. Specific counseling techniques that have been of help with some women include strategies that work on helping a woman reclaim parts of her body that she may have become disassociated from. For example, if a woman does not have sensation or motor control in her legs, she may prefer that they not be a part of her anymore. If the health professional is in a counseling relationship with the woman, she or he might suggest a homework assignment such as, "Go home and simply notice your right leg this week. Notice the color of it and the temperature and the texture of it. Come back and we'll talk about that." Then move slowly through the parts of her body so that she can start to say, "Yes, it's all me and it belongs to me now and not to the people who put me back together after the accident."

One of the things that was very striking to us in our interviews was the wide range of women's feelings about their bodies. Some had developed special competencies, for example, weight lifting or wheelchair racing. They felt these activities improved their appearance and mobility as well. Other women, who perhaps use crutches to ambulate, noticed that just by walking, their chest muscles had become very well developed, which then became useful for singing and voice projection. These activities changed their original feeling of "my body's always in the way" to "I can use it to my own advantage." Developing realistic body competencies and control is important in developing a good body image.

It may also be relevant to do some assertiveness training with disabled women to avoid discounting the positive messages that they do get from others. Almost all of us have trouble with accepting compliments, but especially so when we feel that the barriers in life are insurmountable, when we aren't feeling good about ourselves. If someone does say, "Gee, you look great today," it's hard to even hear that message. This can be especially true for persons with disabilities. As helping professionals, listening and assertiveness skill development are areas where we can really help our clients.

In a medical setting the women that we talked to found it tremendously valuable to have professionals say, "This part of your body is in great shape. I just did a pelvic exam; your vagina, uterus, vulva, the whole area is looking just fine." Women found a great deal of comfort in hearing positive comments like that. Once again, it is getting rid of the "body as enemy" stigma. It is a positive affirmation of "my body is still me, it's part of myself."

Incorporation of dreams and fantasies is an important process to encourage in disabled women. They can begin to feel that "Even if I don't choose to be sexual, even if I'm not in a relationship with anyone right now, I know that I'm sexual because I'm still thinking and dreaming about sex; I'm still fantasizing about sex, and it is an undeniable part of me." Professionals can help with this self-acceptance process. We have found that many women had very sensuous dreams and reported an orgasmic experience in their dreams, even when they were not experiencing it in the rest of their lives. Confirmation that this is part of being a sexual person can be reassuring.

One last way of helping is behavior rehearsal. For clients who are concerned about how a new partner is going to respond to her catheter or respond to other parts of her body, it is often appropriate to do a behavior rehearsal with them. The counselor can help by saying, "Let's pretend that I'm a new partner. I'm somebody you've been going with for awhile, and we are on our way to the bedroom. How are you going to explain your catheter to me? And what are you afraid of? What's the worst thing that he or she can say to you?" Have the woman talk in a safe setting about what she fears hearing to determine how she feels and how she can prepare herself for it.

Many disabled people who enter into new sexual relationships develop brief descriptions to explain bodily functions or limitation, for example, "This is what it means when I get a spasm during sex." Having this explanation prepared contributes to one's sense of control in a sexual relationship. It is probable that there may be some potential sexual partners who don't deal well with appliances or with bowel and bladder problems or who do have a somewhat negative reaction to the person's body. It may be appropriate to prepare a client for that. However, you can also tell the client, "Out of my experience, I can reassure you that many disabled people that I've talked to and worked with do have partners who learn to accept and appreciate their bodies. In fact, people can often accept disabilities with humor, dignity, and affection. That is something that you can look forward to experiencing." There needs to be a balance between gentle reassurance on the one hand and realism about individual differences and reactions on the other.

♀ ABOUT THE AUTHORS ♀

Jane Elder Bogle, M.P.A., is public health advisor at the U.S. Public Health Service, Department of Health and Human Services, Seattle, Washington, where her professional activities and interests focus on improving the delivery of health care services to rural areas. She has had training in and is concerned with reproductive health care for physically disabled women and with the sexual implications of family planning and body image. With Susan L. Shaul and others, she is co-author of *Toward Intimacy: Family Planning and Sexuality Concerns of Physically Disabled Women* and *Within Reach: Providing Family Planning Services to Physically Disabled Women.* Her degree in public administration is from the University of Washington. She herself has had a mobility impairment from birth.

Susan L. Shaul, Ph.D., completed her doctorate in educational psychology at the University of Washington with research interests in counseling, loneliness, and sexuality. She is currently the education and training coordinator for the Family Planning and Disability Project in Seattle, Washington, a national demonstration project on the delivery of family planning services to persons with disabilities. She is co-author of the two publications mentioned above, is an AASECT-certified sex educator, and does consultant work as a trainer and writer in Seattle and nationally.

15 Women's issues

A PANEL DISCUSSION

Jane Elder Bogle, Susan M. Daniels, Susan L. Shaul, Barbara F. Waxman, and Julie A. Wysocki

SUSAN L. SHAUL AND JANE ELDER BOGLE

This article will discuss some perspectives of our work on women's issues and disability, subjects which have not been adequately addressed in the past. Susan is a training coordinator with the Family Planning and Disability Project in Seattle, Washington, which is funded by the National Office of Family Planning. This project has a national focus, and we are glad to be able to spread the word about what we are doing. A few years ago, four of us published two booklets[2,4] on the sexuality of disabled women and how to make sexual health care services more accessible to them. As we did research for the booklets with the help and support of other disabled women, it became clear to us that there was a tremendous need for information about disability among family planning providers specifically, although all health care providers should be more aware of these issues. We have been fortunate to have received funding to study ways of making medical clinics accessible to people with disabilities.

We have also been working with rehabilitation agencies and sexuality programs to train health professionals to deal with sexuality and disability issues. We have funds available to help disabled women get to family planning clinics, as well as for interpreter services for the deaf. Currently we are preparing some public service announcements showing disabled women using family planning services. These will be made available for national distribution.

We have also completed a manual called *Family Planning Services Are For Disabled People Too.** In contrast to our earlier booklet, *Toward Intimacy,*[4] which focused on physical disability, the family planning manual addresses all of the major disability groups. We are also developing a national resource center, looking at what is available in the literature and other resources, such as films on sexuality,

*Available from the National Clearinghouse for Family Planning Information, P.O. Box 2225, Rockville, Md., 20852.

family planning, and disability, so as to better respond in an individualized way to requests from disability groups and sexuality and family planning agencies.

Another service is provided by a nurse practitioner on our staff who can go into people's homes and residential centers and give reproductive health care services such as pelvic examinations. We hope this will help disabled women who have had difficult or traumatic experiences in the past during these examinations.

A counseling experience

We often do short-term counseling, from one to three sessions, in an expanded sex education format. For example, a woman with arthritis called us. She was newly single, in the process of divorce. Her husband was the only man with whom she had ever been seriously involved. They were married for several years but had a rather unsatisfactory relationship, especially sexually.

Some of the most poignant and pressing issues in regard to disability are those which face single disabled women. We asked this woman to make a list of concerns that she had. She wondered what were reasonable goals for herself.

She had been seeing a counselor to deal with her feelings about the divorce, and told the counselor that she was interested in going back to school for a doctorate degree. The counselor told her, "You are just overcompensating for your disability by wanting to do that." He didn't acknowledge that this was his opinion and not necessarily the truth. She was left confused and discouraged.

She had sexual questions as well. "How do I meet people at a party and let them know that I am a sexual person and interested?" This woman's husband had taken a parting shot at her by telling her that she was a "lousy kisser." She had no way to put that into perspective, and this then became a very disturbing concern for her.

She also wanted to know, "How do I alert a new sexual partner that my body looks different under these clothes?" She had arthritis and had had a lot of joint replacements, so sometimes people didn't know that she was disabled when they first met her. She wanted to know if she should tell someone that she had scars on her legs, for instance, before undressing in front of them.

How could she alert a new partner to the limitations of her body? Should she say, before they ever get in the bedroom, "Well, actually I can't have intercourse in the way that you might be used to having intercourse. We are going to have to try some different things." Or should she wait and try to subtly slip that information into the experience once it starts?

She also discussed having had a couple of brief sexual encounters. We talked about getting used to being single and how one develops standards for what one wants as a single person. She decided it was legitimate to say to a partner, "I'd really like to be close to you tonight, but I don't feel like having intercourse." She asked if it hurt men *not* to ejaculate if excited and if she had any responsibility for providing a "release" for them.

She also wondered how she could communicate to a relatively new sexual partner that she liked oral sex. She had had a couple of experiences where that was something she did to her partner but didn't know how to ask it for herself in return. One of the complications of this woman's disability was that she had some arthritis in her jaws. She was also concerned about how that would affect her sexual pleasure in giving oral sex to her partner.

Her most basic question was, "Will I be able to find any man who will be willing to commit his future to me, especially since my disability is progressive?" She also wanted to know about disabled men. It initially seemed incomprehensible to her that her disability along with a man's disability would be manageable. Yet she had seen couples where both partners were disabled. Was that something she could expect for herself too?

There are clearly no easy answers to questions like these. We try to listen actively, be supportive, and create an environment where the person can keep asking questions. We share any information that is relevant, but when we don't have the answers, we say so, and then we try to find resources for the person that may be more helpful.

JULIE A. WYSOCKI

My professional training has been in rehabilitation counseling, and I have worked with disabled clients in a rehabilitation setting. What I want to do is to discuss some of my personal experiences as a disabled woman. I would like to share with you a sort of potpourri of things that I have been thinking about.

First, let me tell you something about my disability. I am 39 and have been disabled since I was 11. I have a spinal cord injury from an automobile accident and have been married for 4 years.

One of the quotations that came out of the booklet to which Susan referred, *Toward Intimacy*, is my favorite, and we use it a lot. The quote is: "The main issue for disabled women is not sexual, it is social. It is establishing social and sexual eligibility within our societal system." I believe this is one of the main issues for me and most disabled women. There have been a lot of comments about the movie "Coming Home" and about John Voight. Many people feel that he was "a little too good to be true." These comments are made mainly by nondisabled people who have had very little exposure to disabled men. I know a lot of sexy disabled men. I don't think John Voight is an exception to the rule. But I think that in our society it is a lot easier for disabled men to project sexuality than it is for disabled women. It's more acceptable for them to be sexually aggressive, and I think it's the rule rather than the exception that many disabled men are fairly sexually aggressive. Women are supposed to be subtle, nonverbal, and just be there. When you have limitations in using body language or when you are surrounded by metal equipment or braces or other kinds of apparatus, being subtle and nonverbal is more difficult.

Women need to talk to each other about promoting sexual opportunities for themselves. Susan has talked about disabled women's limited access to information. This is certainly true in my own case and in the case of many women who have had congenital disabilities or who became disabled early in life. Twenty years ago there was virtually nothing in the literature on sexuality and disability. Ten years ago there was very little in the literature. The last 5 years have seen some good things emerge in the literature specifically for the disabled woman. But I remember as an adolescent pouring through anything I could, trying to find a piece of information that related to my disability and sexual functioning. I found nothing. What I did find related mainly to spinal cord–injured men. If there was a sentence or two about women, it said, "Yes, you can still have children," or, "Yes, you can still be the same passive partner that you were before you were disabled." That's not where my head was. I was interested in intimacy issues. I was interested in how to meet people. I was wondering if anyone would ever be able to accept my disability. I was wondering how I could get close to someone. Those are the kinds of things that I wanted to talk about. I would have been really grateful for *Toward Intimacy*,[4] *Sexual Options For Paraplegics and Quadriplegics*,[3] or *The Joy of Sex*.[1] But there wasn't anything.

However, there is only so much that can be accomplished through reading. One of the most helpful things I have observed is better communication now among disabled women. We are beginning to share with each other what our sexual fears are, what our hopes are, what our expectations are, and what specifically are our sexual experiences.

We can be very helpful to each other if we are more open and sharing. One thing I would have liked to talk to other women about, related to my disability, was that in our society sensation and movement are equated with sexual eligibility. If you can't move, and you can't feel most of your body, are you then sexual? Can you be sexual? I would have liked to have talked to someone about disabled versus nondisabled partners and about sexual positions, especially with a disabled partner. I was very concerned about the effect of sexual activity on body functions. I would have been very reassured if someone had said to me, "Yes, there are people in this world who can accept your disability with respect, with humor, and with dignity and really just matter-of-factly." That was something that took me a long time to learn. I would have been very grateful if another disabled woman would have told me that orgasm is not the only sexual goal. There can be a lot of joy, pleasure, and satisfaction in sex for disabled women.

For many disabled women, especially those with severe spasticity or limitations in range of motion, options for birth control may be limited. For spinal cord–injured women, the Pill is often contraindicated. But many women do use it because it allows for ease of use. We need some good research on birth control and ways in which disabled women can independently prevent pregnancy.

I think also that the option of sterilization needs to be looked at much more carefully for the disabled woman. This option should be more available for women who choose it. I know of disabled women who have had to search for a doctor who would perform a tubal ligation.

As a final note, my own personal opinion is that the best method of birth control for a disabled woman is the vasectomy of her partner. No offense to males intended! But this requires a willing partner and implies having only one steady partner. It also implies that you don't want children.

BARBARA F. WAXMAN

I work in the field of family planning and sexual health care. Traditionally, that field has focused on the needs of heterosexual women, while virtually ignoring the concerns of lesbians and women with disabilities.

A few years ago an article on gay and lesbian people with disabilities appeared in a local paper. In that article several disabled lesbians talked about how they were socialized and how they saw themselves, their relationship to the feminist community, and to the disabled community as well. One woman talked about going through rehabilitation with a number of other women, some of whom were lesbians. Each asked the staff about their sexual potentials. They were told, "You can do what you did before; just sort of lay back and let the man do it." Besides assuming these women were all interested in male partners, the staff also assumed that they wanted to be passive in a sexual encounter, and weren't interested in exploring more of what they could do on their own. No one acknowledged that women can like other women, want relationships with women, and love other women.

Relating to women sexually is an option for disabled women. An example of this is a woman in Los Angeles who has been a paraplegic for about 5 years and is bisexual. After she became injured, she needed to explore what was out there for her. She was paralyzed below her waist. Before her injury she always related to men, had many lovers, and was very sexually active. After her injury she felt cut off. What could she do? She started to relate to women, to develop support systems with women, and to be sexual with women. She began to feel secure in expressing her sexuality with a woman and developed the ability to learn about her body. Women often love each other with much more support than they receive from men. Lesbianism may be a viable option for some of us with disabilities. We can develop a support system with other women and explore ourselves in a less threatening way.

The next topic I feel is important to address is rape. We know that rape is not a sexual act, but an act of violence. The people who are violated are often people who are easily victimized. In some way they are vulnerable at the moment that they are attacked. As women with disabilities, our societal image transmits that we are vulnerable targets. There are very little data on the incidence of rape against the disabled in institutions, schools, or homes (where 50% of rapes occur in this country).

I have a colleague who has worked with two rapists, both of whom raped women with disabilities. One rapist she interviewed said, "I wanted to give her something that nobody else wanted to give her." He basically saw the woman he raped as asexual and thought he was doing her a favor.

It is important to discuss acquaintance rape—rape committed by someone around the block or next door, or by a teacher, a relative, or someone we know. At one school, a young woman of 14 who has a developmental disability was seduced by her teacher. He fondled her and had intercourse with her. Because she had had no sex education or values clarification, she didn't know that she didn't have to submit to this, and so she just went along with it. That is rape. That is coercion. As women, we are taught to be passive. But if you are disabled very early or when you are born, then the passivity is enculturated into what it means to be disabled and into the role of the disabled person. If you are disabled much later in life, you are not as subject to those pressures, and you have a different kind of resource to draw on.

There is a feeling among some disabled people that it is hard to say no to someone who wants to have sex with us because we may never get a chance again. My first sexual experience was coercion, but I figured nobody was ever going to want to do it with me again, so I'd better get it now. I feel now that that was rape. Rape is not always walking down the street, getting thrown in the bushes, and being threatened with a knife. Rape, 75% of the time, is premeditated by the rapist. This person is watching us, and we are very easily victimized.

If we, as disabled women, are easily victimized, we have to take a very hard look at the messages that we give out to other people. We have to feel more powerful and feel good about ourselves.

SUSAN M. DANIELS

I had polio when I was young; so I grew up disabled. In my professional development I have worked with a variety of people. I recently have done counseling with mainly disabled women and nondisabled women and their partners. I have a perspective on these two groups and some concerns about sisterhood and what it is like to be a woman.

Sexism is a double-edged sword for disabled women. On one hand it exempts you from many things that you may not want to be involved in. Sexism "protects" you from having to compete in a lot of ways that may be difficult for you. Sexism says that there are certain things that you cannot do and cannot be because you are a woman. Then disability comes along and says there are many other things that you cannot do and cannot be. This leaves you with a very limited range in which to work.

When we talk about disabled women in relation to things like rape and sexual options, we are talking about people who have limited freedoms to explore who they are and who they want to be. So when we talk about a disabled woman who might be living at home and is dependent on her family, we are talking about a woman who is not only sexually vulnerable, but economically vulnerable as well. She is vulnerable in a whole host of ways. The problems of women with disabilities are problems of life-style issues, not just problems of genital organs or of opportunities for education. I believe the section 504 regulations, which mandate access to education, employment, and public buildings, affect sexuality because if you can't get into places where you can work, meet people, and recreate, you don't meet sexual partners.

In contrast to the limits of sexism, we have the current emphasis on role expansion for women. Women now have the opportunity to be career women, to work, and also to run homes and to take care of children and to be loving, supportive wives. How do they manage all of this without being thoroughly exhausted? In other words, when we start knocking down sexism, we don't just change our roles, we add more roles to what we have. Now we not only have to be interested and delightful sexual partners but also wonderful, caring mothers and great homemakers and keep our houses spic-and-span, and be intelligent and vital on the job. That is just too many roles for most women, disabled or not. Many disabled women must use some of their energies for basic self-maintenance. Having to encounter the problems of architectural barriers or communication barriers is often too much. I would like to know who is going to call a halt to all these expectations.

For the most part, medical rehabilitation does not look on sexuality as an activity of daily living. I don't know why we are willing to spend thousands and thousands of dollars on weird gadgetry for wheelchairs and super electronics for communications when we are not willing to spend $2.50 on a vibrator for sexual activity. I don't know why vibrators have to be bought in dirty book stores and why they can't be bought through an orthopedic supply house. I'd like to know why we are not training people in the medical profession to look on sexual health care, sexuality, sexual functioning, and sexual hygiene as activities of daily living. I would like to see occupational therapists trained to teach options in sexual positioning, the kinds of joint energy-saving ways women and men can relate with each other and women can relate to their own bodies.

One of the best experiences I had was working with an occupational therapist building sexual devices. She wouldn't actually teach people how to use them; she left that to me. But she would build them, and she knew a lot about how to teach people to minimize their spasticity and what to do to make sex easier. We need to demand that our professionals pay attention to sexuality as an important rehabilitation issue.

Most disabled women know that there are men who have fetishes about them.

We may be victims of fetishists, and how we handle that and the shame and guilt associated with that is an important issue. It's often hidden and not talked about. Fetishists are called hobbyists, by the way. Fetishists of disabled women have underground newspapers; they photograph disabled women in public places; they may circulate names and phone numbers. It is important to learn to handle the suspicion that builds in you about nondisabled men. After a while you may get suspicious of a man who "comes on" to you. How do you sort out the fetishists from just regular men? Disabled women need to figure out what is the difference between a man who is *turned on* by disability and the man who will go along with disability.

The able-bodied person who has a relationship with someone disabled is often seen as being with a "devalued person," and is himself devalued by association. I have been going out with a certain man for 3 years. There were times at first when I wondered if he was a hobbyist. "What is wrong with him that he would want to be close to me? Why would he choose a disabled woman?" I think he finds my disability as annoying as I do. He likes me enough to put up with that; so for the goodies, he has to put up with the limping, the slowness, and that kind of stuff.

Another little-discussed topic is disabled women and casual sex. We all talk about how wonderful it is to have a loving partner who gets to know you, one with whom you can relate, who understands you, and who can modify his usual techniques to go along with yours. All the books seem to promote these wonderful, knowing, gentle souls out there. But many women want to have options for casual sex. What are the options for casual sex, and how do we handle the barriers that come between that freedom and a disability?

SUSAN L. SHAUL

Many disabled women experience a scarcity of available men. That shapes an incredible amount of behavior. If I think that there are only one or two men out there for me, that means that I have to do everything I can to hold on to a person. I've got to bend myself out of shape to try to become what I think that person's expectations are. If I am constantly on the lookout for an available man, I will be constantly disappointed when a man I meet is not one of them. This is a real position of weakness.

BARBARA F. WAXMAN

The myth that I was socialized with all of my life is "You are going to meet a very special, nice . . . boy." If someone is interested in me, he *must* be special. I must mold into his image. By accepting these notions, I may lose a really integral part of myself. Sometimes I wonder if I am being unrealistic. Maybe I should settle for something a little less. This guy is a nice man, and he is interested in me.

Maybe he and I don't have that many interests in common, and maybe we don't think in a lot of the same ways. But he is here, and God knows, that is what I have been waiting for—somebody to be warm and comforting, and if no one is going to be there or nobody meets my standards, maybe I should settle for this.

SUSAN M. DANIELS

Many middle-aged women who find themselves single face the same thing, because they know men die earlier than they do. Women live longer, and this lack of potential partners is not just a problem for disabled women. It's a problem that many women in the midyears find. I know that my mother was completely astounded about 4 years ago when I had been living with a man for 2 years and left him and went on to North Carolina. She was completely astounded that I would pack up and leave a man. For awhile I was totally miserable, but it was the best thing that I did for myself. I am so much better off now, but it's a surprising notion that you would let a man go if you are disabled.

One of the things that we have to remember when we talk about disability is that it's not a unitary experience. It's not like being a man or a woman, one or the other. Being disabled ranges from having a little limp and inconvenience to being severely handicapped and in a nursing home with no options and no freedoms. There is a wide range of difference. Recently I was going through a hotel lobby on the way to the bar to meet some friends to have a drink. I passed a man sitting in an electric wheelchair who had severe cerebral palsy. I got in the bar, and I said to my friends, "Lord, help me! Why do I always have to pass the one guy sitting alone in the lobby of the hotel who has cerebral palsy? Why do I always have to see that? Why can't I just *not* notice it?" It's bothered me—the loneliness that people have when they can't communicate with other people, when they look different, when they look ugly in other people's value judgments. That loneliness is a killer. It is what was going to kill that man eventually. Loneliness is going to be the killer of severely disabled people, men and women, who are out there alone. They have no options. The life-style issue is really important—we are not a unitary group of people. We vary in our education, in our financial freedoms, and in our ability to move about. There are some women out there who have had little experience in the world. They are like the man in the movie "Being There." They are out there with the notions that men and women are like soap opera characters. When you start talking to them and start listening to what they say, they aren't talking from an experiential basis, but from some kind of fantasy level. Then they find out that real men are not like television people, and that people just don't flow into sex. People have conflicts about sex. They become confused, get depressed, and withdraw. So there is a real difference between people who have had no experience in the world and no or few options and those who have had options and all of a sudden have them limited.

I had been going out with a nondisabled man for 3 years and only recently got involved, for the first time, with a person who has a disability. I have learned some things I didn't think I even needed to learn. There were some things I thought I knew already, that I absolutely did not know. One of them was how nice it is to be with someone who understands, nonverbally, the disability experience. The man I have been dating for 3 years understands it verbally. He understands me at that level, and the context of the relationship is very different. But one of the things I found out is how easy it is to communicate with a disabled person who takes things for granted and also how much fun it is for me to be able to give in a different way than I have been allowed to give before. My disabled friend, by the way, wears braces so he can't jump up and go get something like a glass of water, so I do the jumping up. I'm a very good jumper-upper, so I jump up and get things. I've never done that before because previously my nondisabled partners would do that for me. I have learned so much in just these last 3 months. I can't even begin to express what an important experience it was for me to know that it is no hassle to give like that. It is no trouble. I always thought my able-bodied partner was making a special effort because he was nondisabled and I was disabled. Then I found out it's no trouble, and I would have never known that had I not been on the other side.

JULIE A. WYSOCKI

I live in a very cooperative family. My husband has two children from a former marriage, both of whom have the same disability that he does; so there are four of us. The day I became a wife, I became a mother. I had been single all of my life, footloose and really fancy-free. The logistics of trying to work out a career, a marriage, and child rearing when you have never done that combination before are just one hell of a job. The organization that is necessary just to fit everything into one day is very complex, and so there is some guilt associated with that. I am working full-time now, whereas I was working part-time when we first got married. I get up and make breakfast, or our 16-year-old son does. Since he took home economics, he discovered that he could make eggs. The division of labor is just a lot different than I was raised to believe as a 1950s girl: you grew up, got married, and your husband took care of you. I don't live in that scene at all. That is an adjustment, but it is a choice I have made.

REFERENCES

1. Comfort, A.: The joy of sex, New York, 1971, Fireside, Simon & Schuster.
2. Hale-Harbough, J., Norman, A., Bogle, J., and Shaul, S.: Within reach: providing family planning services to physically disabled women, New York, 1978, Human Sciences Press.
3. Mooney, T., Cole, T., and Chilgren, R.: Sexual options for paraplegics and quadriplegics, Boston, 1975, Little, Brown & Co.
4. Shaul, S., Bogle, J., Hale-Harbough, J., and Norman, A.: Toward intimacy: family planning and sexuality concerns of physically disabled women, New York, 1978, Human Sciences Press.

♀ ABOUT THE AUTHORS ♀

Barbara F. Waxman is an AASECT-certified sex educator. She is presently coordinator of education to the disabled community at Planned Parenthood/Los Angeles, working to access and make available family planning and sexual health care services to men and women with disabilities. She is also chairperson of the Committee on the Sexual Rights of Persons With Disabilities for the California Association of the Physically Handicapped. Ms. Waxman has had arthrogryposis, a mild mobility impairment, since birth.

Julie A. Wysocki, M.Ed., is a certified rehabilitation counselor, has worked with clients in a rehabilitation setting, and more recently, has coordinated a training project in rehabilitation social work. She is currently working in a consultant capacity for the Family Planning and Disability Project, a national demonstration project involved in the improvement of family planning services to disabled persons. Ms. Wysocki is herself paraplegic as a result of an automobile accident when she was a child.

SEXUALITY AND ATTENDANT CARE

16 Sexuality and attendant care

A PANEL DISCUSSION

Pamela Finkel, Melanee Fishwick, Kathryn L. Nessel, and Debra Soliz

MELANEE FISHWICK

When I first got out of the hospital, I moved back in with my parents. They were not going to assume the role of personal caretaker for me all the time. They were willing to take on the role after they got home from work and my mother would help me during the night, but they were not going to stop work to stay home with me. As a quadriplegic requiring a lot of care, I did not feel that the role of caretaker should fall on my sister, either. So when I came home from the hospital, a lady from the neighborhood stayed with me, and it was nice to have her there. I would go to school for a few hours, and then I would come home. But all we would do together was watch television; we didn't have a whole lot in common.

The next people that I had perform these tasks for me were friends of my sister. I started to hang out with my sister; she was my contact back into socialization and back into being with young people again. Her friends became people who would fill this role for me. Unfortunately, they perceived themselves first as friends and second as employees. They would take many advantages: not come on time, skip a day without much explanation, and they would easily take advantage of that relationship because, as I say, they first saw themselves in the roles of friends.

Later I hired a friend of my own as my attendant, and the same kind of problems happened. Our relationship lasted a really long time, but we had difficulties. We would go out to bars together, we would meet the same men, and a lot of the jealousies and conflicts that often go on between friends would occur. This would seep over into our relationship as employer and employee, and, again, this dual relationship was not very successful. When I was going away to school and needed someone to live with me in the dorm, it became apparent to me that I should hire someone who was not my friend to be my attendant. Then I became afraid because I thought if I put up an ad on the bulletin boards around school or in the paper that I was a disabled individual looking for an attendant, I was sure people would read it and go, "Yuch!" I couldn't imagine anyone would want to work with someone who was disabled. But I mustered my courage anyway and wrote out a short statement that said, "Disabled woman, mid-20's, looking for female assistants in personal care activity" and stated where I could be found and such. Well, I had a few women come, and the one person that I did choose was somebody who had similar interests to mine. I was in graduate school and wanted a lot of time to study; I didn't want to have a lot of partying going on. She was a senior and had the same kind of goals; so we lived together. That relationship went really well.

An interesting aside to this situation was that a few weeks later I was going down the hall at school, and a couple of guys came up to me individually and said, "Are you still looking for someone to help you out?" I said, "Oh, no, I filled that already." They told me, "Oh, you know, I was really thinking of coming and talking to you about it." I didn't know if these guys were kidding me, or if they were serious. They did seem sincere, but because I had devalued myself and didn't think I was very attractive or sexual, having them come up and say that was an ego booster. It added to my self-esteem.

After living with this one woman, I went home at summer to live with my parents. Again I knew I needed another personal care attendant, and, because I'd had this positive experience, I put an ad in the newspaper. I stopped taking applications after 20 calls, interviewed all 20 women, got resumes and references from them, and chose the woman who best suited my interests.

Again, I looked for someone who would be able to entertain herself because being a personal care attendant is a 24-hour job, but one that doesn't take 24 hours. It takes some time in the morning to assist me getting out of bed, some assistance with hygiene, dressing and bladder care, and some assistance with making meals; then the person is done until I have to go to the bathroom again. Although the person has to be around much of the time, each task doesn't take that long. Therefore I like to hire a student or someone who has some activity he or she can do at home to keep busy—I don't want to have to entertain my care attendant.

When I'm counseling my clients who are disabled about using attendants, I talk to them about knowing what they want in someone who is going to be around them a great deal. I found for myself that when I hired someone, right from the beginning I was the employer, and this person was the employee. Our roles were definite and defined. From the beginning there were boundaries to our relationship, and we did not change our roles. We did not go out together socially. We would go shopping together for clothes and such, but we would not go to bars together; we would not date together.

It adds to my self-esteem to see myself in the role of somebody who controls an interaction, who controls the flow of monies, and who can ask a prospective employee for references and resumes. That's a really good position to find myself in. I encourage my clients to explore this role for themselves.

Besides hiring one personal care attendant who would come in every day, I also hired people on a relief basis if my primary attendant became ill and for weekend shifts. I have never had to write a contract with a personal care attendant. I've always had oral contracts, which always stated explicitly that I would need at least 2 weeks notice before they left the position. I now see this transition and movement toward becoming an employer as growth, a manifestation of how I was dealing with my disability. I have come from feeling thankful that that woman in the neighborhood would help me out to the role of seeing myself as an employer, a confident individual who could be in the superior role in a business relationship.

DEBRA SOLIZ

It is important that the relationship between an attendant and a person with a disability be a good one. This necessarily involves open communication. When establishing an employer-employee contract with an attendant, I like to always express that "if there are disagreements, it is my hope that we can talk about them together." It is important that this kind of openness be established early in the relationship.

It is necessary to look at what attendant care means to a person with a disability. I consider my personal care needs to be as basic as the need for food, shelter, and clothing. I have to know that these basic needs will be met before I can begin to think about personal development. For example, I need to know that my bowel and bladder needs will be efficiently met before I can go out and seek and actually obtain employment. To grow as a person, I must live in a safe and secure environment.

The relationship between an attendant and a person with a disability is an intimate one. My attendant bathes me, takes care of my bowel and bladder needs, and touches all of the intimate parts of my body, which I was not accustomed to sharing with anyone before my spinal cord injury. I have no privacy in that area of my life. For example, when I am menstruating, my attendant is directly involved with the care this requires.

Sometimes a close relationship develops between an attendant and the individual with a disability. This can be a caring relationship on both sides. At times there is a breakdown in the employer-employee relationship. When this relationship becomes a friendship, I begin to expect less from this person as a friend than I do from her or him as an employee. It is often very difficult, but I have found it necessary to try to keep the friendship and working relationship separate—although this is not always possible.

The attendant job is very demanding, both physically and emotionally, to both people involved. It can be restrictive and frustrating. The attendant may often just sit down to relax, when I have some need which requires her or him to get up again. I feel guilty, and I sometimes feel like a burden to my attendant and to the world in general. These are feelings I have had to struggle with for years.

The issue of dependency is continuously present within this relationship. Many of the personal care needs that I have are similar to those required by an infant. For example, my attendant is directly involved with bathing me and with my bowel and bladder needs. My attendant also dresses me, which includes putting diapers on me. Since in many ways I have the physical needs of an infant, my attendants have the tendency to psychologically infantilize me as well. Sometimes a parent-child relationship is established between an attendant and a person with a disability. It is important for me to deal with the potential development of such a relationship early. I have to communicate to my attendant that "although you take care of many of my physical needs, I still have the ability to make my own decisions and to be responsible for myself." This is such an important distinction that I think it is necessary to express it to my attendants. Usually such a discussion leads to us feeling much more comfortable with each other.

I find that it requires continuous effort and energy to always be considerate of my attendant and to realize that my attendant has feelings too. Sometimes I want to be selfish, and I do not want to have to think about this other person. Sometimes I feel if I have to say, "PLEASE do this," or "PLEASE do that," and, "THANK YOU for doing this or that" one more time I will scream! Sometimes I want my attendant to be my hands: "I don't want you to have feelings, I don't want you to make 'helpful' suggestions, I don't want you to think or be anything except my hands!" When I was in college, a questionnaire was passed around that asked, "Would you like a person or a robot as an attendant?" I remember checking the robot category because, if my attendant were a robot, I would not have to deal with human feelings. I would not have to deal with the relationship. But I have learned that because this is such an intimate relationship, it must be dealt with on a daily basis. As I think more about this, I see some similarities between this relationship with an attendant and a deaf person's relationship with an interpreter.

There are many feelings that come up between an attendant and a person with a disability. One of the most difficult emotions to express within this relationship is anger. When angry with my attendant, I would rather sit in my urine all day long than have to ask my attendant to change my diapers. I do not want to have to interact in any way with my attendant when I am feeling angry. One part of me is afraid to be angry with my attendant because of the physical care that I fear could be potentially withdrawn. At these times, I feel powerless and helpless because I cannot meet my own physical needs.

The other side of this dilemma is that between the disabled person and the attendant there may exist a love relationship. I honestly feel that I love my attendant and that my attendant loves me. We care about each other. Often a relationship develops in which my attendant takes care of my physical needs and we both take care of some of each other's emotional needs.

I think it is very important to make compromises with my attendant and to be aware of my moods as well as my attendant's moods. I must also remember that my attendant also has needs and that we both require time and space in which these needs can be met. I have found that one of the best ways to deal with feelings like anger and other problems that seem to recur is to use humor. Humor has been one of the best ways to release tension in my relationships. If my attendant and I can laugh together about something, it helps to get us through another difficult time, and it brings us closer together as a result of the mutual understanding that comes with laughter.

KATHRYN L. NESSEL

My situation is also unique. Before Ken had his stroke, we had known each other for 11 years and had been married for 4 years. An important part of our relationship had always been our communicating on verbal and physical levels.

We're very physical people, both with each other and with friends. So when he became ill, we had to adjust to continue our relationship. At first after the stroke, Ken wasn't able to talk but he could move his eyes a bit and blink. One of our friends and I devised a chart: it had the alphabet on it and was numbered across and down. We'd point across, one, two, three; then we'd point down, one, two, three, and he would blink when we came to the letter he wanted, and in this way he could spell words out to us. Because I had known him for a long time, he would start spelling, and I usually could figure out what he needed. Perhaps because medically there was not much that could be done for Ken, the hospital staff was particularly sensitive to his emotional needs. They usually restricted the visiting hours in the intensive care unit, but permitted me to stay there basically 12 to 13 hours a day. They let all our friends come in and even allowed infants. It may sound odd, but we even carried on parties in intensive care. Mobiles that friends had made hung from the ceiling. Later we took over a conference room in the hospital to be able to include many of our friends. In those ways, Kenny and I could keep emotional contact with other significant people in our lives. Even in intensive care, we were able to have physical involvement with each other. The staff let me bathe and massage him and would let me help move him. They even taught me how to stick a tube down his throat and help suction him out; that was an important way for me to help and be involved with him.

After Ken got out of intensive care, we had even more time together. We started working out how we were going to be involved sexually again. We both needed physical contact. In the hospital there were often a lot of visitors. Although I didn't sleep there, I really felt I was in the hospital too because of all the time I spent there, including having all my meals with Ken. At times we would put a sign up on the door that said, "Ken's asleep, don't come in." Sometimes we would wait until "after hours"; then I could get into Ken's bed with him, and we could be physical with one another. All of this was done with the permission and support of the nursing staff.

We celebrated our wedding anniversary when Ken was in the hospital, and for that night we got a private room. We told our friends that we didn't want any visitors after a certain hour that night, but until then people brought gifts, flowers, and food. The nurses took care of his physical needs earlier in the evening and again let us be together. They even ordered an anniversary cake for us.

All of that went quite smoothly, but what we didn't anticipate were the problems that occurred when Ken came home. While in the hospital, his needs such as bowel and bladder care were attended to by the staff, and we could still carry on the romantic part of our relationship. Ken's emotional well-being while in the hospital had been very good. The doctors and nurses kept telling me, "Be prepared, he's going to change, he's going to be much more difficult at home." That never happened, I think, because a lot of his emotional needs were met. But when Ken came home, he did have other needs that I hadn't anticipated. With little preparation, I suddenly became his nurse and personal attendant, in addition to being wife, wage earner, cook, and housekeeper.

At that time Ken was still paralyzed and was totally dependent. I was working and also took his job so that he would have a job to go back to when he got better. I was tired and angry at the situation and didn't quite know what to do; we didn't have the money to hire an attendant. Even if we had been financially more able, we felt we could and should handle this situation ourselves. Many of our friends visited often; that helped out, but it was still just the two of us dealing with it.

Our sexual relationship became very difficult also. We had been teaching sex education and had been doing sex therapy for a number of years, so we thought we were supposed to have all the answers. We didn't, and the disability put us in a very different situation than before. We weren't sure who to go to to talk with. We tried discussions with some of our friends about the difficulties we were having. One of my issues was that I was afraid of the consequences of Ken having an orgasm. His disability had come about when a blood vessel broke in his brain stem. My fear, naturally, was "My God, I don't want him to get too excited because another blood vessel will pop, and I'll have been responsible!" During this time of difficulty, we did enjoy a lot of hugging and kissing; eight pillows also joined us in bed because Ken used them for support.

I was told by nurses, doctors, and physical therapists, "Don't let him get a bed sore." I didn't know what a bed sore was and no one ever showed me one, so every 15 minutes I'd wake up and turn him. You can imagine how well either of us slept! I remember being afraid one night when I saw a little red mark somewhere on his body. I got hysterical and called his physical therapist, who had become a good friend, and she said she'd come over and see for herself. She took a look at this little red mark, laughed, and said, "No, I don't think you have to worry about it."

When Ken was first in the hospital, sex wasn't a big concern of mine—his life was. I remember thinking that if only he could put his arm around me one day, that would be a gift. Affection always had been a major way we related; so it was very easy to maintain physical caring in our relationship, even after Ken became disabled. Lovemaking to orgasm was more difficult to reestablish. I was fearful of what that kind of excitement would do to Ken. He had his own worries—he was having to deal with performance anxieties. His body had taken on a new meaning for him, one he wasn't entirely sure of. We went to one of his doctors with our questions about sex, and he responded by talking about bowel and bladder control. Ken said, "I don't have trouble with bowel and bladder control; I want a little more information about sex." The doctor's reply was essentially, "You were totally paralyzed, all your limbs were affected so don't count on anything." We left there feeling momentarily discouraged, but we vowed to experiment ourselves. From there we decided to speak with a sex therapist who specialized in disability issues. This also was discouraging, since the therapist dealt more with ways Ken could pleasure me and avoided the importance of Ken's own sexuality.

During the first year of Ken's disability, we avoided heavy passion because of our fears. Once I accepted that Ken was all right and not fragile, fears started to dissipate. Once Ken rid himself of the notion that he had to "perform" sexually, we were able to initiate passion back into our sexual relationship. This was not easy and happened only after a great deal of talking honestly with one another. We needed reassurance from each other concerning our fears.

Before Ken's disability, sex had many meanings for us. We tried to keep our relationship, including the sexual part, exciting in many different ways. We have learned that that is still possible after the disability. We are constantly looking at making our lives fulfilling, both independently and together. In some ways Ken's disability has set up more of a challenge. Fortunately, we both find challenges exciting.

DEBRA SOLIZ

I would like to talk about two of my relationships in which my sexual partners also acted as my attendant and how this affected our sexual relationship. The first relationship involved a man who was my full-time, live-in attendant. The second relationship, my current relationship, involves a man who did not act as my attendant when we first began living together, but through a transition became my nighttime attendant.

When I was in college, I lived in the dorms. I had a female attendant with whom I shared a room. Gary, who later became my partner, lived on a separate hall of the same dorm. I remember the first time Gary began exploring my body. I felt insecure and frightened but curious. Since the onset of my disability, I was physically unable to explore my body, and consequently I did not know what I would be able to do or feel. Gary had been a hospital orderly, and he also had experience as an attendant for someone with a spinal cord injury. I felt comfortable with him and trusted him with my body. It is important to me that my sexual partner have knowledge about my body and the care that I need. This helps me to feel physically secure, and it also helps my partner to feel more comfortable with my disability. I remember not wanting Gary to fully undress me and find that I wore diapers. I had a poor body image, and I remember thinking that if Gary saw my atrophied body I would be unattractive to him. In short, I was afraid my disability and all that came with it would turn off any potential sexual partner.

My attendant would undress me and help me to bed. Then Gary would come to our room and spend the night. It was then that Gary and I (quietly) had sexual intercourse for my first time. I was surprised that I had pleasurable genital sensations. I had been convinced by persons in the medical profession that, because of my spinal cord injury, I would feel nothing.

After a while Gary and I decided that it would be better if he were my attendant, since we wanted to spend more time together, and it was difficult finding privacy, since I shared my dorm room with my attendant. Although we had better access to each other, Gary's attendant role in our relationship created many more problems than it resolved.

I became very demanding as an employer and expected much more from Gary than I had expected from previous attendants because we were in a love relationship. I often gave Gary the message verbally or nonverbally that loving me meant physically caring for me, which also included the necessary household chores. If Gary did not take care of me the way I wanted, if he did not wash the dishes, if he did not wash my diapers when I thought they needed washing, or if he did not wash my hair the "right" way, I would get angry and think that he did not love me. Overall, Gary and I had an unhealthy, dependent relationship. I was dependent on him, and he was dependent on our relationship. I wondered why he didn't pursue a relationship with a "normal" woman, and this attitude affected our relationship.

It was difficult for Gary and me to separate our employer-employee relationship from our love relationship. There were many confusing emotions for both of us. We could not deal with our anger, and we did not communicate well; so the relationship ended. However, I feel that our relationship was an excellent experience for me because it helped to improve my sexual self-image. Gary was not turned off by my physical care even during preparation for sexual activity. This improved self-image helped me to have the confidence to pursue other relationships.

My second relationship was with Jim. We lived with each other for a year before he became my nighttime attendant. During that year, I had a morning attendant and a nighttime attendant, neither of whom lived with me. The household was somewhat chaotic with all of the people coming and going, but it was nice for Jim because he could get up and go to work without the interruption in his life of caring for my personal needs.

It is important to understand that Jim and I are not in a two-way relationship, but that my attendant(s), Jim, and I are in a three- or four-way intimate relationship. For example, my nighttime attendant knew, because of the position I chose to sleep in, whether or not Jim and I were going to have sex on a particular night. This also necessitated that Jim and I decided, each night before going to bed, whether or not we were going to have sex. This certainly decreases the possibility of having a spontaneous sex life, which is something I currently believe to be a myth anyway.

My attendant, Jim, and I deal with potentially embarrassing situations by laughing together. One of my attendants, when she was helping me to bed, even went so far as to place me in an obviously sexual position and then called Jim into the bedroom saying "Okay, she's ready; come and get her!" For these reasons, when I hire an attendant, it is important for me to consider whether this person and Jim will get along.

After Jim became my nighttime attendant, our life-style became less chaotic. As my attendant, Jim does all the presexual preparation, which includes undressing me, emptying my bladder (using the Credé method: tapping on the bladder), birth control, and positioning. The majority of these tasks I require help with, whether or not I want sex on a particular night. But I also realize that sometimes after the "work" there is no energy left to play. When Jim and I are both feeling romantic, there is a lot of sex play that we enjoy as part of all the necessary preparation. Jim accepts my disability and does not feel that it negatively interferes with our sexual activity. He does not even mind if I occasionally urinate on him, considering I have no bladder control. Sex can be whatever one chooses to make it, and Jim and I make it fun! Jim and I have a good relationship in which we can communicate effectively. After living together for 4 years, we have learned to be patient with each other and to take the time to explore and share ourselves with each other sexually. Jim and I decide together what is best for us, and what is best for our relationship. We are currently talking about having children. But who is to take care of the children? We will need a live-in person to take care of a child. So currently we are seeking a live-in attendant who will care for me in the morning and in the evening. We will first see how having a live-in attendant affects our relationship. If it works out well, we will begin trying to have a child.

PAMELA FINKEL

I've had several different kinds of attendant situations, but mine is a little bit different from those who have already shared their experiences because I was born with a disability. From the beginning there was never any question about taking care of my needs. My family made me feel, not disabled, but part of the family. I never really had to go through the transitional period of saying, *now* I need all this help; I've always needed it. I always knew that I would need it, no matter what happened. So when I went to school, I just advertised for an attendant because I needed one—my mother couldn't go to school with me, and I didn't want her to. Advertising wasn't as hard for me as for some of the previous speakers. I got a live-in attendant/roommate. A lot of the issues that Debbie brought up about having an attendant and anger never came up with me and my first attendant because I didn't know how to deal with these feelings. I could get angry with my mother, and she would just love me anyway. With the new attendant, I had to learn how to work out those feelings—it took a long, long time. I moved out of the dorm and into a house with five other roommates who, in the process of our getting to be friends, all knew how to take care of me. If someone wanted to go out at night and didn't want to come home to do my attendant care, somebody else would take care of me. The responsibility was shared among four people and one main person, whom I paid.

It is very hard for me to maintain a business relationship with my attendants. I tried to a million times. I even wrote up a contract once. It's hard for me to say, "Hey, listen. You have to do these things." I find that flexibility is an important part of the attendant relationship. I stress my needs to my attendants/friends. It's important for my life to be able to plan on getting up at a certain time. If it doesn't happen, I just can't deal with it. If my friends don't want to be responsible for my personal needs—that's fine. If our friendship includes being responsible for my personal care, then my attendant/friend must remember that I still have to get up in the morning.

With regard to sexuality, I've never been comfortable with my partner being my attendant. I like sex to be a little bit more romantic (if that's possible). My partner has been around when my personal care is being done, but he knows he's not responsible unless there's an emergency. This arrangement works pretty well. Sometimes my partner has a glass of wine or listens to an album while waiting. I used to be uncomfortable with this situation, but sex got a lot better for me when I realized that sexual spontaneity is a myth. People just don't float from the living room to the bedroom without some kind of preparation.

Having an attendant as part of a sexual relationship is not as impersonal as it sounds. The most important thing for me is to find an attendant who sees me as a whole person and who acknowledges that my sexual needs are as necessary as my other needs.

This would be especially true if I were to bring home a new friend. When my sexual partner has been around for a while, my care becomes rather routine. With a new person, however, it is often my attendant's attitude toward me and toward the situation that makes my new partner more comfortable.

Physical dependence is never easy to deal with, but believing in my worth has helped me find attendants who support me and help me reach my life goals.

MELANEE FISHWICK

Now, I'll give the opposite side of this whole issue because the person who is my "significant other" is also my personal caretaker. When we met, I was already disabled. When we started dating a bit, it was difficult because he lived in Michigan, and I lived in a small city in New York. After we courted over a long distance, we decided that perhaps it would be better to move in together and see if this relationship would work. When that decision was made, I told him that there were a lot of things that he would have to do for me, and I felt that he should know about them before we got together. He needed to know about my bladder and bowel care. I wanted to make sure that he knew that this was going to be difficult, that it was going to be time consuming, and that I would make a lot of demands on him as a person. He felt that it was all pretty silly that I put myself through talking to him about all this because he said anybody with any power of observation would be able to see what was necessary to take care of my needs: I took the great leap and moved to Michigan.

We feel that as long as we can talk about all that's going on with us, we can continue to maintain our relationship. We communicate on what's happened, what I need; we communicate about how he's feeling, how I'm feeling; is he able to keep doing this; does he want a break; all those kinds of things. In terms of responsibilities for personal care with bathing, I do my own grooming. He helps me into the tub, but once in the tub I'm able to take care of turning on the shower, the water, getting my shampoo, and all that. He assists me with most of my dressing. He does all my bowel and bladder care.

It seems that my part in the relationship is that I take care of all the business. He's never dealt with banking institutions, so I take care of all the banking, all the bills, all the money that comes in, and all the money that goes out.

He's a student, and I go to work every day. He goes to school in the evening; so he does all the dishes and the groceries and the laundry—he does all that stuff, and he's a real good cook, too. When he was working, though, those were my responsibilities. This is how our relationship is. When I'm working, he does this; when he's working, I do it. As soon as we're both working full-time, then we'll be able to hire someone to do household chores. He has said that he would not want anyone else to do my personal care, however, because this is a very deep and strong part of our relationship, part of our loving, and part of our sexuality and sensuality; and a large part of how we are in our relationship combines with the care. It's just a very natural part of what our relationship is. He would feel very uncomfortable if someone else were to come into our physical relationship. These are his feelings.

I've read some articles about severely disabled women who say women should always have attendants or else their partners will not be able to see them as sexual beings if they have to take care of their bowel and bladder care. Well, I think that's another myth. Maybe it fits with some disabled women, but I think personal care is a very individualistic thing that you figure out with the person who fills this role for you.

A sense of humor is so very necessary in our relationship; we goof about everything that goes on. You can't get too serious about incontinence. We allude to it in our lovemaking; we talk about "golden showers." Even though we empty my bladder before intercourse, there's no guarantee that I won't be incontinent while we're having intercourse because of the stimulation of pushing on the bladder. If I should wet, well, that's a normal and exciting part of our relationship.

I don't know if he's atypical or not, but he's a Vietnam veteran, and his attitude is that he has seen so much that being disabled is nothing. He doesn't even consider me disabled. Recently I asked him, "Is it always hard for you to have to do these things for me?" He said, "You know, I never think about it in those ways." He really doesn't. It's part of being with me, and that's okay. We have a lot of conflicts over finances because I'm the breadwinner, so to speak. He doesn't create any money, so he's always spending mine. We've thought about different things such as, at the beginning of the month, he should get a check for his work, then he could deposit that in his own account and that would be his own money. That seemed too formal for us. He's not on my checking account, but he has a 24-hour banking card so that's his access to money; he just uses that whenever he wants.

Our apartment is inaccessible, but he's strong enough so that carrying me into the house and up seven stairs is not a problem; he doesn't mind that. Accessibility is another issue that we talked a whole lot about. As long as he's comfortable with carrying me and helping me with these things, then our current situation is all right. But if we begin to feel strongly otherwise, we'll get an electric lift outside. I don't think his having to help me with bowel care is a strain on our sexual relationship. He said to me, "If I can't deal with your body and the natural processes of elimination, then what does that say about how I feel about my own body?" He feels this all has to do with how you feel about yourself. This determines how you deal with another person's needs in these areas.

We get into fights, and we yell and all, but we don't stay angry very long because the reality is he is going to have to help me do something. It's hard; he'll be carrying me, and I'll be looking away from him with clenched teeth, but in those circumstances we can't stay angry very long.

♀ ABOUT THE AUTHORS ♀

Pamela Finkel is a graduate student in rehabilitation counseling at San Diego State University in addition to completing training in sexuality and disability offered by the University of California, San Francisco. She facilitates support groups and presents lectures about sexuality, does telephone counseling for rape victims, and is actively involved in increasing community awareness of the rights of disabled individuals. Since birth she has had a physical disability that is diagnosed as nonprogressive muscular dystrophy.

Melanee Fishwick, M.A., is a licensed psychologist and is completing training in sexuality and disability at the University of California, San Francisco. She is presently employed as a staff psychologist at the Rehabilitation Institute in Detroit, Michigan. Ms. Fishwick has been a quadriplegic since 1968.

Kathryn L. Nessel, M.Ed., is a marriage and family counselor specializing in sex therapy and sex education. She is presently teaching classes in human sexuality and does counseling in private practice and at a social service agency. In addition to her individual work, she is a cotherapist with her husband, Kenneth Lane, who is also a marriage and family counselor. At this time, they are both involved in a training program in sexuality and disability at the University of California, San Francisco. Ms. Nessel presently resides with her husband in Tucson, Arizona.

Debra Soliz, M.S.W., graduated with a master's degree in medical social work, with an emphasis in the rehabilitation of newly disabled individuals. She was trained in sexuality and disability at the University of California, San Francisco. Ms. Soliz is presently assisting in the development of a sexuality and disability program at San Diego State University. She acts as a community consultant and facilitates a sexuality group for women with disabilities for the Resource and Educational Network for the Equality of Women with Disabilities (RENEWD). In 1969, she incurred a spinal cord injury from a diving accident, resulting in quadriplegia.

PART II

PROFESSIONAL ISSUES

David G. Bullard

During the past decade, health and education professionals have begun to acknowledge the need to learn more accurate information about human sexuality, especially the experience of sexuality for persons with physical disabilities or medical conditions. Much of the available literature addressing these topics has been infused with value judgments exemplified by the use of the word "problem" in the titles of many articles ("The Sexual Problems Associated with Z"). Such reports stress helplessness rather than hopefullness, a sickness rather than wellness orientation, and a problem-obsessed rather than enhancement-centered response to sexual issues.

The "Personal Perspectives" section of this volume points out that many people with disabilities and medical conditions arrive at a comfortable and enjoyable sense of their sexuality *in spite* of their experiences in the health care and educational systems, rather than because of support from them. However, the articles in this next section show that many creative and dedicated people *are* concerned with the quality of sexual health care and education; they *will* make a difference.

If there are commonalities among the following articles, one of the most important in my view is that the authors have listened to the true experts in this "field"—persons who themselves have a disability. Many of these authors have had their own experience with disability, and all have learned from the people they attempt to serve.

I hope that this section provides sufficient information to heighten your curiosity about the mystery of sexuality and how it is experienced uniquely by each of us, that you find pragmatic approaches and techniques for helping those you work with or love, and that the attitudes expressed cause you to reflect on your own beliefs and on those of the people around you.

125

OVERVIEW

17 Sexuality and disability in the United States

Mary S. Calderone

In January 1974, the Sex Information and Education Council of the United States (SIECUS) published its first lead article on sexuality and the handicapped.[1] (We didn't know any better than to call it that in those days.) In 1976 we took all the information we had on the topic and prepared a special issue on "Sexuality and the Handicapped"[2] (there went that word again!). Through the generous offices of Sol Gordon, 1600 extra copies were printed and sent down to the White House Conference on the Handicapped (look who was also doing it!) for distribution. The powers there informed us it could not be distributed because it was "inappropriate." Can you believe that? The information was just exactly what the people they were concerned about wanted. Well, there were many nice people in wheelchairs and on crutches who were happy indeed to be of service. The 1600 copies *were* distributed, so people got them just the same.

I later found out from someone who had worked on a committee what had happened: The Ford Administration sent work trickling down to avoid "controversial" issues. The discussions were therefore restricted to the topics of curbs, stairs, accessibility, jobs, handrails, education, and other truly important things, and the central topic of "sexuality and disability" was not mentioned. It's a subject that has commanded increasing attention in the past few years as many people, including those who themselves have disabilities, have demanded more humanistic services for those born with, or who have acquired, what were formerly known as "handicaps."

We cannot consider the individual human being wholly human until his or her sexuality has been completely recognized. I'm proud that SIECUS was among the earliest to begin to think in terms of the *resexualization* of certain groups of people who, up to then, were being desexualized by the society because of some condition—a learning disability or a sensory or bodily disability, whether acquired or congenital. This desexualization also affected those with other conditions who were "too old," whatever that may mean, or "too young," simply by reason of being a child. Those who were too old were (and still are) being desexualized by those who were younger, and those who were children were (and still are) being desexualized by those who were older, always by the people in power.

To counteract such oppression and denial of human rights, the Quakers have a good phrase, "Speak truth to power." The truth about the importance of sexuality in all human lives needs to be addressed.

I believe that we are becoming more aware of this need. For example, in 1979, in San Francisco, I spoke at a 3-day conference for physicians and other health workers about body image, self-esteem, and sexuality in cancer patients.[3] That was really a breakthrough. The pediatricians who were there heard speakers discuss the sexual needs of all cancer patients and of adolescents, specifically, whose self-esteem, body image, and sexuality were threatened not just by the disease itself, but by the treatment modalities used against it, whether surgery or radiation or chemotherapy. What is the impact on an adolescent girl when she loses all of her head *and* body hair because of medical treatment? You can't put a wig on the pubis. Think of what that means to your self-image as a female when you're an adolescent—or when you're an adult for that matter.

At that conference we were privileged to hear Dr. Jordan Wilbur, a medical oncologist who is director of the Children's Cancer Research Institute in San Francisco, who spoke on the topic of sexuality and body image in the teenager with cancer. Two weeks later I got him to come down to a 4-day international symposium on adolescent medicine, cosponsored by the International Society for Adolescent Medicine and the American Academy of Pediatrics in Washington, D.C. Five hundred physicians spent a full day discussing adolescent sexuality. Dr. Wilbur was wonderful, just as he was in the San Francisco meeting. He discussed the social ambiance in his cancer institute, where adolescents must spend varying periods of time. He talked about the jukeboxes, the dating, and the fun and play activities that adolescents so dearly love and could initiate there. He also showed slides, including urine specimen bottles decorated with the guys' own logos. If you have to have cancer therapy, this would be a marvelously warm ambiance in which to have it.

In speaking of self-image, he projected slides of a young girl with a tumor of the upper palate, which, of course, was not operable because of its location, and could only be treated with radiation. The slides showed an improvement in the tumor, but they also showed marked narrowing of the mouth opening. At both meetings Dr. Wilbur said: "The narrowing interfered with talking, oral sex, and eating." How wonderful to include oral sex as just one more important activity. I hoped that all the male physicians listening didn't block it out. We all should realize that even 5 years ago, such a meeting would not have been held, nor could such a remark have been made; so something really has been happening.

My cochairman at the session on adolescent sexuality was Dr. Murray Kappelman, professor of pediatrics at the University of Maryland School of Medicine. During years of counseling troubled adolescents and their parents, he has recognized the right of the adolescent to sexuality. His message is "Parents, you had better accept your adolescent's sexuality. It exists. They are going to be sexual. You just have to understand how to be *with* it, not *against* it." He also said another very important thing: "They are sexual in a way that you weren't sexual; it's a fact of life for them, different from the way you were sexual, so you can't handle them in the same way you were handled or mishandled."

So we find that the extraordinary complexities due to disability itself are piled onto a part of life that is already notable for its complexities and its own particular disabilities. A good example is the emerging interest in the sex education of deaf children, so much of whose energy must specifically be focused on extraordinarily difficult techniques of communication. In their case, the sex-related difficulties seem even greater than with visually handicapped people who have their own special difficulties, of course, in learning about sexuality. With sexuality we must deal not just with facts, but with concepts of subtlety. How do you communicate these to hearing-impaired children who already have difficulty coping with subtle concepts in verbal language? How do you help a visually impaired boy "see" breasts, or a girl "see" a penis?

The case of the hearing-impaired person becomes mind boggling when, in addition to deafness, there is blindness from birth or early childhood, as with Helen Keller. How do people manage their sexual lives without two primary means of personal and sexual communication such as the tender and meaningful glance that says, "Hey, I like you, let's get together," and the tender whisper meant for the hearing of only one person. How can we help deaf and blind persons enjoy and feel secure in their sexuality? That is our job, no matter what the circumstances are.

The World Health Organization has defined sexual health as "the integration of the somatic, emotional, mental and social aspects of sexual being, in ways that are positively enriching and that enhance personality, communication and love." We should be aware that not all influences will actually serve to enhance our sexual health. In becoming aware of our individual sexuality, not all of us are able to redress all of the negative influences or enhance the positive ones. We need to become convinced of the two great endowments to being human that differentiate us from the lower animals: our intellect and our sexuality. The animal responds automatically to certain climatic, seasonal, or other physical conditions to behave reproductively. But the human mind makes it possible, indeed imperative, for us to learn, to choose, to evaluate, to postpone, to enjoy, and to use or *not* to use or to misuse the sexuality that was programmed in us—whether for procreation or for pleasure.

As I have so often asserted, we must deal more realistically with preadolescent or early childhood sexuality to prevent its being damaged. To promote these goals, SIECUS will establish a learning center (not an education center; education is something you do *to* somebody). We'll have a *learning* center, where people, ordinary people, parents and kids can come to learn about their own sexuality. We will have an "A program" for consumers, and a "B program" for training those providers who will be meeting with the consumers at their own levels. We've already begun this project by looking for the money to do it,* and a special grant will be sought for a sex and disability component as one important part of the learning program. If parents don't know how to deal with the sexuality of nondisabled children, consider how much less they know how to deal with the sexuality of a child with a disability.

Thus we must not be satisfied with the sex education of adults or even adolescents with disabilities. Right now we really have to begin to think about the needs of children with disabilities. They don't need a real handicap such as fear about sex; that's a double bind. It is essential that we develop materials and programs to help parents in terms of the sexuality of their disabled young children.

Remember what Victor Hugo said: "More powerful than the tread of mighty armies is the idea whose moment has come." We need your help in attaining this goal.

I'm paraphrasing what Thoreau said: "All it takes for evil to survive, in the face of lies and distortions deliberately maintained, is for one good person to fail to stand up and be counted." SIECUS and the people in SIECUS have stood up and been counted, as have many others. I'm asking us all to stand up and be counted in support of the rights of the child before the age of 12 to have his or her sexuality recognized and honored as early as possible. I encourage you to enlist your friends and colleagues everywhere to support these rights wherever you are. Be with us; you are needed because the time has come.

---

*In August, 1980, SIECUS received a grant to begin work on this program in the Philadelphia area.

REFERENCES

1. Bidgood, F.E.: Sexuality and the handicapped, SIECUS Report, **2**(3):1-2, 1974.
2. Cole, T.M., and Cole, S.S.: The handicapped and sexual health, SIECUS Report, **4**(5):1-10, 1976.
3. Vaeth, J.M., (editor): Body image, self-esteem, and sexuality in cancer patients, Front. Radiation Ther. Oncology **14**:1-133, Basel, Switzerland, 1980, S. Karger.

♀ ABOUT THE AUTHOR ♀

Mary S. Calderone, M.D., M.P.H., received a medical doctorate from the University of Rochester in 1939 followed by a master's degree in public health from Columbia University in 1942. From 1953 to 1964 she was medical director of the Planned Parenthood Federation of America, resigning to cofound SIECUS (Sex Information and Education Council of the United States) in 1964. Its first executive director, she is now president. Its goal as originally stated was "To establish human sexuality as a health entity." Its success is evident in the present existence of 20 scientific periodicals in the field and the American College of Sexologists, of which she is a charter member. Her work has earned eight honorary doctorates and numerous awards, most recently the American Public Health Association's Edward Browning Award for Prevention of Disease, and the Margaret Sanger Award of the Planned Parenthood Federation of America. In her middle seventies, she still flies all over the world to speak on human sexuality, its nature and importance to all of us.

18 Sexuality and disability: the international perspective

Emanuel Chigier

INFORMATION

Until 1970, there really wasn't any growth at all in the field of sex and disability, and then there were various stages of development in Europe. The first stage was a kind of awareness—special sessions at professional meetings and papers here and there proclaimed that there was something special about sexuality and the disabled.

The next stage was advocacy. Various publications appeared, such as one from Sweden in 1970 called *Life Together*,[5] a publication in England by Dr. Wendy Greengross called *Entitled to Love*,[2] and a book published in Holland called *Not Made of Stone*.[3] The Spastic Society of England made the film *Like Other People*.[4] You can see from the titles of these materials that the message essentially was that disabled people are sexual beings and are entitled to their sexuality.

In 1972 I had the privilege of presenting a paper on sexuality and disability at the World Congress of Rehabilitation International in Sidney, Australia. This was the first time this topic was discussed in a plenary session of that international body, then celebrating its fiftieth year of existence. Basically in line with the advocacy feelings of that period, I delineated six sexual rights for the disabled:

1. The right to receive information
2. The right to be educated
3. The right to sexually express oneself
4. The right to marry
5. The right to be parents
6. The right to receive sexual health services from the community, such as genetic counseling, family planning, and sex counseling

These may appear fairly obvious, but they are still very controversial, especially when we deal with various forms of disabilities such as mental retardation.

The next stage was the drawing together of information. It is not enough to go around waving a flag and saying the disabled have a right to various things. How do they function, and what are their problems as sexual beings? A study in Sweden in 1972 indicated three things that were *not* creating problems. The severity of handicap did not create sexual problems necessarily. The age of onset of disability was not necessarily a factor, nor was the age of first sexual experience. What did indicate that a problem was present was whether a person considered that his or her sexual problems depended on their handicap or not, and if they thought their handicap limited their possibilities for sexual relations. In other words, the question of whether a sexual problem existed depended on the attitude of the disabled person, rather than on the physical circumstances of their situation.

In 1974 the British Council for Rehabilitation ran a survey called Sexual Problems of Disabled (SPOD), in the city of Coventry. They interviewed every seventh person on a list of those with physical disability between the ages of 15 to 65 to see whether they had sexual problems. The first question that arose was what *is* a sexual problem? Their definition was a very good and beautiful one that I would like to bring to your attention. They came to the conclusion that a sexual problem is "an obstacle to the satisfaction of sexual needs." That's all. The nature of the problem could be physical, psychogenic, sociogenic, or a combination of these. In that study with 212 interviewees, they found 54% currently had a sexual problem in one of these categories, and an additional 18% had experienced such problems in the past and had overcome them or given up, so therefore they didn't see it as a problem. The other point that was very clear was that, as I think happens in the United States, none of them had had any medical or other professional advice on sexual matters.

We, as health professionals, were very ignorant and needed to collect more facts. For instance, a practitioner in England named Dr. Katherina Dalton tried to find out the situation with blind adolescent girls. She found some very interesting things for which we do not necessarily have an explanation. For instance, it's been found that those who are blind from birth become physically mature earlier than the average: they have an earlier menarche, they have a shorter menstrual cycle than other girls, and they also have a shorter menstrual period, which is regarded as an "adult pattern." She also observed that being blind meant you are unable to learn from visual experience the very basic things as to how people look, genitally or sexually. The third finding was fear in sexual matters—the fear of being observed. A blind girl (there's no equivalent research with blind boys or men) cannot see if anybody's around watching, especially in an unfamiliar environment. Fourth, these girls had an enhanced sense of smell; their first sexual experience involving the odor of semen was for them rather surprising or unusual, and could have been handled better if there had been some understanding of that beforehand.

Let's take another area where information is slowly being put together: cardiac disability. Of people who've had a cardiac infarction and go back to work (by definition 5 to 7 hours a day, doing the work they were doing before), how many also go back to sexual activity? The percentage is much less than those who go back to work. It's kind of paradoxical that a person feels that he can work a 5- to 7-hour day, but he or his spouse is frightened that having a sexual climax may be dangerous. We are again at the question of fears. Another study of 39 people who had angina pectoris before having a full-blown myocardial infarction found that 19 of them developed chest pains during intercourse, and four had abstained altogether from intercourse. After specific sexual counseling, all had reestablished enjoyable sexual relations within a year.

EDUCATION
Parent education

The next development was that of education. Education can be divided into various categories. First, I would indicate the need for the development of parent education. There are many people who are born with, or at an early age acquire, a disability, and the best way of getting parents to help out is to educate them. Because of the enormity of the disability as such, whether it be retardation, blindness, deafness, or severe physical disability, most parents are so overwhelmed by the disability, as are often the professionals who counsel them, that they tend to regard disabled children as being sexless. They are often called "an epileptic, a retarded, a deaf"—not even "a deaf *girl*, a deaf *boy*." When they become teenagers, because of the physical changes that occur, parents may be confronted with what they think of as almost bursting sexuality in their retarded or disabled girl or boy. The same phenomenon, the need for parents to get help with their anxieties, is demonstrated by my own experience in working with parents in places as diverse as Mexico, Brazil, Singapore, Israel, and Japan. It does seem to be a pretty universal phenomenon, and I think the time has come for those working in sexuality and the disabled to get into the preventative level of working with parents and children with a disability before they become clients for counseling programs as adults.

Professional education

What about professional education? Apart from national symposia that have been held in the United Kingdom, United States, Sweden, Australia, and other countries, for the last 8 years there has been an international clearinghouse centered in Sweden, with material and bibliographic references on sexuality and the disabled. It is run by a very charming woman named Inger Nordqvist, who has been a pioneer in this field. In terms of international meetings for professional people, in 1973 in Israel we had an international symposium on the disabled adolescent that devoted about 40% of the time to sexuality. In 1976 we had our first international seminar on sex and the disabled in Tel Aviv, and in 1981, as part of the U.N. International Year of the Disabled Person, we had an international symposium on sex and disability in Israel (following the World Congress of Sexology held in Jerusalem in June, 1981).

I'd like to bring to your attention a special journal, *Sexuality and Disability*.* The editors are Dr. Ami Sha'ked, an Israeli who spent 8 years in the United States, and Dr. Susan Daniels. This journal is an excellent resource of relevant articles.

The next area of importance is staff education for people who are working in clinics or other agencies where there are disabled people. These people require specific inservice training. These training sessions have been held in Sweden, Holland, and the United Kingdom for some time. One of the things that is significant in dealing with the physically disabled is that there is a demographic imbalance. If you look at spinal cord injury units or other areas of severe physical disability, most of the patients are males, usually of a fairly young age, and most of the care providers are young female nurses, social workers, and physical therapists, etc. There is a need for working with staff about their reactions to patients, especially when dealing daily with their bodily needs. Staff themselves need to deal with their feelings.

One question that comes up in chronic, long-stay situations is "How far does nursing or health care go?" For instance, it has been debated whether a severely disabled person who cannot use his or her own hands is entitled to get help from a nurse for masturbation. The argument is that if nurses help you with bed pans, urinary problems, feeding, and every other basic physiological need, what is so wrong with helping the patient masturbate? On the other hand, is the objectivity of being helped to masturbate the same as the objectivity of a nurse helping with toilet problems? These are issues. There is a very interesting movie in Holland that we showed in 1976 in Israel about helping couples (where at least one of them is disabled) get together to have sexual intercourse. In this movie they demonstrate that, if two adults agree that they would like to have sex in a long-stay rehabilitation center, and yet, because of a disability one cannot get into the bed of the other, the nurse will help. This takes the form of arranging for the man or the woman to get into the bed of the other person, both of them being nude, and helping them to position themselves comfortably. After a discreet length of time, the nurse returns and takes the man or woman back to his or her own bed. Again, this is the kind of thing that, when you think about it, is really not so wild or radical. I just wonder how many nurses or doctors are prepared to accept this as part of health care service.

---

*Published by the Human Sciences Press, 72 Fifth Ave., New York, N.Y., 10011.

Consumer education and counseling

The last aspect of education is consumer education, as in the United States where therapists are working with adults in groups, couples, groups of couples, individual counseling, and also with adolescents. How about services? England and Sweden have had some counseling services for disabled people, but these are fairly minimal at this stage. An interesting program that has been described in Holland makes use of volunteers. There is a Dutch Society for Sexual Reform, which, according to their statistics, has about 30,000 members who are tackling various sexual issues in a less polemical manner than is the case in the United States. What can be done with volunteers to help disabled people get more comfortable with their own sexuality? There are "cells" or small groups directed by the national center that are scattered all over Holland in big cities and small places where people sit around, four or five nondisabled and four or five disabled people, and talk about their feelings and what they can do to be happier sexually. It seems to work very well, and in the description of their program they mention that there are three phases in considering the problem. The first phase is what they call the *"I"* phase: "I am the problem, I have a disability, I have sexual needs, I have sexual frustrations." After the meetings continue a while, the second phase, or the *"we"* phase, develops; "We have problems; we as disabled people, we as a certain age group, we as people in a certain environment have problems." The final phase is the *"they"* phase. Not *"we* have a problem," but *"they* have a problem; other people have a problem about our sexuality as disabled or nondisabled people." There is a movement away from your own ego-centered concern toward the idea of a group phenomenon, and finally to a situation where you have a sufficient belief and confidence as a group and as an individual to be aware that "we" are not the problem, which helps you focus on the real social issues.

In Europe, a major concern of spinal cord–injured people is the question of fertility. It surprised me that up to now in the United States, a lot of the emphasis has been on being a sexual person, getting pleasure, and relating to that. But being a parent is also an instinctive, gratifying, and enjoyable experience for most. I don't know if this is the effect of zero population growth in the United States, but in Europe and most countries many paraplegics who have reached the stage of having a feeling of enjoying sex are also very concerned about having a child of their own.

In Holland mechanical sexual aids such as vibrators and artificial penises are used more often than in other cultures. In countries like Israel, my impression is that use of sexual aids is regarded as a very poor substitute, and I think that most people would rather use their finger than use a mechanical device. It would be interesting to see some cross-cultural comparisons of countries like the United States and Israel, for example, to determine whether there is a need at all for the advancement of technology in the use of sexual aids or devices.

Another topic that I think is worth mentioning when discussing the field of physical disability is arthritis. In Oxford, England, the Nuffield Foundation's center for the treatment of arthritis has been paying special attention to the problems of sexual functioning when one has a painful hip, knee, or back. What they've done there is really a simple extension of what is generally called "activities of daily living" (ADL). Their philosophy is that sexual activities should also be included as part of daily living and is therefore a logical extension of the ADL concept. So what they have done in Oxford is to have a room or apartment like those in rehabilitation centers in Israel and the United States with a kitchen, bathroom, and bedroom so people can learn under guidance how to adapt to functioning in their homes in relation to their specific disability. They suggest that when a person has a sexual partner, he or she also should come into the program, maybe on weekends or for a couple of days. The little apartment is thus available for them to learn how to adapt to their arthritic condition; what kinds of positioning to use, when to use medication—all these subjects are addressed. This helps people who have arthritis leave a rehabilitation center with better sexual functioning.

In Sweden and Holland live models are provided for teaching blind adolescents about sexuality. Since it is quite respectable for nude models to be paid for being drawn or photographed by artists, there is no reason why the blind adolescent shouldn't have a chance to learn about the body of the opposite sex through a tactile experience. This has been demonstrated beautifully in a short movie by Dr. Whalan from Sweden. There is also a physiatrist in Vancouver, Canada, who uses live models to teach medical students how to conduct sexual examinations and to know what the genitalia are like, not only on the cadaver but on people themselves. This seems to be a good idea because for a small investment there is a good learning experience.

As part of the services of the Tokyo Metropolitan Rehabilitation Center, there is a person who arranges marriages for disabled people. This person gives them sexual advice and counseling as part of the matchmaking process: "Now that you have agreed that you want to get married, let's work during the engagement period on how to function sexually, how to use contraception properly, etc."

As far as surrogates are concerned, I don't know of any such programs for disabled people in Europe, but they may exist. It is of interest whether this is an area that should be developed. In Sweden the use of erotic movies was presented at the Tel Aviv Seminar of 1976. As compared to Sexual Attitude Restructuring (SAR) programs in the United States, which are ostensibly given to desensitize and resensitize people, there is at least one program in Sweden using erotic movies as a sexual instrument. In other words, people who have difficulties in erectile performance or feel that they are not capable of sexual response are shown erotic movies for about 30 minutes to increase their sexual interest. I don't know if there is an equivalent in the United States, but this is a sexual tool that certainly can be used.

Sweden uses disabled volunteers to give talks. For example, there is a young man in a wheelchair who goes around with a kind of script: "I want you to imagine this is Mary and John and they are going to go out for an evening. One of them is disabled. Through using fantasy, try to imagine how they get undressed and function sexually." They conceptualize this to get both disabled and nondisabled people to understand the road to sexual experience. Another approach that is being explored in Sweden (where they have had compulsory sex education since 1958), is that they are now including a section on disabled people as part of general sex education for young people. One learns that people have sex in different ways. This is part of a move that I think is significant; that is, teaching children as part of their general education that the disabled are what I call "different but not strange." If we can get that across, we can indicate to people who are not disabled before their ideas are formalized that, just as we enjoy and think there is value in the variety of geographic natural landscape, people who have different physical characteristics are part of the human landscape.

Let me turn to what has been done in my own country, Israel. One study I conducted compared the sexual adjustment of a group of disabled veterans with above-the-knee amputation as compared to those of the same age and socioeconomic and cultural background who had paraplegia. We found that those with paraplegia had many sexual problems, and the amputees had none. We thought the latter group would have some problems in mobility and self-image because of the difficulties with above-knee amputation. When should we intervene with sexual counseling? I do think we can overdo this and come on too strong sometimes with people who are in a life-threatening situation. If you have just broken your back, I am not sure that that's the time to say, "Well, what about your sexual functioning?" However, I do not mean to say that counseling should be avoided until the person has become buried in his or her own anxieties and frustrations. We need more research on the optimal timing for intervention in sexual rehabilitation.

We have also had an interesting study on survival in marriage of paraplegic couples. A follow-up of 14 to 16 couples in which the males were paraplegic showed what happened to their marriages. (There have been other studies, but these have been retroactive.) Although 7 out of 14 had considered divorce, only one did become divorced; that's a very low proportion. Despite these figures, we have to regard the onset of severe disability as putting a spouse in a high-risk category about the whole marriage as such.

In client education in Israel, we have conducted some small programs for adolescents with cerebral palsy, for children with mental retardation, and for the deaf. We also have a program for teenagers in a psychiatric unit. They are severely disturbed youngsters in a closed unit, and we give a sex education program that is integrated with their individual and group therapy. Our study indicated that not only did sex education *not* disturb them, but it seemed to facilitate their therapy as psychiatric patients.

Another area that is not regarded as disability at all, but I think is in some ways, is the lack of sex education programs for prisoners. For the last 2 years we have had a sex education program for young male prisoners in a short-term (1 to 3 years) prison. We found not only that there is a general lack of information, but there are very specific things that bother people who are in prison. One is the relationship between drug use and sexual performance. Second is homosexual experiences while in prison: "Does that mean that I'm going to be a homosexual when I get out?" We try to immunize them against this concern: "If you wipe out your prison record, then why be obsessed because you've been in some homosexual experience which you did or didn't like; it doesn't have to have an aftereffect unless you allow it to." The third concern is being away 2 years or so without any real opportunity to maintain a relationship with a woman: "What is she doing out there, and is she going to stay with me?"

In Israel, apart from various international symposia I have mentioned, the continuing education program at Haifa University has a special course on sex counseling for the disabled so that social workers and rehabilitation workers have the opportunity to get a credit course in this area. The major rehabilitation center in Israel began by having a voluntary program for sex counseling. It now has a central institute for sex counseling for the disabled in which we have four full-time people and 5-year funding. The center provides all services for all groups of disabled people within the hospital setting, the rehabilitation center, and the community. My last point about the situation in Israel is that because of the development in the field of sex education, the demographic center, which is linked with the prime minister's office and Ministry of Labor and Social Welfare, is planning to set up a national institute to train all kinds of professionals in family life and sex education. This is because we've found that, although 3000 teachers have received sex education training in Israel, doctors, nurses, clinical psychologists, and others have not yet had training to become better sexual health care providers.

In conclusion, I believe that the situation in the rest of the world in regard to sexuality and disability is similar to that in the United States. Various issues need to be tackled in a scientific and objective way: Where do we put the center for counseling? Whose responsibility is it? How do we deal with doctors and rehabilitation people as compared to sex therapists? What kind of research is needed? How can we assure a continuity in programs? The length of many programs is dictated by availability of funds and persons interested. When the persons move, the program collapses.

Finally, I think it is very clear that it is no longer possible to ignore the fact that there cannot be quality of life without the opportunity for sexual fulfillment.

REFERENCES

1. Chigier, E., editor: Sex and the disabled: an international seminar, Isr. Rehab. Ann. 14:1-108, 1977.
2. Greengross, W.: Entitled to love, National Fund for Research Into Crippling Disease, 1 Springfield Rd., Horsham, Sussex, Great Britain, 1976.
3. Heslinga, K., Schellen, A.M., and Verkuyl, A.: Not made of stone, Springfield, Ill., 1974, Charles C Thomas, Publisher.
4. Like other people, film, 1825 Willow Rd., Northfield, Ill., 1973, 60093, Perennial Education, Inc. (film, 16 mm, sound, color, 37 min.).
5. Nordqvist, I.: Life together, Stockholm, 1972, Swedish Central Committee for Rehabilitation.

♂ ABOUT THE AUTHOR ♂

Emanuel Chigier, M.D., is national secretary for the Israel Society for the Disabled; lecturer in human sexuality at Tel Aviv University Medical School; consultant, Institute of Sex Counseling for the Disabled, Sheba Medical Center, Tel Hashomer, Israel; and director, International Institute for Sex Education and Therapy, Tel Aviv, Israel. Dr. Chigier has directed a number of research projects involving sexuality and disability in addition to holding several positions dealing with adolescent medicine. He has been chairperson of several international workshops and symposia, and has recently been appointed to the Expert Advisory Panel on Rehabilitation of the World Health Organization.

SPINAL CORD INJURY

19 Neurophysiology of sexual response in spinal cord injury*

Robert C. Geiger

An understanding of the impact of spinal cord injury on the neurophysiology of the sexual response cycle is essential for effective counseling. Awareness of physiologic problems and potentials can help to demystify and demythologize this often misunderstood area. Comfort and willingness to deal with problems can be increased with knowledge of what is expected at the physiologic level.

On the other hand, it is a mistake to impose expectations of physiologic potential or limitations on any individual. While statistical data may help us predict the effects of a given lesion at a given level, there are far too many exceptions in all the studies to allow rigid application of the physiologic concepts. More importantly, human sexual activity is never a purely physiologic event. Even with apparently isolated behavior such as masturbation, nocturnal emission, or the reflex activity of a person with a total cord transection, the entire individual ultimately participates. In general, the totality of the physiologic, interpersonal, and socioeconomic milieu has more to do with sexuality than do the neurophysiologic specifics.

A significant area of deficiency is neurophysiologic knowledge about women. For various reasons, except in regard to pregnancy, there are little data, even of the gross statistical type, that define the changes in women imposed by spinal cord injury. Because the sexual response cycle is so similar in men and women, however, it is assumed that one can safely analogize with the male in predicting the female response following spinal cord injury. Information gleaned from histories given by cord-injured women and their partners have so far born this out.

The description of the sexual response cycle used here for the noninjured as well as the cord-injured male was developed in order to avoid some of the erroneous assumptions implied by the standard description popularized by Masters and

*Preparation of this chapter was supported, in part, by grant MH 14346-03, NIMH, and it was previously published in Sex. Disabil. 2:257-266, 1979.

Johnson[4] and used by most sex therapists. In describing the female, I will use the standard terminology and will make an effort to correlate the two descriptions. Although there are some sources describing the neurophysiology and sexual responses in detail,* in this chapter both male and female descriptions have been simplified in hope that a more easily applicable concept will emerge. Working from the model of the noninjured person, one can pretty well construct the impositions anticipated by a given level of cord injury.

MALE RESPONSE CYCLE
Erection

Erection occurs as a result of engorgement of the corpora of the penis. This is usually a result of hyperemia due to vasodilatation and to the opening of arteriovenous shunts. This may be mediated by either the sympathetic or parasympathetic divisions of the autonomic nervous system. Occasionally, as in some malignancies, erection occurs as a result of mechanical obstruction or vascular sludging in the outflow from the penis.

Psychogenic erection. As a result of psychogenic stimuli (visual, auditory, or olfactory stimuli; dreams, memory, and fantasy; in short, "whatever turns you on"), the autonomic nervous system is activated, and impulses course from the brain down and out of the cord in fibers that synapse in the lowest sympathetic ganglia at the eleventh thoracic to second lumbar levels. Postganglionic fibers carry impulses to the penis, which cause vascular engorgement. It is likely that parasympathetic fibers from the sacral segments participate in this as well.

Reflexogenic erection. As a result of local stimulation either internally, as with a full bladder, or externally, as with stroking, or pressure, erection can occur. This is a result of activation of a reflex arc with sensory fibers in the pudendal nerve, innervating the genitalia and other perineal structures and coursing to the second, third, and fourth sacral segments of the cord, where they synapse with motor fibers of the parasympathetic nervous system. The motor fibers return via the nervi erigentes to supply the blood vessels of the penis.

It is a mistake to think of psychogenic and reflex erections as two entirely separate entities. In the noninjured male the two are mixed and usually must remain mixed for the erection to be maintained. For example, maintaining a psychogenic erection may be difficult unless some external (reflexogenic) stimulus is applied. This external stimulus may then feed back into the psychogenic activity and get further reinforcement. A reflexogenic erection may also be difficult to maintain unless the psychogenic aspects are appropriate. Anxiety can certainly overwhelm satisfactory external stimulation. Sudden shifts of attention such as appearance of a

---

*References 1-4, 6, 7.

child or some other unwelcome visitor on the scene can be devastating to the best erection!

Ejaculation

For the sake of simplicity, the term ejaculation is adequate. From a physiologic standpoint, however, it consists of two phenomena.

Emission. As a result of increasing tension, there is rhythmic contraction of smooth muscle in the vas deferens, seminal vesicles, and prostate. Semen is thus propelled into the prostatic urethra. This is essentially a function of the sympathetic nervous system.

Ejaculation. Several intense contractions of the bulbospongiosus and ischeocavernosus muscles, as well as the other muscles of the floor of the pelvis, move the semen out of the urethra. This activity is mediated by the somatic nervous system via the motor fibers to striated muscle carried in the pudendal nerve and originating in sacral segments 2, 3, and 4.

Retrograde ejaculation occurs when semen is pushed into the bladder rather than out through the urethra. This can result from failure of the sympathetic nervous system to cause contraction and closure of the bladder neck during ejaculation or from mechanical factors such as resection of the bladder neck to allow for better urinary drainage.

Orgasm

The use of the terms "orgasm" and "ejaculation" interchangeably by both professionals and the general public is unfortunate. Ejaculation is a pelvic event, in so far as any activity can be isolated to a single part of the body. Orgasm is essentially a cerebral event. It may be associated with ejaculation in the male, but this is not essential to experiencing the sensation. Of course, for most noninjured men the inevitable association of orgasm with ejaculation has been a lifelong assumption. Like many assumptions, it is inaccurate. Finally, the labeling of this purely subjective phenomenon as a "phantom orgasm"[5] when it occurs in paraplegics is also inaccurate.

Involution

Detumescence and the return to the flaccid state of the penis along with some degree of general body relaxation usually follows ejaculation.

FEMALE RESPONSE CYCLE

The female response cycle is mediated by the same pelvic nerves as in the male, consisting of fibers from the lowest sympathetic ganglia, the presacral parasympathetics, and the sensory and motor fibers of the pudendal nerve.

Excitement phase

The excitement phase can be initiated in similar ways as in the male. In the pelvis the physiologic response is similar: vascular engorgement. This results in vaginal lubrication, labial engorgement, and clitoral erection.

More obviously than in the male, the female response involves areas other than the genitalia. There is often nipple erection and beginning breast engorgement, in addition to general body phenomena such as changes in pulse, respiration, and blood pressure. Changes in blood pressure, pulse, and respiration occur in the male as well, as can nipple erection, but in our culture the focus in the male has been primarily genital, essentially ignoring other events in the response cycle.

Plateau phase

As the excitement phase continues, augmented either by continued excitement or stimulation of erogenous zones, there are further changes. The inner two-thirds of the vagina dilates and begins to form the seminal pool. The outer third and the labia minora become more engorged and tend to constrict. The erect clitoris retracts upward away from the vaginal entrance and against the symphysis pubis.

Breast engorgement increases, and there is also engorgement of the areola of the nipple. As a result of increased blood flow to the skin, a light rash, "the sexual flush," may be seen across the upper chest and face.

Orgasmic phase

By usual terminology, "orgasm" is used to describe ejaculation in the male and its physiologic analogue in the female together with associated subjective sensations. As noted previously, this is unfortunate because using the word "orgasm" for either sex does not specifically distinguish between the physiologic events and the subjective perception of those events.

The physiologic events in the female are rhythmic contractions of the uterus and vaginal introitus, contractions of the anal sphincter, increased skeletal muscle tension, and peak pulse, respiration, and blood pressure levels; all these responses also occur in the male or have specific analogues.

Resolution phase

As with the male, the female experiences a gradual detumescence of the pelvic organs as well as the other areas involved with vascular engorgement. One difference is that although there is usually a latent period in the male before erection and ejaculation can again occur, some women can achieve repeated or multiple orgasms without a significant time interval.

EFFECTS OF SPINAL CORD INJURY

Although much of the knowledge of human sexual neurophysiology has been gained from observations of cord-injured persons, an approach to understanding the effects of spinal cord injury on an individual's physiologic response is to use the noninjured model and assume from it the alterations in function that would result from interruption of various neural pathways. Again, it is essential to remember that the basic premises are based on statistical data replete with exceptions. Also, the predictability is greater given a complete transection of the cord or cauda equina, while in actual practice partial or incomplete lesions are far more common.

Because of the similarities in the neurologic pathways and the basic phenomena that result from their activation in both sexes, it is possible to discuss men and women together. Focusing on the similarities rather than the differences may not only help avoid some of the misconceptions implied by the standard terminology, but may also serve as a useful therapeutic tool in helping people overcome rigid misconceptions regarding differences between male and female sexual responses.

Lesions of the cervical cord

Psychogenic (excitement) stage. A complete lesion of the cervical cord can result in certain predictable changes. Autonomic (sympathetic and parasympathetic) impulses coming down the cord from the brain cannot pass the level of the lesion. Therefore during the psychogenic or excitement phase, there will be neither erection nor vaginal lubrication. On the other hand, the manifestations of this phase of the sexual response cycle activated by those fibers above the level of the lesion may occur; thus changes in blood pressure, pulse, and respiration are common. Because structures of the upper chest receive some innervation from the cervical roots, lesions of the cervical spine often allow for breast changes during the response cycle. The so-called "sexual flush" may occur. Sensation is also often preserved in this normally erogenous zone; that sensation, augmented by the tactile hypersensitivity commonly encountered at the level of the lesion, can make this a valuable source of erotic stimulation.

Reflexogenic (plateau) stage. Reflexogenic erection occurs in over 90% of men with complete lesions of the cervical cord. The reflexogenic phase may be initiated by stimulation below the level of the lesion. Stroking of the penis, particularly stimulation of the glans or frenulum, catheter changes, or a full bladder all may result in "reflex erection." If this is the result of some internal bodily event, the term "spontaneous erection" is sometimes used. Similarly, vaginal lubrication and pelvic engorgement can result from stimulation of perineal structures.

Thus from a neurophysiologic standpoint, sexual excitement may occur from cerebral or other stimulation above the level of the lesion but with no manifestations in the genitalia, or genital manifestations may occur from stimulation of structures below the level of the lesion, often with no subjective awareness on the part of the individual. However, in some people, particularly those with complete cervical lesions, the stimulation of pelvic structures may result in "autonomic dysreflexia" with marked or even dangerous increases in blood pressure level, which may result in headaches or other manifestations of elevated blood pressure.

Ejaculation. Ejaculation is a relatively rare occurance with cervical spine lesions. Considering that this is probably a combined function of sympathetic and parasympathetic activity and input from the somatic nervous system, it is reasonable that ejaculation is more difficult for the isolated cord to mediate than simple erection. There are no studies available referable to specific responses in a cord-injured female during this stage of the response cycle. By analogy, however, one could reason that similar responses might occur, and counseling regarding the symptoms and hazards of autonomic dysreflexia is appropriate.

With incomplete lesions of the cervial cord, sexual function, from a standpoint of physiologic performance, is improved. When the spinal cord is not obligated to independently mediate the entire process, more men are able to ejaculate. Depending on the pathways that are open, more men have psychogenic erections.[3] A higher percentage of these males also reports "orgasm."

Orgasm has been described as a cerebral event. For most people most of the time this occurs in association with ejaculation (or its equivalent in the female). We know from various studies, particularly with women but also as noted in the dreams of paraplegic men and women as well as in our own studies with cord-injured persons, that orgasm can occur as a purely cerebral event without any genital or tactile stimulation at any level whatsoever. This awareness is crucial in the sexual rehabilitation of many people. The sexual pleasure of the quadriplegic or paraplegic need not be limited to the satisfaction gained by gratification of a partner.

Lesions of the thoracic cord

Lesions above the tenth thoracic level impose essentially the same results as lesions in the cervical spine. The great difference is the amount of skin surface available to act as a source of erogenous pleasure. In women it is sometimes important to be aware that the sixth thoracic vertebra is the sensory level for the uterus. A pregnant woman with a lesion above that level can be totally unaware of when she is going into labor.

Lesions of the cauda equina

Because they are below the spinal cord per se and hence are below the synapses in the cord, cauda equina lesions are also called "lower motor neuron lesions." This can be confusing, since not only lower motor neurons are involved but also sensory and autonomic fibers.

Using the model of the noninjured person, one may be able to predict the effect of lesions at this level with some accuracy.

Psychogenic erection. At least one pathway described for psychogenic erection is from the cerebrum via the lowest (thoracolumbar) sympathetics to the penis. Impulses pass down and leave the cord above the injury, although no input upward from the genitalia is necessary. Therefore psychogenic erection or vaginal lubrication, for example, could be predicted with lesions at this level. Indeed, in a high percentage of cases, statistics support this.

Reflexogenic erection. Reflexogenic erection is literally the result of activation of the reflex arc. This requires stimulation of the sensory leg (fibers from the genitalia running in the pudendal nerve) that returns to the cord and synapses with fibers, forming a motor leg (parasympathetics at S2, 3, 4 levels), which returns to the blood vessels of the penis. With complete lesions of the cauda equina, both legs of the reflex arc are interrupted. Therefore reflex erection should not occur. Indeed, it does not occur in about 75% of cases. The fact that it does occur in 25% of the cases underscores the fact that although these data may help us to understand in a broad sense, they must *never* be applied to an individual.

Ejaculation. The sympathetic nervous system is thought to play a crucial role in ejaculation. Since the sympathetic pathways are intact with lesions at this level, ejaculation can be anticipated more frequently than with higher cord lesions where the thoracolumbar sympathetics have been interrupted. Statistical data also support this; however, as with all levels and degrees of lesion, there are far too many exceptions to allow predictions with any one individual.

As with lesions in the cord, incomplete lesions of the cauda equina more commonly allow for successful physiologic functioning. Also, with incomplete lesions at this level, more men report "orgasm" associated with genital stimulation and ejaculation. The force of these ejaculations seems to be related to the amount of motor involvement; a dribbling type of ejaculation occurs when motor involvement is profound and the muscles of the floor of the pelvis are flaccid.

We have no specific data regarding the response cycle in the female with cauda equina injury. By analogy, we can predict psychogenic lubrication and engorgement but little reflexogenic augmentation.

FERTILITY

At all levels and degrees of injury in the male, fertility is profoundly affected. In addition to problems with erection and ejaculation, hormonal influences may alter sperm formation and vitality. It suffices to say that *no* specific prediction can be made with a given individual unless a thorough fertility work-up is conducted. Even the conclusions of such an evaluation must be viewed only as tentative in that history may prove us wrong. Techniques such as electroejaculation may be of help in the future.

In regard to women, one must assume that a young woman's fertility has not been altered. The potential for normal pregnancy and delivery exists. Urinary tract infections and thrombophlebitis, both potential hazards of pregnancy in the noninjured female, are hazards of the cord-injured woman, pregnant or not. Significant renal insufficiency can be a contraindication to pregnancy.

SUMMARY

A neurophysiologic model of the sexual response cycle has been presented. The terminology used is intended to help clarify some of the areas of confusion and mythology that surround human sexual activity. Also, although there are sufficient data to afford some understanding of the neurophysiology and the alterations imposed by spinal cord injury, there are far too many exceptions within the data, and human sexuality is too complicated a response system to allow for application to a given individual. As with the nondisabled, persons with spinal cord injuries should be encouraged to become their own experts by experimenting and exploring the wide variety of options for attaining sexual pleasure and fulfillment. Also, we feel it essential to stress that while sexual activity may or may not involve genital sensation, sexual gratification is invariably a cerebral event.

REFERENCES

1. Bors, E., and Comarr, A.E.: Neurological disturbances of sexual function with special reference to 529 patients with spinal cord injury, Urol. Surv. **10**:191-222, 1960.
2. Comarr, A.E.: Sexual concepts in traumatic cord and cauda equina lesions, J. Urol. **106**:375-378, 1971.
3. Horenstein, S.: Sexual dysfunction in neurological disease, Med. Aspects Human Sex. **10**:6-11, 1976.
4. Masters, W., and Johnson, V.: Human sexual response, Boston, 1966, Little, Brown & Co.
5. Money, J.: Phantom orgasm in the dreams of paraplegic men and women, Arch. Gen. Psychiatry **3**:373-382, 1960.
6. Tarabulcy, E.: Sexual function in the normal and in paraplegia, Paraplegia **10**:201-208, 1972.
7. Weiss, H.D.: The physiology of human penile erection, Ann. Intern. Med. **76**:793-799, 1972.

♂ ABOUT THE AUTHOR ♂

Robert C. Geiger, M.D., is an assistant clinical professor of orthopaedic surgery and of ambulatory and community medicine and is medical director of the Sex and Disability Unit, Human Sexuality Program, Department of Psychiatry, University of California, San Francisco.

20 Sexuality counseling of women with spinal cord injuries*

Carla E. Thornton

> Since my accident I have been constantly struggling to deal with my handicap. I am having to give birth to a new person—develop new goals, adjust to new limitations. This is harder for me than anything I have ever done before in my life. Every day I am experiencing something I have never done. I've had to relearn how to tie my shoes, go to the bathroom, open doors. The whole process has been one of experimentation.

The preceding quote was written by a 27-year-old woman 4 months after she sustained a spinal cord injury at the T5-6 level. What she did not write is that she also was going to have to adjust and experiment sexually. Sexuality information, education, and counseling for women with spinal cord injuries has only lately become an area to be given serious consideration.

REVIEW OF THE LITERATURE

Until recently, there has been a paucity of information regarding the sexual attitudes, behaviors, and adjustments of women who have spinal cord injuries. Griffith and Treischmann[18] stated:

> A review of the available information might lead to the erroneous conclusion that women have no sex drive, that they engage in only one sex act (intercourse in the supine position) and that their sexuality is defined as the ability to conceive and deliver babies.

Cole[10] agreed:

> What do we know about how a paraplegic or quadriplegic person responds to sexual stimulation? The research on paraplegic women is abominably lacking. We know of no literature that describes the secretions from the wall of the vagina during sexual arousal in a woman with complete cord transection. Nor does the literature tell us what happens to the swelling and opening of the labia, contracting of the

*Preparation of this chapter was supported by Department of Education Grant No. G007601869 and was previously published in *Sex. Disabil.* 2:267-277, 1979.

uterus, and ballooning and expanding of the vagina. We know that the clitoris may become reflexly tumescent; the nipples may indeed swell, as may the breasts. Breathing, blood pressure and pulse rate may increase. Muscles may go into spasm, and a characteristic sex flush can occur.

Instead of any defined research, authors seemed to assume that it really does not matter how a woman with a spinal cord injury sees herself sexually because she can "continue" to be a passive partner in sexual intercourse, thus ignoring all other avenues of sexual expression and assuming that she was a passive partner before her injury. One writer described the sexual expression of the woman with a spinal cord injury as follows:

> In brief, coitus to a paraplegic female would be the equivalent of an above-the-waist petting party, plus the psychologic gratification of knowing that the male was obtaining coital satisfaction.[31]

Cottrell viewed the primary sexual concern of the woman with a spinal cord injury as "whether ankylosis with atrophy of the leg and abdominal muscles prevents proper positioning for coital penetration."[13] Romano[29] stated:

> We must remember that the disabled woman is first a woman and second disabled; she has desires, needs and feelings just like any other person and has the right to express them in ways that are acceptable to her. Sexuality is composed of many things, has many ways of expression, and requires the possibility of compromise just as other facets of life do; it offers satisfaction in giving, as well as getting, and while its expression may present certain problems, these problems need not be hopeless.

In contrast to the limited amount of information available to women with spinal cord injuries, there is the voluminous amount of information on men with spinal cord injuries and their abilities to attain erection, ejaculation, and orgasm.[1] Though many of these studies refer to "paraplegics" in their titles, many of the authors seem unaware of women with spinal cord injuries. For those who do discuss women, it is usually one paragraph concerned with fertility. Additionally, little has been written about the sexual expression of men with spinal cord injuries other than through coitus.

A number of reports have been made on the fertility, pregnancies, labor, and deliveries of women with spinal cord injuries.* Fertility of women with spinal cord injuries is the same as that of able-bodied women; the woman with a spinal cord injury is more likely to have anemia and bladder and kidney problems during pregnancy; labor and delivery may be complicated by premature or rapid labor, dysfunctional uterine contractions, and autonomic dysreflexia (a condition which occurs in spinal cord injuries above T4 and causes a high increase in blood pressure, sweating, flushing, and severe headache). Unsupervised deliveries at home may

---

*References 12, 14, 17, 26-28.

occur if the woman's injury is above T6, since she may not be aware of her uterine contractions.

Recently, several reports of women with spinal cord injuries have been published.[4,5,16,33] In all these studies spinal cord–injured women were interviewed about their sexual feelings and behavior. The most common information these women wanted others to know is that they continue to be sexual beings. Their descriptions of orgasms to Bregman were similar to those of able-bodied women. She stated, "It is interesting to note how much potential people still have to experience orgasm and sexual pleasure despite the fact that significant parts of their bodies are sensationless and motionless."[5]

Helsinga found in a discussion group of people with spinal cord injuries that the first question after surgery for the spinal cord trauma was "Am I going to live?" The second question was "What are my sexual responses like now?"[21] Cole and his colleagues stated, "For some, regaining sexual performance is more important that regaining the ability to walk," and "in the vast majority of patients, psycho-sexual content remains substantially normal in spite of loss of sensation."[11] Trieschmann added that "the onset of a physical disability does not eliminate sexual feelings any more than it eliminates hunger or thirst."[34]

When one's sense of self is seriously disrupted by the trauma of a spinal cord injury, it is more important than ever to reestablish a positive self-concept. Diamond believed that "meeting an individual's sexual concerns can go a long way in re-establishing a general feeling of self-worth conducive to general rehabilitation."[15] Hohmann found a "great improvement in the self-concept" of the paraplegic men he counseled when they discovered they *could* be a meaningful sexual partner.[22] Women interviewed by Fitting "stress that although they were involved in sexual relationships now and felt good about themselves, this had been an evolving process."[16]

People with physical disabilities are beginning to demand that their sexual rights, like those of all people, be met. Chigier[7] outlined the sexuality rights of people who are physically disabled:

1. The right to be informed
2. The right to be educated
3. The right to sexually express oneself
4. The right to marry
5. The right to be parents
6. The right to receive sexual health services from the community

To provide sexual education and counseling for women with spinal cord injury, professionals themselves need to understand and be comfortable with the range of experiences and options available for sexual expression and satisfaction.

Cole has suggested that hospitals should provide the opportunity for more privacy in exploring one's sexual response after the traumatic event of a spinal cord injury, and concluded that "we should encourage sexual rehabilitation in the hospital as well as outside of it."[9] One facility that has available a private room for patients has found it greatly benefited patients and their partners in coping "with interpersonal aspects of the disability and particularly the sexual aspects."[19] Rooms such as these should be more widely available.

Sexuality information and counseling have not been widely available for people with spinal cord injuries either in their initial hospitalization or in the rehabilitation center. Women interviewed by Fitting et al. commented that "health professionals could have been more helpful in terms of sexual counseling and treating them as human beings and not bodies."[16] In 1974 only three education and counseling programs on sexuality and disability had been described in the literature.[11,22,30] More programs do exist today,[8] and one book is available to assist family planning and sexuality clinics in becoming accessible to women who are disabled.[20]

SPECIFIC ISSUES IN SEXUALITY COUNSELING OF WOMEN WITH SPINAL CORD INJURIES

One of the most important things a woman with a spinal cord injury needs in sexuality counseling is permission to acknowledge that her sexuality is an integral part of her being, not just what she does. Women who become injured often share the stigma that the general public has for disabled people. Part of the stigma is the false assumption that one who is disabled is also asexual; if she has shared this thinking, she may be confused at finding she continues to have sexual feelings or desires. She may fear that she will be unable to respond sexually. She may need permission to explore and reaffirm her sexuality.

Communication skills are important in all sexual relationships and assume more importance when one is looked at as "different." The newly injured woman needs to be able to meet and relate to other people and to deal with the stigma often directed at her. If she can learn to relate her needs, desires, and feelings in a confident, assertive manner, it is believed that others will respond in a more positive way.[29] She also needs to "check out" her feelings such as her hopes and fears with her partner so that she can find out "what is and is not possible, and what is or is not acceptable."[15] Role playing can be useful in expressing feelings or trying out new situations or experiences.

Experimenting and relearning

The woman with a spinal cord injury must be encouraged to experiment with her sexual expression, to try new positions, new caresses. There is not enough information currently available to say, "This will work," or "This won't work." Instead we need to say "Try out anything you can think of." Diamond[15] wrote:

> Private acts have no standards that are immutable or written in stone. As we ourselves don't ask society's blessings in our private activities, let's help our clients

to be encouraged at arriving at their own acceptable solutions, regardless of how novel, but we must encourage experimentation so that many possibilities are attempted to achieve a maximum of satisfaction.

Helsinga pointed out that "in the world of the nonhandicapped, people keep thinking of new things to do and new ways of doing them" and encouraged people who are disabled to do the same.[21]

Sexual enhancement and preorgasmic group programs such as those described by Ayres et al.[2] and Barbach[3] can be adapted and used for women with spinal cord injuries. These programs contain specific exercises that can assist the women in exploring her body and learning her current sexual responses. Some women with spinal cord injuries have spotty or breakthrough feeling or may respond to pressure in paralyzed parts of their bodies. When she explores her own body, she then may be able to communicate to her partner specific likes and dislikes or learn to reach orgasm herself. Ayres et al.[2] also include exercises to do with a partner. Again, these can be adapted for the woman with a spinal cord injury and will encourage experimentation with her partner. Schanche's group work with four women with spinal cord injuries was based on an adaptation of Barbach's program and used fantasy work, body-mirror imaging, and much experimentation in sensation exercises.[32] Vibrators were used first on parts of the body that had sensation and later on the rest of the body. The two women who were orgasmic before injury experienced orgasm once again by the eighth session with a partner. The other two women reported heightened sensations and increased feelings of satisfaction.

A counselor should not assume that genital functioning is absent; many people with spinal cord injuries need 4 to 6 months for recovery from spinal shock, and 2 years is not an unreasonable amount of time to anticipate some genital function and/or sensation to return. Women with spinal cord injuries definitely need an explanation of spinal cord physiology as an adjunct to understanding their sexual responses after injury. They also need to know that people can have orgasms (generally from sensory input to areas of the body other than the genitals and through psychological components) that are not genitally based. Women who have had the reflex arc interrupted by the injury may find that lubrication of the vagina is impaired and will need advice on appropriate use of vaginal jellies or lotions (e.g., K-Y jelly, which is water soluble); those with intact reflex arcs may need manual stimulation to activate lubrication. Only time and experience will determine what is possible for a woman with a spinal cord injury.

For many women with spinal cord injuries, it is important to use the whole body, rather than just the parts of the body that have sensation, in sexual activity. The fact that part of the body is paralyzed does not mean that another part of the body no longer exists.

With an injury below T6, women can be very sensitive to breast stimulation and should be encouraged to take advantage of this. The area around the injury in the back sometimes becomes very erogenous; some find new erogenous areas after injury (e.g., shoulders, neck) or find that areas that were erogenous before injury (e.g., mouth) become more sensitive to stimulation. Vibrators can be useful in determining where sensation exists and as part of sex play. All this should be discussed with the woman, and she should be encouraged to experiment and discover which areas react pleasurably to touch.

Some women experience pain or burning in the paralyzed parts of their bodies for some time after the initial trauma. If the woman has pain, it will have to be dealt with in whatever way is acceptable to her; some find sexual excitement "overrides" the pain. Conversely, sexual partners may fear hurting a cord-injured woman during sexual activity. Again, communication between the partners is essential, and the woman needs to be able to tell her partner what and what not to do. There are many positions in which coitus and other sex play can take place.

The woman who has severe adductor spasms (thus preventing coitus in the usual "missionary" position) needs to be aware of alternative positions such as rear entry. Some spasms can be reduced with medication (e.g., diazepam [Valium]), and some women may want to try this.

If two people who are disabled wish to engage in sexual activity together, they may need the assistance of an attendant (a trained person hired by the disabled person for personal care, housekeeping chores, and transportation) in positioning. For some the addition of a third person in sexual activity is an impossible barrier; for others it is accepted with ease.

Besides genital intercourse there are other methods of sexual expression. Oral-genital sex, digital stimulation, cuddling, and massage can be exciting and fulfilling. Since many, if not most, able-bodied women do not experience orgasm through vaginal-penile thrusting alone,[2] this would also seem to be true of women who are paraplegic. The paraplegic woman's pretrauma sexual experience and knowledge should be explored in counseling, and various methods of sexual expression should be discussed. Knight stated, "By using sexual expression other than intercourse, she is able to maintain an active role in sexual activity and gain more physical sensation from contact with her partner."[23]

It is known that people with spinal cord injuries can experience orgasms in dreams.[24] Since the ability to fantasize to orgasm in able-bodied persons has been reported, the use of fantasy as an adjunct sexual activity should be suggested to people with spinal cord injuries. Some authors have suggested that people with spinal cord injuries have "phantom" or "para" orgasms.[24,29] Knight stated, "The human being is too complex in his or her repertoire of physical and psychic responses to stimuli to discredit any experience as 'phantom.'"[23] I believe that an orgasm is an orgasm is an orgasm. It is a disservice to classify the orgasm of a person with a spinal cord injury as "para" or "phantom," and I believe that whatever good feeling a woman with a spinal cord injury gets, she may consider it an orgasm, and it should be accepted as that.

Some women with spinal cord injuries find their sexual gratification in pleasing their partners, and this may be satisfactory to some women. Other women feel their own physical fulfillment should not be denied and see no reason to participate in sexual activity if they receive no physical pleasure from it. Gratifying a partner and receiving empathic gratification from doing so can be positive and should be discussed as one possibility with the woman who has a spinal cord injury, but this should be discussed *only* as *one* possibility.

Bowel and bladder control during sexual acts need to be explored and perhaps planned for. Many people find a bowel or bladder "accident" unesthetic and disruptive; others seem less bothered or learn to cope with it. This is one aspect that definitely needs to be verbally explored between sexual partners. Indwelling catheters can either be removed or left in during sexual activity without harm. If intermittent catheterization or the Credé method is used, voiding immediately before sexual activity may reduce bladder accidents. It is also useful to tell the cord-injured woman that some able-bodied women also void involuntarily during sexual activity. A regular bowel program can greatly diminish or eliminate the possibility of a bowel accident. For those who need attendant care to perform bladder and bowel functions, some advance planning with the attendant can be useful. Positioning for sexual activity with either a catheter or ileostomy bag in place has been well described by Mooney et al.[25] and Shaul et al.[33] The prevention and treatment of bladder infections are important to discuss, especially since bladder infections can cause incontinence in people with spinal cord injuries who otherwise have good bladder control.

Contraception

All women of child-bearing age with spinal cord injuries should have the opportunity to discuss contraception at a counseling session. Women with spinal cord injuries become pregnant as easily as able-bodied women and should have the same rights and information to make knowledgeable choices in contraceptive protection.

There is controversy about whether women with spinal cord injuries should use oral contraceptives. Because they are at risk of thrombophelebitis due to lack of mobility, and because oral contraceptives have been implicated in thrombophlebitis, they may be at double risk if they use oral contraceptives. However, no research has been reported in this area, and whether the risk of a woman with a spinal cord injury being pregnant is greater than taking the Pill has not been determined. If a woman with a spinal cord injury were to develop thrombophelebitis, she might not be aware of the earliest sign (e.g., pain in the calf or thigh) and also might not notice redness or swelling. She should be advised to examine her legs regularly.[33]

For the woman with a spinal cord injury who has some uterine sensation and can cope with the possibilities of increased menstrual flow or breakthrough bleeding, an intrauterine device (IUD) may be acceptable. There is some concern about the woman with no uterine sensation in that she would not be aware of the usual signs (pain, increased cramping) that indicate a problem with the IUD (e.g., puncture of the uterus or infection). She also may need assistance in checking for the IUD strings each month to ensure that the device has not been dislodged or expelled.

Diaphragms and jelly are a reasonable method of contraception, but their use may be complicated by problems of paralysis. A woman with poor hand coordination may not be able to insert and remove a diaphragm without the assistance of her partner or attendant. Some women can use an inserter device, which works well with coil spring diaphragms. The ability of her legs to spread can also interfere with the diaphragm insertion. Diaphragms may be contraindicated for women with recurrent bladder infections. Diaphragms may slip if pelvic muscles are weak or may be dislodged with the Credé method of emptying the bladder.[33]

Contraceptive jellies and foams along with use of condoms is another effective contraceptive method. However, the woman with little hand and arm mobility may encounter great difficulties with their use, unless her partner or attendant can assist her.

For the woman with a spinal cord injury who has decided she has enough children or chooses not to have children, tubal ligation is a viable possibility. For the woman who wishes to postpone having children, reliable contraception can be complex and frustrating.

The woman with a spinal cord injury should understand that her fertility remains undiminished and that if she chooses to become pregnant, she may develop anemia or bladder or kidney problems, which often happens with able-bodied women. As mentioned earlier, she has more potential complications during labor and delivery and may need to be closely monitored at this time. A spinal cord injury itself is not a contraindication to pregnancy.

Social realities

Developing awareness of the reality of the world outside of the hospital is of paramount importance for the person with a new spinal cord injury. There will inevitably be personal questions, stares or negative comments, or the person may be pointedly ignored. Coping with unwanted sympathy, obtaining help when it is needed, and handling help or offers of help when one is capable of carrying out the task independently will have to be learned. It can be useful to share the *Stigma* tape[6] (in which young adults with disabilities discuss living as a disabled person) with the person or to role play some possible situations. Social excursions outside of the rehabilitation center can provide an awareness of the reality of being in the world in a wheelchair, braces, or crutches. Peer counseling in independent living can be extremely beneficial and supportive.

Because our culture values physical "perfection," the woman with a spinal cord injury may find a scarcity of avilable sexual partners. She may be considered asexual by others who see only her wheelchair or crutches or who consider all disabled people asexual. Cole et al. found that "the most serious sexual problems of the spinal cord–injured person were the unavailability of sexual partners (from whatever cause)."[11] The disabled are low on the "sexual market place" in our culture.[23] For the woman who experiences this situation the counselor can provide her emotional support, assist her in working through frustration and anger feelings, and work with her in increasing her communication and socialization skills.

Emotional aspects—depression, lowered self-esteem, changed self-image, grief, performance fears—can also interfere with sexual functioning. It may be difficult to determine if a sexual dysfunction is due to the psychological aspects of a new disability or to the physiology of the disability. Brief therapy can be initiated for emotional problems related to sexual expression and often is successful.

SUMMARY

With more information currently available on the sexuality of women with spinal cord injuries and with an increasing awareness of the rights of those who are disabled, it is hoped that sexuality counseling services will be provided as an integral part of the rehabilitation experience.

REFERENCES

1. Athelstan, G.T., Scarlett, S., Thury, C., and Zupan, I.: Psychological, sexual, social and vocational aspects of spinal cord injury: a selected bibliography, Minnesota Medical Rehabilitation Research and Training Center No. 2, July, 1976.

2. Ayres, T., Lyon, P., McIlvenna, T., Myers, F., Rila, M., Rubenstein, M., Smith, C., and Sutton, L.: SAR guide for a better sex life, San Francisco, 1975, The National Sex Forum.

3. Barbach, L.: For yourself: the fulfillment of female sexuality, New York, 1975, Doubleday & Co.

4. Becker, E.F.: Female sexuality following spinal cord injury, Bloomington, Ill., 1978, Accent Special Publications, Cheever Publishing, Inc.

5. Bregman, S., and Hadley, R.G.: Sexual adjustment and feminine attractiveness among spinal cord injured women, Arch. Phys. Med. Rehabil. **57:**448-450, 1976.

6. Center for Independent Living (CIL): Stigma: what it's like to be disabled: the physically disabled and the world, tape recording, 1973. Available from CIL, 2539 Telegraph Ave., Berkeley, Calif., 94704.

7. Chigier, E.: Sexual adjustment of the handicapped, Intern. Rehabil. Rev. **24:**5-6, 1973.

8. Chipouras, S.: Ten sexuality programs for spinal cord injured persons, Sex. Disabil. **2**(4):301-321, 1979.

9. Cole, T.M.: Reaction of the rehabilitation team to patients with sexual problems, Arch. Phys. Med. Rehabil. **56:**10-11, 1975.

10. Cole, T.M.: Spinal cord injury patients and

sexual dysfunction, Arch. Phys. Med. Rehabil. **56:**11-12, 1975.

11. Cole, T.M., Chilgren, R., and Rosenberg, P.: A new programme of sex education and counselling for spinal cord injured adults and health care professionals, Paraplegia **11:**11-124, 1973.

12. Comarr, A.E.: Interesting observations on females with spinal cord injury, Paraplegia **3:**263-271, 1966.

13. Cottrell, T.L.C.: Sexual problems of the paraplegic, Med. Aspects Human Sex. **9:**167-168, 1975.

14. Daw, E.: Pregnancy problems in a paraplegic patient with an ileal conduit bladder, Practitioner **211:**781-784, 1973.

15. Diamond, M.: Sexuality and the handicapped, Rehabil. Lit. **35:**34-40, 1974.

16. Fitting, M.D., Salisbury, S., Davies, N.H., and Maydin, D.K.: Self-concept and sexuality of spinal cord injured women, Arch. Sex. Behav. **7:**143-156, 1978.

17. Goller, H., and Paeslack, V.: Pregnancy damage and birth complications in the children of paraplegic women, Paraplegia **10:**213-217, 1972.

18. Griffith, E.R., and Trieschmann, R.B.: Sexual functioning in women with spinal cord injury, Arch. Phys. Med. Rehabil. **56:**18-21, 1975.

19. Griffith, E.R., and Trieschmann, R.B.: Sexual function restoration in the physically disabled: use of a private hospital room, Arch. Phys. Med. Rehabil. **58:**368-369, 1977.

20. Hale, J., Norman, A.D., Bogle, J., and Shaul, S.: Within reach: providing family planning services to physically disabled women, New York, 1978, Human Sciences Press.

21. Helsinga, K., Schellen, A.M., and Verkuyl, A.: Not made of stone: the sexual problems of handicapped people, Springfield, Ill., 1974, Charles C Thomas, Publisher.

22. Hohmann, G.W.: Considerations in the management of psychosexual readjustment in the cord injured male, Proc. Veterans Adm. Spinal Cord Inj. Conf. **18:**199-204, 1971.

23. Knight, S.E.: Sexuality and the disabled: a progress report, 1973 (unpublished manuscript).

24. Money, J.: Phantom orgasm in the dreams of paraplegic men and women, Arch. Gen. Psychiatry **3:**373-382, 1960.

25. Mooney, T.O., Cole, T.M., and Chilgren, R.A.: Sexual options for paraplegics and quadriplegics, Boston, 1975, Little, Brown & Co.

26. Oppenheimer, W.M.: Pregnancy in paraplegic patients: two case reports, Am. J. Obstet. Gynecol. **110:**784-786, 1971.

27. Robertson, D.N.S.: Pregnancy and labour in the paraplegic, Paraplegia **10:**209-212, 1972.

28. Robertson, D.N.S., and Guttmann, L.: The paraplegic patient in pregnancy and labour, Proc. R. Soc. Med. **56:**381-387, 1963.

29. Romano, M.D.: Sexuality and the disabled female, Bloomington, Ill., 1975, Accent on Living, Inc., Reprint Series #1.

30. Romano, M.D., and Lassiter, R.E.: Sexual counseling with the spinal-cord injured, Arch. Phys. Med. Rehabil. **53:**568-572, 1972.

31. Rusk, H.A., Covalt, D.A., Fisher, S.H., Marks, M., Sullivan, J.F., and Diller, L.: Roundtables: sex problems in paraplegia, Med. Aspects Human Sex. **1:**46-50, 1967.

32. Schanche, K.: Personal communication, 1978.

33. Shaul, S., Bogle, J., Hale, J., and Norman, A.D.: Toward intimacy: family planning and sexuality concerns of physically disabled women, New York, 1978, Human Sciences Press.

34. Trieschmann, R.B.: Sex, sex acts and sexuality, Arch. Phys. Med. Rehabil. **56:**18-21, 1975.

♀ ABOUT THE AUTHOR ♀

Carla E. Thornton, R.N., M.S., is the director of Family Life Education/Social Skills Development Training for Teachers and Parents of Students With Disabilities in the Sex and Disability Unit of the Human Sexuality Program, University of California, San Francisco. In addition to teaching family life education to students with physical disabilities for three years, she has also conducted a social skills development group for disabled adolescents for 2 years.

HEARING IMPAIRMENT

21 Communication as an aspect of sexuality and the hearing impaired person

A PANEL DISCUSSION

Hank Berman, Howard Busby, Elizabeth Hall, Lizabeth Katz, and Joanne Jauregui

In this panel discussion most of the participants' statements were translated from sign language to spoken English by a registered interpreter and subsequently were transcribed. It should be acknowledged that many of the nuances presented in the original signs are not fully captured by even the best interpreters in making the translation to spoken English. Given this limitation all the participants agreed that the information as presented does an admirable job of expressing their views.

A great deal of this chapter stresses communication, which is an important aspect in dealing with the sexuality of the hearing impaired individual. Communication is not only the first step in initiating a sexual relationship, it is the first step in initiating any human relationship and therefore a significant concern to the hearing impaired person.

LIZABETH KATZ

As a deaf child, I had several experiences that are typical for many other deaf children with hearing parents. Only 10% of deaf children are raised in deaf families by deaf parents, either with or without siblings. I suspect that I was born deaf, but the cause is unknown. My parents discovered that I was deaf when I was 14 months old and then began the process of seeing psychologists to deal with their shock, depression, and, finally, acceptance.

First, my parents were told that they should not learn any sign language because if I were to learn that, I would not be able to learn how to speak. So my parents did not learn sign language and tried very hard to teach me to speak.

I remember once accompanying my mother to a speech therapist. On the therapist's desk was a fork, knife, and spoon. The lessons were very repetitive and boring. To make matters worse, the speech therapist was always very rigid. She

169

would bang on the desk and say, "Look at me, watch, pay attention," while twisting my neck toward her. She would feel my throat to see if I was making sound. She would have me feel her throat and then my own and say, fork, knife, and spoon over and over again. As you can imagine, my attention would often wander away from the lesson. I had a very short attention span and would look all around the room. Finally, I got so bored and numb that I just stared incessantly at the therapist and then blew my tongue heartily at her. My mom started laughing with me about all this. She was a very special person and quickly recognized my emotional needs.

I must emphasize that the way my parents decided to raise me was different from many other families who have deaf children. For example, my parents saw that using a strict oral approach (speech only) would not meet my needs socially and educationally. They were able to accept me for what I am and therefore learned sign language to better communicate with me. In retrospect, it seems a paradox that as I became more involved in an educational environment using sign language, I experienced no decrease in my English verbal language ability. Perhaps this was because sign language gave me the opportunity to so successfully interact with my parents and friends that I became willing to take the risks to develop my oral verbal ability.

HANK BERMAN

I'd like to add something to what Liz said about sign language. It's interesting to note that I know of no schools that teach sign language to deaf kids in a formal academic course like there are courses in English for hearing people. Deaf children have to learn sign language from their peers. That's why there are so many variations in sign languages. There are several sign systems; the American Sign Language (ASL) is used by the deaf culture in this country. Just like verbal languages, ASL is linguistically independent; it has its own syntax and structure. ASL has directionality and movement, as well as hand shapes and proportionality in the language. Directionality means that the distinction between "you" and "me" is in the same index finger. If I make a certain gesture, it means "all of you." However, I can point to each person and say, "you, you, you, and you," as well, so there are many different ways of using this language.

HOWARD BUSBY

What Liz said about the typical reaction of parents who discover that their child is handicapped is similar to my experience. I became deaf at the age of 5. This was a very traumatic occurrence for my parents, partly because my mother was in the hospital at that time giving birth to one of my sisters. I became deaf on the very same day that my sister was born, and my mother almost died from the birth. My father was away during World War II, so it was really a difficult period for our family. A double dose of the mumps hit me in both ears, and I became profoundly deaf, which means that I have almost no functional hearing left.

When I first came to the University of California training program on sexuality and disability, I thought that only Liz and I were deaf—it was not obvious to me that Elizabeth was also deaf at first. Then I realized that there were three of us. The natural inclination of deaf people is to gravitate toward each other, so I went looking for them—you know, "safety in numbers." When I looked at the people in our training program who had a variety of physical handicaps, I wondered, "What possible link could there be between all these different disabilities we have?" I was looking for that link, something for me to identify with, a common bond between myself and the rest of the group. After a while I found one.

Someone pointed out the fact that people do get body sensations even if they are paralyzed from nerve loss, and I started thinking about sensations I got through my ears and through my hearing. Even though I have a hearing loss, I still pick up noises; I've developed a familiarity with them and can identify some things. I'm sure that kind of sensation does go through many people. I can't really give the exact word for this, but it is something in the area of sensations. I don't think we ever really understand the quality involved with the use of words because it's really just sounds. So what you can do is combine sensations and sounds and give them a lot of interpretation. Maybe that's a link; it is for me anyway, at least. So you can join me, link up with me if you wish.

ELIZABETH HALL

My experience is a little different because my hearing impairment happened in my twenties. For all intents and purposes, I am totally deaf in one ear. In the other ear I have almost normal hearing in the lower range (up to 250 frequency), then it drops off until deafness again for all functional purposes. I hear vowels but no consonants, so I can hear you making noise, but it doesn't always make a whole lot of sense. My loss happened overnight. I didn't find out until a month later that it was permanent.

What I want to share with you are the personal and social reactions I went through. I used to consider myself a sharp person who could pick things up very fast. It made me feel stupid to go in a store and have no idea what amount the person at the cash register told me to pay. I tried to find other ways of coping—staring at the cash register to figure it out before they said it. Other times I'd say, "I'm deaf" and show off my hearing aid so that they would know immediately. But sometimes I would try to ignore the whole thing because my speech is good. The problem with good speech is that people are less likely to realize that I have any kind of hearing impairment.

I still have a lot of angry feelings; I don't know sign language well enough to really feel comfortable in the deaf community, and I find that with hearing people, if I identify myself as a hearing impaired person, they also shy away from me. I go to California State University at Northridge, which has about 250 deaf students. When I first got there, no one could communicate with me in sign language. At the same time, hearing people kept putting me in groups with the deaf people. I felt a lot of isolation. I had to become a lot more aggressive, which I alternate with being really passive. I'm still dealing a lot with becoming deaf.

JOANNE JAUREGUI

My experience is different from Elizabeth's, since I was born severely hard-of-hearing and did not realize it until the age of 9. I don't know why I didn't know about my hearing loss. I went to a special school for the deaf starting at age 4 and was forced to use earphones and a large microphone on my chest with two very heavy batteries on my lap. I needed to drag myself around to hear these weird noises. I was very confused from not understanding the words that were going through my ears. I needed to learn to lip-read. My lip-reading skill developed as I grew older, but at the same time I was confused with spoken English. You know, many words in spelling don't come out the way they sound. For example, with the word "doubt," I used to pronounce the "b" in it. I would articulate a word letter for letter because that's just how I thought spoken English was supposed to be, so I was often confused.

At that time I didn't know sign language; our school forbade us to use it. I knew a deaf family who used sign language as a major mode of communication at home, and when their kids went to school and wanted to use sign language in the class they were scolded and their hands were tied up behind their backs. It confused me; I just didn't understand why they did this to them.

When I was 9 years old, my family took a summer cottage, and we went out to dinner with some friends. I was talking to my mother, who was sitting next to me, and I demanded that she look at me when I spoke, the same way that she demanded me to look at her when she was talking to me. Instead she said, "I don't *have* to look at you, I can hear you fine. I understand you fine." I thought, "What's all this?" It really threw me off. Then I asked her why I had to look at her, since she didn't have to look at me, and she said, "Because you can't hear." I said, "What do you mean?" She said, "You have very little hearing, so you have to lip-read." That really shocked and upset me. I asked her, "Why me, why not all of the others, my brother for example?" "Well, you were just born that way," she said. Naturally, I was very disturbed that night. By the next morning I had forgotten all about it and became adjusted to my hearing problem. I would look at people and how they communicated and felt very different from them. I felt better back at school, where I could identify with the other kids, but at the same time I was still confused with writing and developing language until I was 15 or 16 years old, when I learned sign language in just a few months at Gallaudet College. I felt freer there to communicate, and my writing and speech began to improve. My parents were pleased with my speech skills, but I didn't use them very much at Gallaudet College. This, by the way, was the only college for deaf people at that time.

Later on I realized that sign language does help reinforce speech and that you can't teach speech alone without understanding sign language. We realize this now through research that has been done, but I was born before that kind of research gave such evidence. Now teachers believe that sign language is a useful tool to any spoken or written language.

Do not say "deaf and dumb"—the word "dumb" is an old one and is commonly used in England. We borrowed that, but now we've dropped that word. Some people say that they are "deaf-mute"; this is okay only if they cannot speak. I myself do not use that term, I say, "I cannot hear you, please speak clearly and slowly for me to lip-read." Deaf people often point at people and things, which is a taboo in the hearing society. You know you can't point at people—that's awful—but deaf people do that all the time. One time there was a woman who became very paranoid of my pointing in her direction, and all I meant was "over there." Then she called the police to arrest me, and I had to slip away. So there are many different things that seem okay to us but not to hearing society.

I've grown up with deafness, and it's really a part of me. I face many frustrations, but I know how to cope with them. Sometimes people are shocked when I tell them I can't hear and that I need to lip-read them. I try to make them feel comfortable and ease their minds because sometimes people speak with tight lips, which are especially difficult for me to follow, and we have to use writing back and forth.

I prefer to have an interpreter tell me what others are saying because interpreters can give me more information about how hearing people feel and what they mean with their language. Alone, it's hard for me to guess; lipreading can be misleading sometimes. I prefer to have intrepreters to prevent errors and misunderstandings from happening.

Deafness does relate to sexuality. From my past experience, I have had dates with hearing men, hard-of-hearing men, and deaf men to decide where I could fit in. Because of my advanced educational background, I was not comfortable in the company of deaf people who did not have similar interests or education and who did not read very much. I shifted my attention to hearing people, but they were not sensitive to my needs for communication. They left me out or were paternalistic or too sympathetic toward me. So I went back toward the hard-of-hearing group, whose experiences were similar to mine and where I found myself fitting in better. But there are not that many hard-of-hearing people who are willing to associate with deaf people. I have always associated with deaf people because I grew up with them and understand their problems and identify with those problems a lot.

I ended up marrying a man who is hard-of-hearing, just like I was. I say *was* because I am now profoundly deaf. I could use a telephone until the age of 25 and could talk to people who knew how to slowly say one word at a time in a sequence.

Becoming profoundly deaf hasn't broken my heart. I just changed my way of living. I now rely on hearing friends or interpreters to make some of those phone calls for me. What's wrong with that? You can always find a way to substitute for what is lost. That is why I say I coped with my very gradual hearing loss. I knew it was coming, so it didn't really upset me. Because I've seen many people with hearing problems, I know how to cope.

I did not see physically disabled people very much while I was growing up because my school was just for deaf and hard-of-hearing students. However, in 1977 I participated in a demonstration at the HEW building in San Franscisco during the time the Section 504 Regulations were to be signed. There I saw many people in wheelchairs and people who were blind and realized that it would be good to work with people of different disabilities to make the deaf community more aware of their rights.

The deaf community, by nature, has been passive because we do not know about our rights. What we need is visual information, for example, from TV or movies, to be able to see information in picture form. I know this is necessary, but it has not been done enough. Whereas other disabled people have made deaf people realize that we can join them for common political goals, I've noticed that deaf people, including myself, tend to stay in social cliques of other deaf people for most activities because of the language bond that we share. If hearing people wanted to join the deaf community, you would be more than welcome if you could communicate in our community or could bring along an interpreter.

HANK BERMAN

Why the resistance to sign language? Where is that coming from? Why the dominance of oral methods of education? Parents chase about for an appropriate diagnosis for their hearing impaired child and are told either one of two things: (1) with the appropriate amplification, hearing aids, and speech therapy there will be a day when your child will speak perfectly normally and be able to fully participate in the hearing world; this is a very powerful message; or (2) your child is profoundly deaf, will never be able to learn to be a full participant in your family, will never be able to give you the love that you would like from your child; institutionalization in a home for the mentally retarded is suggested.

Those two extremes occur all the time. Today it happens much less in urban areas, but it continues in rural areas. Thus parents become wedded to one message or the other, usually the first. No doctors like to give what they perceive to be "bad news." Very few doctors have contact with the adult deaf world. They don't know role models of successful, well-functioning, normal, happy, deaf adults. Their images may be of the deaf person who sells ABC cards. (ABC cards are those cards that show finger spelling. Some deaf people seem to think that a good way to make a living and travel at the same time is by selling them for maybe 50 cents or a dollar to pay for gas or whatever. This can be a way of life.)

Once parents become "married" to the message, it's very hard for them to disavow it or change. The message also carries with it some side messages such as, "If you let your child use sign language, he'll never learn to speak." That's what Joanne and Liz were talking about. Research has debunked that myth.

Another message that is given is "if your child learns sign language, then he'll probably marry another deaf person, God forbid. They might grow up in a deaf ghetto." Inherent in this view is that it is better to associate with hearing people than with deaf people. The message is very powerful early on and is often coupled with the parents' need for denial.

This prejudice also has to do with the awkwardness most of us who hear have in using our hands. American culture does not appreciate or respect hand and body movement in communication. These same attitudes have been institutionalized and fossilized in schools for the deaf where sign language has often been—and still is—forbidden.

What deaf people understand from this view of hearing people is, "Your language is bastardized English. It's a poor and imperfect form of English. You 'ain't' got any grammar and you have to learn the majority language." Now there's a paradox right there: "You have to learn to speak, *but* you'll never learn to speak well enough because you're deaf." So right away the message is failure. Then the message is, "If you do fail, and chances are you will, you'll have to go to a deaf school, an institution where they allow and use sign language. It's okay to use sign language once you've failed." Right away deaf children learn that what is good, comfortable, nice, supportive, and warm to them, that is, sign language, is failure in their parents' and society's eyes.

There are some stereotypes about the "deaf personality." Stereotypes always have some basis in reality, something that's true about them, but if you understand where it's coming from, it's easy to understand. In deafness, one of the sterotypes that Joanne was alluding to is immaturity, being unsophisticated. Well, if 90% of what you know is overheard, and sign language is not the medium by which most people transmit information to you, then socially, culturally, academically, and so on there's going to be some immature or inappropriate behavior.

Using Erickson's model of developmental stages, we know that communication is necessary to master the developmental tasks. Most deaf children with hearing parents who don't use sign language don't begin to communicate well with their parents until they learn lipreading in school at the age of 5, if indeed that early. The message to parents from the oral school is to talk, talk, talk to the child until one day he or she will talk back. Parents are advised that they have to be teachers, they can't just be parents. If the deaf child can't understand what's being said within the family, such as why Dad is crying or why such-and-such is happening at the dinner table, there will be some developmental delays and difficulties for the child.

LIZABETH KATZ

We wonder why some deaf people are called immature or act strangely. Maybe I can explain this with the fact that hearing children often learn about appropriate behavior by listening, for example, when parents have an argument about deciding something. These children can overhear what it is the parents are saying and thereby learn about decision making in the family. The hearing children pick this up, whereas the deaf children don't hear it. As a result, deaf children often find it difficult to make decisions for themselves. Oftentimes parents (hearing) become too protective, and that can create further problems. Many young deaf people have a problem with self-esteem and may feel less competent than their hearing peers. Often, when there are teachers who are deaf, it is very helpful because they can be models for the children: "Look at me, I can do it; you can be successful, too!"

HOWARD BUSBY

I can follow this up and clarify it with some examples; the first is making change with money. How many people learn to make change at school? Most of us learn at home or at the grocery store, right? Well, deaf kids have to learn that in school because if a hearing child goes to the store with his or her mother, the cashier hands back the change while verbally adding it up. The hearing child knows how it is done then. Deaf children never hear that information. They know after they get to school and learn it from books. It's not done the same way it's done at the store, it's done with subtraction. "Ten dollars, subtract such-and-such," so when they go to the store, they try to make change by the cumbersome method of subtracting, and that is slow.

LIZABETH KATZ

I would like to share my mother's favorite story; she was an educator in the field of deafness and set up a parent organization. She used this story repeatedly; it's in relation to what Howard said: "I see, therefore I imitate." My mom took me to a store where there was a long line of children waiting to talk to Santa Claus. I was watching this with my mother standing nearby, and she said, "Go along, get in line with the other children." I said shyly, "Really? Me?" So I got in line to wait and watched this Santa Claus and how he communicated with the other children. They would sit on his lap and Santa would say, "And what would you like to have? Would you like a toy, or would you like candy?" Each child would say, "I think I'll have candy. Thank you very much," and step down. That was it. When it came my turn, Santa Claus spoke, and I said, "Blahblahblah," and put my hand out, probably for candy. Santa Claus looked at me puzzled and said, "Well, what do you want?" I just wagged my tongue, and Santa Claus didn't understand me. He then gave me something, and I walked away. My mother was amused; she realized I hadn't understood what was being said, I just imitated the movements.

HANK BERMAN

When I consult with schools that are trying to mainstream, I always ask, "Are you ready and willing to pay for interpreters? Are you going to have interpreters during football practice? During the recess and breaks? Are you going to have them at dances? Are you willing to have them in all social things, like the cafeteria and lunchtime?" They never think of that. They say, "What for? We have them in the classroom. The kids are here to learn." Learn what? The importance of learning social skills is often neglected in schools for the deaf. When some of the teachers and administration staff are deaf, there seems to be more social learning going on. There are often problems in schools with regard to the sexual development of the deaf child. Liz brought up the issue of protecting deaf children from experiences in which they might get hurt. This attitude often denies children information about sexuality and social skills.

Personally, I learned about sex on the street through friends and not so much from my deaf parents, although we had full communication. It's just that they felt uncomfortable and didn't want to tell me much about it until the "right time."

HOWARD BUSBY

During my school years I learned about sex from my deaf peers. A large majority of people I went to school with had heard English before they came to school. Today 90% of school-age hearing impaired children are prelingually deaf (deaf before acquiring speech). We were 7 to 10 years old when we came to school, so we had already picked up a lot about sex from hearing peers. I associated with hearing peers a lot, and I learned a lot about sex from them. Over the summer I had no deaf playmates; I lived in a town where there were only about three or four other deaf people, so I associated with hearing people. I was able to lip-read and teach them signs, so I learned some more from them. Hank said he learned about sex on the street; I had a similar experience.

JOANNE JAUREGUI

There was no sex education during my school years. I was very naive, but my peers and friends shared information with me. I did not understand what sex was until I saw homosexual interactions in the dorms where I lived and watched people's sexual behavior. Since I didn't understand what people were doing, I asked my friend and she said, "Oh, they're playing like mothers and fathers do," and I said, "Really?" It was all very vague for me. It didn't make sense to me. One day my parents brought a book full of pictures about sex and gave it to me. There were too many big words in it, but I picked up some information from the pictures. So with all this made up information, these myths and facts that I picked up as a base, I went to Gallaudet College and there learned a lot more from my peers.

For many people, living in college dorms was the beginning of their active sex lives. They just grew up all at once; it's where it really hit them. It almost was like culture shock.

Both in action and information we shared a lot—a lot of gossip. We got into a lot of talk that gave me more and more ideas about sex. I couldn't share this with my mother, who had grown up in England and was very passive about talking with me about sex. She and I didn't feel comfortable talking about sex, not because of her hearing but because of her background. I had a lot of friends who were older than I was, and with them I shared experiences. That was how I grew up knowing how to make the best choices for myself. From my experience of teaching the deaf kids in public schools, I don't think deaf children and adolescents have access to the right information to protect themselves.

LIZABETH KATZ

I find it difficult to remember where I learned sexual information. I guess at college. I got some information from adults, but basically I remember being curious and wanting to know more about sexuality and not knowing how to go about it. I remember the feeling of confusion during my teenage years; I was curious about boys, and whenever I got a chance to see someone change diapers on a child, I'd look and say, "What's that?" Someone would say, "A penis." So I was a very curious child but didn't know much.

I really got all my sexual facts straight by the time I joined a community telephone hotline with a deaf program. We had training, and this helped me get what I was seeking. Some topics in this training were active listening, drugs, sex, suicide, and communication. Also I was glad we got a chance in this training to explore ourselves and our own values and to see how we interact with both the hearing and deaf worlds socially.

HOWARD BUSBY

Using interpreters can affect our getting sexual information. I sometimes resent the fact that I have to depend on an interpreter to be honest with you. I feel that it interferes and cramps my style sometimes. It's a three-way communication process I don't always like or feel comfortable with. So that's one reason why I tend to avoid people I can't lip-read well. It hurts my relationships because I can't know those other people. I do try to communicate with a lot of people, but I intensely miss communicating in a meaningful way. I really feel the limitations of the use of an interpreter. I have to look at the interpreter every once in a while to make sure he or she is saying exactly what I'm signing. So, for me, using an interpreter is unnatural and uncomfortable.

When it comes to talking about sexuality with the use of an interpreter, many deaf people become reluctant. One big problem that I see is that the deaf community is very small. For example, I know Joanne but haven't seen her since 1957. So if she were in a clinic as a counselor, and I walked in as a client and saw her, I'd go right out the back door. I'd be afraid that she might tell the whole world about me. Deaf people tend to gossip a lot. Maybe that's true in the hearing world also, but we don't know about it.

HANK BERMAN

This is very important when we consider the unique relationship that must exist between a counselor and a person talking about a sexually related issue. As a counselor, how do I make you feel? I need to make you feel comfortable, willing to share, trusting, and open. I need to feel that way myself. Even if I am comfortable and you are, as well as the interpreter, where's the relationship? Is the relationship between you and me through the interpreter? Does it get watered down? If the interpreter is not comfortable with sexual material, then you, as the client, get that feeling and generalize that to me, as the counselor. If the interpreter is comfortable, and I'm not, do you then want to say, "I don't need you, counselor, I'm going to talk to my interpreter about my sexual problems." There are many complications that can happen in that situation.

One point that is tangential concerns what I call the "transmitters" in the deaf world. Those are people who have the power over information, for example, teachers, who censored books or movies when they wanted to, or the captioned film business that says, "We'll show some G-rated movies but none that are risque." For a long time they refused to caption some movies: "The deaf don't need stories about drugs and sex. It will pollute them. Protect them from that dirty stuff." Dorm counselors in schools who came fròm strict or fundamentalist religious backgrounds didn't want their students learning about sexuality. Now we see a new phenomenon: the professional interpreter, who does develop relationships with deaf people on the outside; the new dorm counselor who became socialized sexually in the 1960s and 1970s; and the new young teachers of the deaf. These people's attitudes have changed.

HOWARD BUSBY

Recently I talked with someone in a wheelchair, and we discussed communication and the communication process. My friend made an analogy about my using an interpreter in the same way that he uses a wheelchair. We both need them, but why can't I accept an interpreter the way he accepts the wheelchair? First of all, the wheelchair does not communicate with you, it does not socialize with you, and it does not make love to you either; but the interpreter is a human being.

RECOMMENDED READINGS

Fitz-Gerald, D., and Fitz-Gerald, M.: Sex education survey in residential facilities for the deaf, Am. Ann. Deaf **121**(5):480-483, 1976.

Fitz-Gerald, D., and Fitz-Gerald, M., special editors: Sex. Disabil. **2**:159-252, 1979. (Special theme issue devoted to issues of the deaf, blind, and deaf-blind.)

SIECUS Rep. **6**:1-16, 1977. (Special issue on deafness and sexuality.)

Smith, M.S.: The deaf. In Gochros, H.L., and Gochros, J.S., editors: The sexually oppressed, New York, 1977, Association Press.

♂ ABOUT THE AUTHORS ♀

Hank Berman, M.A., is a licensed marriage, family, and child therapist, and his clients are primarily hearing impaired individuals and their families. His parents are both deaf, and he holds a comprehensive skills certificate from the Registry of Interpreters for the Deaf. Recently, Mr. Berman was a trainer at the Sex and Disability Unit of the Human Sexuality Program, Department of Psychiatry, University of California, San Francisco. He is currently active in advocating the mental health needs of the deaf in California.

Howard Busby, M.A., is a counselor and therapist for the deaf and has had training at the Sex and Disability Unit of the Human Sexuality Program, Department of Psychiatry, University of California, San Francisco. He is currently working on his doctorate in counseling at the University of Arizona. Deaf since the age of 5, he has been involved in numerous programs of and for the deaf, including sex counseling for deaf adolescents and adults.

Elizabeth Hall is completing her master's degree in education for the deaf at California State University, Northridge, and works in an outreach program to the deaf community at Planned Parenthood, Los Angeles, California. She has had training at the Sex and Disability Unit of the Human Sexuality Program, Department of Psychiatry, University of California, San Francisco. Ms. Hall has a progressive hearing loss that began suddenly 4 years ago.

Lizabeth Katz is an educator for the deaf community at Planned Parenthood, Los Angeles, California. Deaf from birth, she received her bachelor's degree in community health education at California State University, Northridge, and has had training at the Sex and Disability Unit, Human Sexuality Program, Department of Psychiatry, University of California, San Francisco. She has conducted workshops on the use of interpreters in medical and family planning settings.

Joanne Jauregui has been teaching multihandicapped, deaf, and hearing-impaired children for 17 years and was the first deaf teacher to be hired in a public school in California. Ms. Jauregui has taught American Sign Language since 1971, and for the past 2 years has been coordinator of Deaf Services, Center for Independent Living, Berkeley, California.

SURGICAL AND MEDICAL CONDITIONS

22 Self-image and sexuality after mastectomy

Regina Kriss

Denial, stoicism, and prayer are common defense mechanisms among cancer patients.[8] Denial is the most common defense response to cancer and mastectomy in all studies reported.[6] Not only patients but also their doctors tend to deny the importance of breast loss to the woman's readjustment and quality of life. When weighed against the risk of early death, the amputation, mutilation, and destruction of femininity associated with mastectomy seem of little matter to physicians. Is it any wonder that physicians in general are of little help to women with problems of self-image and sexuality?

The doctor-patient relationship is of primary importance to the women. Typically, however, one hears comments such as, "My doctor didn't prepare me," "After surgery my doctor said that I was doing beautifully. I smiled bravely and didn't show my horror, anger, and self-pity," or "When I told my doctor how I couldn't sleep on the side of the surgery, he said, 'You're only missing a breast.'" There are also stories of compassionate, kind doctors who hold your hand and even have tears in their eyes. However, the majority of doctors are either unaware of the overwhelming psychological effect of mastectomy on a woman's body image or feel so helpless to deal with such problems that they prefer to ignore them.

The single thing that angers a woman most is being told she simply has a vanity problem. She feels dewomanized and mutilated and especially demeaned by wearing a prosthesis where her breast used to be. A woman who has lost a breast feels the way a man would who has lost his penis. Both organs are symbolic of sexuality, and each defines the sex of that person. Not only does she feel inadequate but disfigured and even dishonest in passing for a "normal" woman by wearing a prosthesis. This discrepant feeling can lead to a great deal of psychological pain and discomfort.[3]

The usual emphasis of mastectomy adjustment is placed on outward appearance, often starting with the "Reach to Recovery" visitor who looks charming in her clothes and extending to meetings with women who have reconstructed breasts and are able to show cleavage in a low-cut dress or bathing suit. A woman is very grateful for the perfect outside appearance, but the inconsistency of this with her "real" appearance gives her the feeling of being a fraud: "Everyone says I look fine, but underneath I look terrible." This dilemma, kept to herself, erodes self-confidence and can have a devastating effect on sexuality.

In working with women in groups, I have asked them to go home and take a relaxed bath or shower, dry themselves softly, apply oils and lotions with sensuous touch, and then look at themselves nude in the mirror. They were to report whatever feelings or images came up. One woman with a bilateral mastectomy said, "I looked like an old-fashioned washboard that you could scrub clothes on." Another said, "I looked like a wreck from an auto accident." Another woman said, "I looked like I had been hit with two hand grenades," and added, "I can't even use the word, but I feel asexual." A young single woman who had recently had bilateral breast reconstruction said, "I looked like Frankenstein's monster. One breast is higher by an inch or two, and an ugly scar remains where the nipple was, a gaping hole that didn't heal. The doctors told me it was a perfect job but that sometimes the breasts just don't match up." Her forlorn face told the story: "I look fine to everybody else but me."

The women in the first two groups of a program at Stanford University were asked to respond to a question concerning body image (see Fig. 22-1). They were asked to rate numerically in three different ways (columns A, B, and C) the 17 body regions indicated in the body drawing. Thus an area highly liked in all three ways would rank 3, whereas an area highly disliked in all ways would rank 15. A neutral area would rank around 9.

Fig. 22-2 indicates the mean rank score of the 17 areas. Even in the present small sample there are highly significant differences. Note that a large number of areas were ranked as neutral (range 7 to 11.5) such as eyes, mouth, nose, hand, shoulders, abdomen, and hips. It is clear that although the unamputated breast is highly favored (average rank more than 5.6), the amputated breast is not just a neutral area but a highly disfavored one (average rank about 14.6).

Women who undergo mastectomy suffer manifestations of psychological maladjustment that may result in their feeling rejected, sexually mutilated, and depressed. These feelings often contribute to poor self-image, sense of worthlessness, difficulties in interpersonal relationships, avoidance of social contact, decline in sexual activity, and, in some cases, deterioration of marriage.

Basic to a woman's sexual functioning is an ability to abandon herself to erotic or sexual feelings. Focusing on her surgical scars will interfere with her process of arousal and decrease orgasmic release. Furthermore, the woman's distractions and concerns about performance may be exacerbated by the worry that her male partner is no longer attracted to her. This in itself disrupts sexual pleasure.[4]

The data on sexual behavior of the first 19 women in the Stanford University study show that 16 (84%) are married or involved in a long-term relationship; 2 of the remaining 3 so involved at the time of mastectomy report that the mastectomy

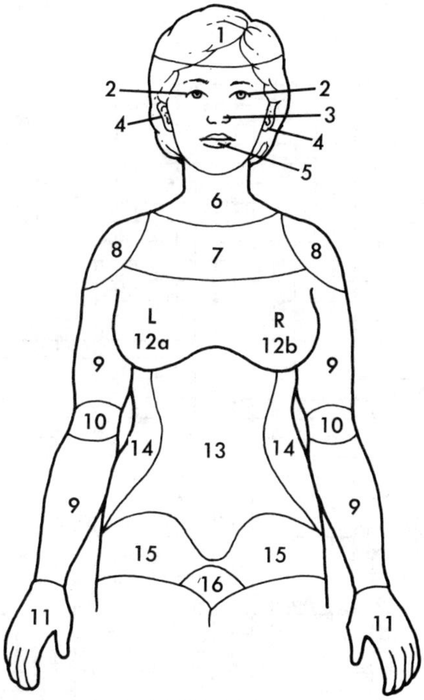

	I like-dislike this area of my body					I like-dislike touching this area of my own body					I like-dislike having my partner touch this area				
	A					B					C					
Body areas	Like			Dislike		Like			Dislike		Like			Dislike		
1	1	2	3	4	5	1	2	3	4	5	1	2	3	4	5	
2	1	2	3	4	5	1	2	3	4	5	1	2	3	4	5	
3	1	2	3	4	5	1	2	3	4	5	1	2	3	4	5	
4	1	2	3	4	5	1	2	3	4	5	1	2	3	4	5	
5	1	2	3	4	5	1	2	3	4	5	1	2	3	4	5	
6	1	2	3	4	5	1	2	3	4	5	1	2	3	4	5	
7	1	2	3	4	5	1	2	3	4	5	1	2	3	4	5	
8	1	2	3	4	5	1	2	3	4	5	1	2	3	4	5	
9	1	2	3	4	5	1	2	3	4	5	1	2	3	4	5	
10	1	2	3	4	5	1	2	3	4	5	1	2	3	4	5	
11	1	2	3	4	5	1	2	3	4	5	1	2	3	4	5	
12a	1	2	3	4	5	1	2	3	4	5	1	2	3	4	5	
12b	1	2	3	4	5	1	2	3	4	5	1	2	3	4	5	
13	1	2	3	4	5	1	2	3	4	5	1	2	3	4	5	
14	1	2	3	4	5	1	2	3	4	5	1	2	3	4	5	
15	1	2	3	4	5	1	2	3	4	5	1	2	3	4	5	
16	1	2	3	4	5	1	2	3	4	5	1	2	3	4	5	

Using the key below, circle the number that best describes your likes or dislikes

KEY
1 Like intensely
2 Like
3 Neutral
4 Dislike
5 Dislike intensely

Fig. 22-1. Body image rating chart.

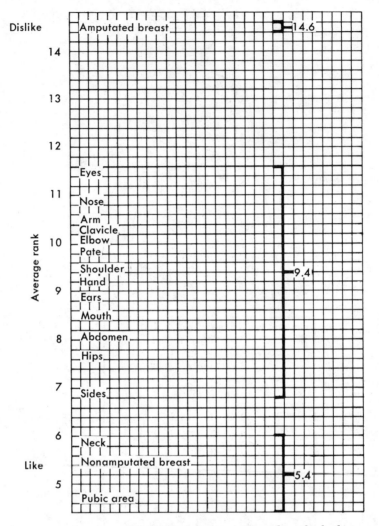

Fig. 22-2. The mean rank scores of the 17 body regions as rated on the body image chart.

disrupted the relationship. Of the women under 50 (n = 10), 50% report their present sexual adjustment as poor or very poor, and 50% report that they have recently had intercourse less than once per week. Of the women over 50 (n = 9), 78% report poor or very poor sexual adjustment, and 75% report intercourse less than once per week with 44% reporting no sexual intercourse at all in the last month. The indications then, even from the preliminary data, are that the women are suffering from a considerable degree of sexual dissatisfaction.

Many women may believe that their husbands will help them recover their previous feelings of sexual wholeness. The husband, however, may also be suffering from shock and reaction to his wife's disfigurement and may need help for himself before he can help her. This is a serious dilemma. In his desire to keep his wife from further pain and hurt, he does not share with her or anyone else how he really feels about her disfigurement. He is not allowed to cry, and he is not able to tell his wife how sad and unhappy he is for her as well as for himself. If the woman asks her husband or lover whether her post-mastectomy body still turns him on, he is likely to answer that the loss of breast means nothing compared to her restored health: "For all I care one, two, or even three breasts are all the same to me." What else could the husband say? Can he tell her he has stopped reading *Playboy* and telling sexy jokes, and he is unable to look at other women's breasts without feeling sad? How does the husband grieve for the loss of his wife's breast, and how does this affect his adjustment?

Perhaps one of the most threatening experiences for either partner is to have negative feelings and no way to express them. From the doctor, family, and friends the patient and her husband are encouraged to think positively. A typical remark is, "How marvelous you look; who would guess what you have been through?" This approach does not encourage expression of negative feelings. A husband is not apt to blurt out to his wife, "I can't bear to look at your washboard chest," or "God, those two hand grenades sure messed you up." We have been taught to thrive on compliments and hide our real thoughts even from ourselves. The ultimate effects can be devastating: "My husband won't come near me. We now have separate bedrooms. When my husband looks at other women, I feel I can't measure up to them." From a single woman: "I used to enjoy being with men. Now I'm afraid of being rejected." Another says, "The friend who usually dances with me at parties seems afraid to ask me to dance anymore. I feel hurt." Some other remarks are: "My husband won't talk about it, but he says he can no longer have sex with me;" "My husband says it doesn't matter, but I don't believe him, because he has rarely initiated sex since my mastectomy;" and "I feel dishonest when a man shows an interest in me. Would he show an interest after he saw my body?"

One of the questions in the Stanford University questionnaire was: Since your mastectomy, has your husband or partner talked to you about:
- The way your body looks to him?
- How he feels about your loss of breast?
- Whether it has affected his sexual desire for you?

The majority of women have answered, "He avoids talking about it totally," or "He seems awkward, but talks about it a little." We also asked the woman if she had talked to her husband about:
- Fear that her body might be a "turn off" to him?
- Fear that she has of being rejected sexually?
- Wanting and needing his love and acceptance?

Again the majority of answers have been "I have never talked to him about it," or "I have but feel awkward."

Witkin[12] described the "mastectomy bind" as a self-fulfilling prophecy:

> The woman feels that the loss of the breast has rendered her unattractive sexually, an object of pity rather than ardor. Not wishing to seem pitiable or act as a "drag" on her husband, she does not share her feelings with him. Fearing rejection because of her ugly wound, she does not generally exhibit sexual interest and waits for the husband to take the initiative. The husband, unsure of his wife's desires and distrustful of his own fear and inability to accept the loss of breast or tolerate the wound, fears he will do something wrong and hurt his wife. The "bind" is that, despite the fact that each desires physical and emotional closeness, each fears to approach the other, and the man and woman move apart.

The marriage that breaks up after mastectomy is labeled as not strong enough or too problem ridden to last anyway. Clearly this may be too simplistic a view.

If diminished sexual activity becomes a problem because the medical condition makes a patient and partner afraid to engage in it, they are deprived of the joy and sense of well-being. This change may contribute to more frustration, unhappiness, and strife in the relationship.[15] When sexual adjustment and activities are adversely affected, women usually feel rejected and avoid sex altogether.[5,10]

Such problems are themselves related to recovery. Cancer patients may have considerable difficulty in interpersonal relationships, and it has been observed that there is a direct relationship between the quality of a patient's interpersonal relationship and ability to cope with illness.[13]

Wabrek states that the reaction to losing a breast is identical to that of losing (by death or divorce) a loved one. The predictable phases of this grief reaction are (1) denial, (2) depression, (3) anger, (4) acceptance, and (5) resolution. However, case histories indicate that some women who do very well in the immediate postoperative period may develop a deep depression later.[9] This finding is consistent with a study of the pattern of change in body image of patients who underwent mastectomy. It may take several months before loss of self-esteem is reported. This phenomenon may reflect the diminished effectiveness of denial as a coping mechanism.[7]

The approach we have chosen to these problems is to shift the focus away from the partner initially and onto the woman herself. *She* must bear the responsibility for removing the barriers that prevent ventilation of negative feelings. *She* must deal with her own negative feelings before she can respond to and help with the feelings of those close to her. Having no one with whom to share feelings outside her family increases the chance of her problems becoming more severe. Therapy groups serve as an outlet for such feelings.

One of the main purposes of group therapy is to discover what feelings are really present and to allow them to surface and be shared with others who have also experienced breast loss. We can grow to accept almost anything if we are given an opportunity to fully explore our feelings about it. In group therapy, women are able to share similar experiences, thus finding out that they are not alone or the worst off. There is a lessening of fears, mutual caring and helping others, learning to ask for help, and an increased enjoyment of intimacy. Communication by speech, touch, glance, smile, or grimace is a powerful tool for dealing with sexual concerns. Frank discussions of sexual matters dispel guilt and myths, which are barriers to satisfying relationships particularly for those who have some form of disability.[2]

This is all part of the unburdening process. As we go deeper into the therapy, we begin to see behavior change. Some examples of this are the way the patients look and dress, weight loss, return to work or improved jobs, and improved relationships with husband and family. We have included specific communication skills for the patients to learn and practice on their doctors, families, and friends to instill confidence and awareness of their goals.

One positive effect of cancer is facing one's mortality, a realization that time is running out. If there are things to change or accomplish or goals to develop, now is the time to formulate and act on them. In a recent newspaper article California Chief Justice Rose Elizabeth Bird wrote, "When you face the fact of your own mortality, you must also face the facts about what you have done with your life. In a peculiar way, death can teach you what life is all about."[1]

A desire to do the most with herself can teach a woman to accept her mastectomy and to learn how to feel fully alive. But first she must have a strong feeling of her sense of worth, and this is not easy to accomplish. Not only must she accept herself, but she must help her husband and family accept her. This means she should learn to see her nude body as it is without feeling demeaned or less of a woman. One feels a loss of innocence when one becomes aware of body changes, aging, fading beauty, poor health, and whatever else a person would rather not face. This loss of innocence can be a way of growing, maturing, and gathering the strength to deal with the problems each woman has to confront.

Many women may feel that facing these difficult feelings would only make them worse and would rather use denial as a way of avoiding change. Anticipation of the future, recurrence of cancer, and further body destruction are overwhelming fears with which to contend. It is understandable that as a natural response to these fears a woman would seek protection from uncomfortable feelings by using denial. We are attempting to employ the group therapy as a means of uncovering these fears, airing them in the group, and restructuring or reframing their meaning in a context that ultimately means changing values, interaction, and communication in the family and marital relationship. If sexuality is viewed as a global feeling, a feeling of vitality and desirability can emerge. To achieve this a woman has no alternative but to see herself as a heroine and survivor of a dangerous battle worthy of the highest respect and regard. She is a beauty in a new form. The task may be almost as difficult as that of the maiden in *Rumpelstiltskin* who wove flax into gold. Somehow this effort must be made if a woman is to become vital, worthwhile, and desirable to herself and others even in full view of her mastectomy.

In our previous experience in group therapy of terminally ill patients, we observed that by openly confronting death, many patients adopted a mode of existence that seemed richer than their previous one. For example, they reported a fuller appreciation of changing seasons, sunsets, love for others, and gratitude for the parts of their bodies that still functioned. Many felt they had radically altered their perspective, and they expressed a sense of liberation and autonomy as a result of this confrontation.[14]

We hope the confrontation with cancer and body image will similarly benefit women. After mastectomy a woman needs to unburden her feelings, fears, and anger, so she can change her attitude and gain a sense of well-being and psychological wholeness, despite a changed body. If it is true that the sexual self-concept supersedes mortality as the primary concern of most recovering mastectomy patients,[11] then the focus on self-image and sexuality should enhance the lives of mastectomy patients and provide the basis for encouraging others to seek this kind of treatment.

REFERENCES

1. Bird, R.E.: Cancer is not an automatic death sentence, San Jose Mercury News, July 20, 1980.
2. Diamond, M.: Sexuality and the handicapped. In Stubbins, J., editor: Social and psychological aspects of disability, Baltimore, 1977, University Park Press.
3. Goffman, E.: Stigma: notes of the management of spoiled identity, Englewood Cliffs, N.J., 1963, Prentice-Hall, Inc.
4. Kaplan, H.S.: The new sex therapy, New York, 1974, Brunner Mazel, Inc.
5. Maguire, P.: The psychological and social consequences of breast cancer, Nurs. Mirror 140:54, 1975.
6. Meyerowitz, B.E.: Psychosocial correlates of breast cancer and its treatment, Psychol. Bull. 87:108, 1980.
7. Polivy, J.: Psychological effects of mastectomy on a woman's feminine self-concept, J. Nerv. Ment. Dis. 164:77, 1977.
8. Shands, H.C., Finesinger, J.E., Cobb, S., and Abrams, R.D.: Psychological mechanisms in patients with cancer, Cancer 4:1159, 1951.
9. Wabrek, A.J., and Wabrek, C.J.: Mastectomy: sexual implications, Primary Care 3:803, 1976.
10. Wells, R.W.: Body image and surgical operations, Am. J. Organ. Reg. Nurs. 21:812, 1975.
11. Witkin, M.H.: Psychosexual counseling of the mastectomy patient, J. Sex Marital Ther. 4:20, 1978.
12. Witkin, M.H.: Psychological concerns in sexual rehabilitation and mastectomy, Sex. Disabil. 2:54, 1979.
13. Wortman, C.B., and Dunkel-Schetter, C.: Interpersonal relationships and cancer, J. Soc. Issues 34:120, 1979.
14. Yalom, I.D., and Graves, C.: Group therapy with the terminally ill, Am. J. Psychiatry 134:396, 1977.
15. Zilbergeld, B.: Sex and serious illness. In Garfield, C., editor: Stress and survival: the emotional realities of life-threatening illness, St. Louis, 1979, The C.V. Mosby Co.

♀ ABOUT THE AUTHOR ♀

Regina Kriss is a doctoral candidate and a licensed marriage and family therapist and was trained at the Human Sexuality Program at the University of California, San Francisco. She is presently collaborating with Professor Helena Kraemer at Stanford University Medical Center in a 3-year research project involving 100 women after 1 year of group therapy to study the effects of mastectomy on self-image and sexuality. Previously, she worked with Dr. Irvin Yalom, professor of psychiatry at Stanford University, treating group therapy patients who had breast cancer and metastases. She has had two mastectomies herself over a period of 24 years.

23 Sexual functioning following creation of an abdominal stoma

Victor Alterescu

Throughout most of history, illness was a clearly definable and distinct entity. One either died or got well; there was little in between. It was not until the years after World War II that the disease burden within the United States had taken on a different character. Illnesses previously called "terminal" are now giving way to "chronic" and "debilitating" illnesses. Indeed, as advances in medical technology continue, there is the paradoxical result that the numbers of chronically ill increase. Therefore in greater numbers than ever before our society is composed of persons with disabilities of one sort or another that require some changes in life-style. In addition, disabled people are requesting health care professionals to address themselves to issues concerning the "quality" of life as well as "quantity."

A type of surgery that necessitates altered functioning and could be considered disabling is ostomy surgery. It entails a change in one's bowel or bladder habits. Usually the change is permanent, though it can be temporary.

An "ostomy" is a general term that describes an opening in the body. The prefix to the term "ostomy" designates into which organ the opening is. Therefore a "colostomy" is an opening into the colon. An "ileostomy" is an opening into the ileum (the final segment of the small intestine). "Urostomy" is a general term referring to any diversion of urine. In all cases, either urine or feces (or sometimes both) are diverted from the intestine or bladder to a surgically created opening on the abdominal wall. The actual portion of intestine or urinary tract that is firmly sutured to the abdomen, usually in the lower left or right quadrant, is called a "stoma." Abdominal stomas can be created for any number of reasons.

The colostomy, the most usual of the three general ostomies, is usually performed on persons middle-aged and older. The most common indication is cancer of the rectum or large intestine. However, it may also be performed to alleviate severe diverticulitis, in which case the ostomy is usually temporary. A colostomy may also be performed on a newborn. Congenital anomalies, such as Hirschsprung's disease and imperforate anus, may necessitate a colostomy (usually temporary). As a rule, however, a colostomy may be essential when the fecal stream

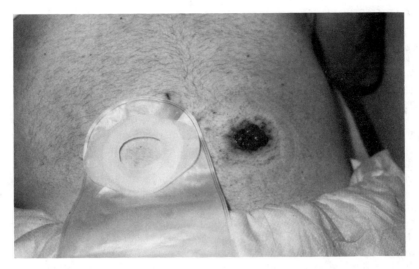

Fig. 23-1. Photograph of a 44-year-old man with a permanent colostomy. The portion of intestine, which is exteriorized in the lower left quadrant of the abdomen, is the stoma. The patient is holding the pouch that he wears: a plastic, polyethylene plate with a odorproof, clear pouch attached to the plate. The whole appliance adheres to the skin around the stoma. For additional support, the patient may wear a belt that attaches to the polyethylene plate.

has to be diverted. It is a lifesaving procedure. Adjustment to this altered form of elimination can be difficult (see Fig. 23-1.)

The ileostomy is usually performed in conjunction with a total colectomy. The colon and often the rectum are removed, and an abdominal stoma is fashioned from the remaining ileum. Such surgery is indicated when a person has some fulminant form of inflammatory bowel disease such as Crohn's disease or ulcerative colitis. Persons who usually require an ileostomy range in age from teenagers to persons in their early thirties. The most severe phases of bowel disease usually occur during this period of the life span. There are situations, though, when a middle-aged or older person may need to have an ileostomy. Bowel disease is rare, though certainly known to be present, in infants and children. Because persons with inflammatory bowel disease are so ill before surgery, and because surgery may result in a cure, an ileostomy is often looked on as a welcomed relief.

The urostomy is most commonly performed as a treatment for cancer of the bladder. The bladder is removed, and the urine is diverted, usually via an isolated segment of small or large intestine through an abdominal stoma. Other diseases that may require a urinary diversion or urostomy are neurogenic bladder, urinary incontinence, or birth defects such as myelomeningocele and exstrophy of the bladder. Persons with urostomies are at both ends of the age spectrum; elderly persons and children are the two age groups that most often undergo urostomy surgery.

TYPICAL CASE STUDIES

♂John is a 55 year-old-professional. On Thursday he notices some blood in his stool. Realizing that this could be an early sign of cancer, John immediately sees his doctor. He does have cancer. He is admitted to the hospital on Sunday and has a sigmoid colostomy on Tuesday. The physician explains that John may experience some sexual dysfunction postoperatively.

♀Susan is a 22-year-old graduate student. She has had inflammatory bowel disease for 8 years. She can no longer continue her studies because most of her time is spent in the hospital or the bathroom. It is suggested that she have a total colectomy, including removal of the rectum, and an ileostomy. After attending a meeting of the United Ostomy Association and discussing an ileostomy with several other women, she decides to have surgery. Even though Susan has tried to prepare herself for the surgery, she is still very frightened. Her physician may indicate to her that he expects her to feel much better after the surgery than she felt previously.

♂Mike is a 62-year-old truck driver. He has a cancer of the bladder that can be removed only if he has a cystectomy and ileal conduit (that is, removal of the bladder and formation of a urostomy by using an isolated segment of ileum and implanting the ureters into it). The surgery is performed. Mike will undergo radiation treatment before surgery as well as chemotherapy after the surgery. He will be out of work for several weeks. The physician has explained to him that removal of the bladder also includes removal of the prostate and seminal vesicles. Mike will be unable to ejaculate or achieve an erection. After surgery the physician indicates to Mike that he thinks "he got it all."

From these short sketches one can compile a list of possible concerns that may run the gamut from being passing thoughts to consuming obsessions. Any number of known and unknown variables may determine which concerns become prevalent, if any, and which not. The following is an overview of specific sexual questions:

1. Will the patient's significant other(s) still consider him/her desirable and attractive?
2. Will the patient be capable of maintaining social usefulness such as working, mothering, or fathering?
3. Will the male patient continue to be capable, assuming he was in the past, of maintaining and/or achieving an erection and ejaculation?
4. Will the patient need to make adjustments in the types of clothing worn?
5. Will the patient experience pain during intercourse?
6. Will the patients who have had the rectum removed mourn the loss of this sex organ?
7. Will the pouch interfere with sexual activities?
8. How will the patient explain the existence of a pouch to a new partner?
9. Will the person who had/has cancer be overwhelmed by fears of death?
10. Will the patient feel that the whole experience is not "worth it"?
11. In short, will the ostomy keep the person from being/becoming the person that he or she wants to be?

As a result of such questions and scenarios, I have compiled the following outline that describes the most common sexual concerns of people who have undergone ostomy surgery*:

A. Mechanical
   1. Appliance is unattractive.
   2. Appliance does not adhere.
   3. Patient can no longer wear certain types of undergarments and outer clothing.
   4. Patient fears that appliance is discernable under clothing.
   5. Patient fears that there is an odor.
   6. Pouch gets in the way during sexual activities.
B. Physiologic
   1. Dyspareunia may occur in women due to scarring of perineum.
   2. Men may be unable to achieve or maintain an erection due to S2-4 parasympathetic nerve damage.
   3. Retrograde (or nonexistent) ejaculation may occur due to damage of L1-3 sympathetic nerves.
   4. Postoperative weakness may exist.
   5. Medications (antihypertensives, phenothiazines, etc.) may have side effects.
C. Psychologic
   1. Depression results.
   2. Regression results.
   3. Stress is put on an already strained relationship.
   4. Patient fears death.
   5. Patient experiences natural grieving process.
   6. Patient responds with anger.

Mechanical problems are those which pertain to the wearing of a pouch itself. They are similar to those concerns which are attendant on the wearing of any prosthetic device. The additional factor, however, is that ostomy pouches contain bodily wastes and therefore have an inherent repugnance, since most persons, except possibly very young children, establish a distaste for excrement and urine early in life.

The physiologic problems that may accompany ostomy surgery can be due directly to the surgeon's knife, such as nerve damage and scar formation, or may be the results of any major surgery, such as weakness and pain medication.

Last, it is in the psychologic realm that the majority of concerns exist. For example, depression will inhibit one's ability to perform and to enjoy sex. Regression to a dependent state, a phenomenon often seen by nursing staff, can result in an apparant lack of interest in sex. Stress on any relationship, and ostomy surgery certainly is stressful, can separate couples as well as bring them together. Surgery of any sort, and especially body image–changing surgery, can create a chasm between partners, family, and friends. The number of reactions is quite limitless and the reader is encouraged to consider as many possibilities as imaginable.

---

*This outline is not designed to exhaustively delineate all the items that may fall within the categories of mechanical, physiologic, and psychological concerns. It also is not meant to imply that an individual necessarily will have any particular concern listed.

A FRAMEWORK FOR APPROACHING A CLIENT WHO HAS SEXUAL CONCERNS

The following outlines an adaptation of the first three components of the PLISSIT (Permission, Limited Information, Specific Suggestions, Intensive Therapy) model[1] to the needs of someone whose sexual concerns revolve around ostomy surgery.* The reader may note that the aspect of "Permission" is actually quite universal and not in the least particular for the person with an ostomy. Such a situation is understandable and points out the fact that people with ostomies have much in common with other people who have sexual concerns. On the other hand, there is some very specific information that is unique to the person with an ostomy.

A. Permission
  1. To discuss sexual concerns openly and honestly
  2. To engage in those sexual practices which are of concern
  3. Not to engage in those sexual practices which are of concern
  4. To expect a listener who is comfortable discussing sexual matter, accepting of those sexual matters which are the object of discussion, and free from judging
B. Limited Information
  1. That it is common to be depressed postoperatively
  2. That depression, regression, postoperative weakness and the like will affect one's ability to function sexually
  3. That scarring of the perineum may make intercourse painful for females
  4. That nerve destruction (both sympathetic and/or parasympathetic) may have occurred
  5. That erections, ejaculation, and orgasms are all each independent of the other
C. Specific Suggestions
  1. Kegel exercises
  2. "Squeeze" technique
  3. Selecting an ostomy pouch with the aid of an enterostomal therapist
  4. Sensate focusing
  5. Noncoital forms of sex play, e.g., fellatio, cunnilingus, masturbation
  6. Penile implants

The ultimate adjustment of persons with ostomies, including sexual adjustment, will depend to a great extent on the acceptance they receive from those who are closest to them. This point not only crystallizes the direction one's efforts toward adjustment must take, namely, in the continuance or establishment of healthy relationships, but it also points out the difficulty of dealing with someone who is isolated. The isolated person undergoing body image–changing surgery is most often at risk for developing emotional and sexual difficulties.

When counseling someone who has an ostomy, the health professional must consider several items: the reactions of those persons closest to the client; any mechanical problems the client may be having with the wearing of the pouch; the

---

*From Annon, J.: Behavioral treatment of sexual problems, vol. 1, New York, 1976, Harper & Row Publishers, Inc., pp. 45-119. This outline is not designed to exhaustively delineate all the items that may fall within the categories of "permission," "limited information," and "specific suggestions."

possibility of actual physiological changes resulting from surgery; and, most importantly, the psychological state of the individual. Indeed, identifying which issue is at the forefront of one's difficulties may require a great deal of very thorough investigation.

TWO CASE STUDIES RECONSIDERED

Now let us go back and assume that John and Susan are visiting us to discuss some sexual concerns. We have gathered our data by asking them how they perceive the situation, how long it has been an issue, what they think would make it resolve, or what keeps it from resolving. In short, we try to get as complete a perspective as possible of how they view the situation that concerns them. We are careful not to label the "problem," jump to conclusions, or make value judgements and to remove ourselves as therapeutic persons should we find ourselves unable to accept the sexual practices of our client.

John has been back to work for 3 months. He looks healthy, and all his tests are indicative of cure from disease. He believes he is free of cancer at this time. He has been able to maintain his job, his income, his role as a father, but not "my role as a husband."

Interviewer: What do you mean?
John: Although I can perform many of the functions of a husband, I cannot have sex.
Interviewer: What do you mean by sex? Are you referring to intercourse?
John: Yes, I cannot have intercourse.
Interviewer: Why?
John: I cannot keep an erection.
Interviewer: Were you able to maintain an erection before your surgery? When did your not being able to keep an erection begin?
John: I have had this problem ever since my surgery. Not before, or at least, not all the time before. Now, I never can get an erection.
Interviewer: Why do you think you cannot get an erection now?
John: I think it is because of my surgery. The doctor said this could happen.
Interviewer: Is it important for you to have intercourse?
John: I think my wife wants it.
Interviewer: How do you feel about it?
John: I have not been too interested lately.

Note that the interviewer assumed very little. It could have been possible to jump from John's not having sex to assuming that it meant intercourse, was obviously related to his surgery, and was organic, since nerve interruption was highly likely. However, by not leaving out any step in the process of gathering data, the interviewer has given John, by asking the appropriate questions, permission to explain his circumstances as he sees them. Should nothing further be done, the interviewer has already been of help to John. Should the interview, or rather the relationship, continue, then the interviewer could move from the "permission" phase to the "limited information" aspect of John's situation. One could explain the following to John:

1. It can take several years for nerve regeneration to recur, if indeed, any destruction has taken place.
2. If John gets an erection at any time, then it is likely that the physiological apparatus is intact.
3. His major surgery was not so long ago, and even though he is back to work, he may still need some more time before his sexual interest and abilities will return.
4. When interest is lacking, it is difficult for anyone to be sexually responsive.
5. Many people are depressed after ostomy surgery, even though they would not describe themselves as such, and this is a normal, reactive depression that can diminish sexual interest and is usually self-limiting.

Going on to the area of "specific suggestions":

1. John could discuss with his wife his feelings revolving around his desire to please her.
2. He could attempt noncoital forms of sex play or simply nonsexual touching and caressing.
3. He could discuss with his wife her feelings regarding his recent surgery.

As the relationship progresses, data and circumstances may indicate an organic etiology to John's erectile difficulties. However, a therapeutic relationship will have been established and other specific suggestions could then replace the current ones.

In Susan's case, let us assume that she explains in an interview she no longer feels feminine; she is unable to have casual affairs as she did in the past; her pouch is odiferous; she fears rejection; and she is no longer able to experience multiple orgasms. Again, by providing a certain amount of information, one can supply a context for her experience. For example, one could indicate to Susan the following: changes in orgasms have occurred to other women and sometimes resolve after about a year; there are pouches that are impermeable to odor; her fears of rejection are understandable; and people usually respond to a person with a stoma in the same manner as that person feels about herself. Specific suggestions could include seeing an enterostomal therapist, addressing herself to the legitimate grief she feels as a result of surgery, acknowledging her feelings about wearing a pouch, and continuing to have relationships even though she fears rejection.

CONCLUSION

Although I have primarily addressed myself to sexual difficulties, I do not wish to give the impression that all persons who have undergone ostomy surgery will have them. I would say that most persons who have had major surgery, debilitating disease, cancer, or anesthesia will probably experience feelings of loss and a chronic, low-grade depression for at least 3 months. In some cases, sexual dysfunction may be superimposed over some other primary concern, for example, fear of death. In other cases, sexual functioning may be *the* issue. I would caution the interviewer to assume nothing and expect the data to be consistently changing throughout the first year after surgery. By providing suggestions and information, and, most importantly, by being an empathic listener, the interviewer can help alleviate some of the experiential loneliness that the client may be feeling. By helping the client to express feelings of loss and grief and to frankly talk about sexual concerns, one is then in the best possible position to make informed and increasingly more specific suggestions.

RESOURCES

Enterostomal therapists are nurses who have received specialized training in the care of persons who have undergone ostomy surgery. Most graduate from a school of enterostomal therapy that has been accredited by the International Association for Enterostomal Therapy. Not only do such therapists receive specialized training in the mechanical aspects of stoma care, but they also receive instruction in the rehabilitative needs of stoma patients, including grief and sexual counseling.

The United Ostomy Association was founded as a self-help support group to provide emotional support to persons during the early adjustment phase after surgery. Chapters of the United Ostomy Association exist in almost every large city, and the groups usually meet monthly. Such chapters are often listed in the phone book. Additionally, the American Cancer Society may be able to direct one to the nearest chapter.

REFERENCE

1. Annon, J.S.: Behavioral treatment of sexual problems, vol. 1, New York, 1976, Harper & Row Publishers, Inc.

SUGGESTED READINGS FOR THE PROFESSIONAL

Bernstein, W.: Sexual dysfunction following radical surgery for cancer of the rectum and sigmoid colon, Med. Aspects Hum. Sex. **6:**156-163, 1972.

Druss, R., et al.: Psychological response to colectomy. I. Arch. Gen. Psychiatry **18:**53-59, 1968.

Druss, R., et al.: Psychological response to colectomy. II. Arch. Gen. Psychiatry **20:**419-427, 1969.

Gallagher, A.: Body image changes in the patient with a colostomy, Nurs. Clin. North Am. **7:**697-707, 1972.

Gruner, O.P., et al.: Marital status and sexual adjustment after colectomy, Scand. J. Gastroenterol. **12:**193-197, 1977.

Littlefield, V.: The surgical patient's sexuality, AORN J. **26:**649-658, 1977.

Lyons, A.: Sex after ileostomy and colostomy, Med. Aspects Hum. Sex. **9:**107, 1975.

Montague, D.K.: Sex after cystectomy, Med. Aspects Hum. Sex. **11:**91-92, 1977.

Murray, R.: Principles of nursing intervention for the adult patient with body image changes, Nurs. Clin. North Am. **7:**697-707, 1972.

Roy, P., et al.: Experience with ileostomies: evaluation of long-term rehabilitation in 497 patients, Am. J. Surg. **119:**77-86, 1970.

Schoenberg, B., editor: Loss and grief: psychological management in medical practice, New York, 1970, Columbia University Press.

Wirsching, M., et al.: Results of psychosocial adjustment to long-term colostomy, Psychother. Psychosom. **26:**245-256, 1975.

SUGGESTED READING FOR THE CLIENT

Mullen, B.D., and McGinn, K.: The ostomy book—living comfortably with colostomies, ileostomies, and urostomies, Palo Alto, Calif., 1980, Bull Publishing Co.

♂ ABOUT THE AUTHOR ♂

Victor Alterescu, R.N., E.T., is coordinator of ostomy services at John Muir Memorial Hospital in Walnut Creek, California, and is a consultant to the Sex and Disability Unit, Human Sexuality Program at the University of California, San Francisco. He holds degrees from the University of California at San Francisco and at Berkeley. Additionally, he is a graduate of Harrisburg Hospital's School of Enterostomal Therapy in Harrisburg, Pennsylvania. Mr. Alterescu himself underwent ostomy surgery.

24 Issues of sexuality in head-injured adults

Sheldon Berrol

The primary rehabilitation issue for the head-injured population is the significant loss of intellectual function as opposed to physical impairment. In contrast to the persons with mental retardation, the head-injured population will demonstrate cognitive and behavioral changes over time. In the past it was felt that positive change would occur within a maximum of 6 to 12 months, but studies have demonstrated that improvement can continue for many years. It does appear true that physical changes begin to slow down after 6 to 12 months, but the cognitive changes, particularly psychosocial adaptation, and the behavioral changes do continue over long periods of time. We therefore need to recognize that our approach as health professionals must constantly change as the clients continue to improve. If we lock them into a model of "no possible change," as we have done with the mentally retarded, then I do not believe that we will be able to take advantage of behavioral strategy changes that can take place over time.

As stated, in addition to physical changes as a result of the injury, thought processes and behavioral manifestations, including the previously developed sexuality of the individual, are frequently altered. Frustration is frequently increased, whereas tolerance is decreased. The family usually has a difficult time dealing with these behavioral changes. Thus what we have is not only an altered form but an alteration of one's ability to perceive and interact within the family.

The role changes of family members over time have been evaluated by Mary Romano at Columbia University. If a man was injured, the wife of that partner had to change her role to assume even greater responsibility for the family unit. In terms of sexual interaction, these women were fearful that the man might become even more injured as a result. In addition, they were not sure they even wanted to engage in sexual activity with him in the first place because essentially, from an intellectual and behavioral point of view, he was not the same person that they initiated their relationship with. "Intellectually, I can't even talk to him. Why should I want to go to bed with someone I can't talk to? I never would have done it before, and I have difficulty doing it now."

The children in the family face a striking emotional change. Most frequently they evidence fear of the injured father because of his short temper and intolerance. Thus the children increase their dependency on their mother. The family's usual social activities are frequently altered, both because he may not want to go anyplace and because the family may be embarrassed to be seen with him. As a result, friends and family contacts begin to dramatically decrease. Sometimes the mother of the patient will become frustrated because she thinks that the wife "isn't taking care" of her son's needs. No matter how near or far removed the mother is geographically, this can be a problem further alienating the major caretaker.

It is important to point out that head injury can occasionally result in purely a motor effect without interference in cognitive function. This will occur most often in focal or mass lesions as a result of an acute hematoma. Unfortunately, the vast majority of severely head-injured persons (those who have been in coma for 6 hours or more) have more diffuse cortical damage with its resultant cognitive and behavioral effects.

Virtually all the patients with a severe head injury will have some memory deficits. At the very least, an amnesia for the time of the injury to some point in the future is manifested. Just as frequently, there may be a retrograde amnesia with some loss of memory for events preceding the injury. It is not surprising, therefore, that when patients come out of coma, they frequently do not understand that they are in a hospital, or why they are in a hospital. As professionals dealing with these injuries, we need to understand the information limitation that these patients have. Imagine if you woke up someplace tomorrow not remembering, or at least unaware that there was a period of time that you did not remember, were told that you were in a hospital and that you had been severely injured in an accident. You are dressed in peculiar clothing, told what to do, when to do it, and how to do it. You are pushed, pulled, pinched, twisted, and turned. You are hurt physically and continuously. The logical assumption is that you are being punished for something. It would be the only assumption that would make sense, and this appears to be the most frequent conclusion of severely head-injured patients coming out a coma. We are then faced with a period of reality orientation, bringing them back to a level of awareness and comprehension, to integrate reality with what happened.

It is essential, therefore, early in the process of recovery, that significant loved ones be allowed to interact on a personal, touching basis with the injured party. Dr. Verduyn in Wisconsin has developed a program that allows for such family intervention early in the recovery from coma phase, when reality orientation is a prime necessity. This restoration of family contact allows the significant other to become a vital part of the rehabilitation team. Dr. Verduyn's program could never have been established in many university hospital settings, where psychosocial and cognitive needs are considered too unimportant to consider; unfortunately, it is too often believed that significant others are a burden to the delivery of adequate medical care.

HEAD-INJURED PERSONS AND SEXUALITY

Perhaps the major sexual performance problem that the head-injured person encounters is a loss of libido, a disinterest. However, there is generally no problem in obtaining an erection with stimulation. It is, I believe, important to restore the balance of the sexual relationship early in the rehabilitation program. Therefore we must develop privacy areas in acute hospital settings. More and more hospitals are adapting motel facilities adjacent to or even within the hospital building. It is essential that we involve the family early in reestablishing their relationships and validating sexuality as a legitimate concern for both parties, particularly noninjured spouses, since it often becomes their responsibility to integrate and foster closeness and physical contact. As health professionals, we need to promote touching, feeling, and being together and alone for some period of time to reestablish the relationship and to promote the reality orientation of the brain-injured individual. We need to encourage the right of families and injured individuals to close the door to a hospital room and to expect hospital staff members to respect their right to privacy. Unfortunately, in most hospital settings that I know, the individual is never allowed to close a door, and certainly if the door is closed, one never knocks when entering.

It is important for families to understand the specific cognitive deficits that the brain-injured individual has. I treated a patient not too long ago who had a severe head injury. He and his wife had been married for approximately 20 years, and following the head injury, he would always call his wife Mary, Rose, Margaret, Sandra, or Louise. Her name was Roxanne, and to her his inability to remember her name was the most disturbing result of his head injury. It took some time, but we were finally able to impress on her that he did not have a problem with memory and that in fact he knew quite well who she was. He had a very specific aphasia, and it was impossible for him to come up with the right name. When she became aware of the organic nature of the problem, their sexual difficulties began to resolve.

Occasionally there are problems with what appears to be hypersexuality. There are some very specific syndromes such as the Kluver-Bucy syndrome that result in true hypersexuality. Not uncommonly, however, the issue is one of memory. Another patient of mine was constantly badgering his wife to engage in sex six, eight, and ten times a day. Every time she tried to do the wash he wanted sex, and she had a room full of unwashed laundry. In fact, his problem was one of memory. He had a very severe short-term memory problem in addition to retention memory deficits. He knew that he wanted to have sex but could not remember that he had had it. This is frequently expressed in terms of eating behavior rather than sexual appetite. It is not uncommon to see severely obese head-injured patients constantly eating. There are cognitive retraining tools and specific remediation programs for memory deficits.

Essentially what I am saying is that every brain-injured adult needs comprehensive neuropsychiatric evaluation to assess specific cognitive deficits and to develop specific cognitive retraining programs. It is essential that the significant others of the individual are involved in the program and that they specifically understand such a program.

The discharge of injured individuals to the home environment does not necessarily result in the development of independence. There are some family situations that promote more dependency than even a convalescent hospital. Once the person returns home to the community, it is important that he or she become reintegrated into the family unit. We need community programs that encompass not only cognitive retraining, but social skills development for long periods of time for individuals with significant cognitive and intellectual problems. Currently, some isolated, transitional living facilities that promote the redevelopment of cognitive skills and positive behavioral strategies are being developed in the United States.* The traditional psychiatric or psychologic halfway houses unfortunately are not generally geared to individuals with cognitive deficits. Transitional living facilities need to incorporate the family unit; reintegration and normalization of sexual expression must be an integral part of the rehabilitation process.

Medications

The question regarding medications in sexual function has been raised. There certainly are some medications that interfere with sexual functioning. However, just as importantly, many of the medications that interfere with sexual functioning also interfere with the individual's ability to learn and to remember. These are exactly the cognitive deficits that are so devastating to the reintegration of this individual back into society. Medications such as tranquilizers and sedatives need to be used sparingly if at all in the head-injured population.

Social skills

The key to constructive remediation over time, which in fact does occur in head injury, seems to be the development of a structured environment that changes as the patient changes. It is important in the normalization process that social skills development be an integral part of the program. Such basic skills are necessary for

---

*The following people are involved in developing cognitive retraining modules: Dr. Yehuda Ben-Yishay at New York University; Dr. Bill Lynch at the Veteran's Administration Hospital in Menlo Park, California; Leanne Michael at Santa Clara Valley Medical Center, San Jose, California; Jeanne Fryer at the Ralph K. Davies Medical Center, San Francisco; and Craig Muir at Casa Colina, Pomona, California.

sexual interaction for all of us. We need to interest local mental health departments in the specific needs of the head injured, which are often more long-term than they are used to dealing with. We need to develop programs in community colleges for the development of social skills that allow for effective positive reinforcement of one's sexual identity.

RECOMMENDED READING

Dimond, S.J.: Neuropsychology: a textbook of system and psychologic function of the human brain, Woburn, Mass., 1980, Butterworth Publishers Inc., pp. 80-99.

♂ ABOUT THE AUTHOR ♂

Sheldon Berrol, M.D., is chairman of the department of physical medicine and rehabilitation at the Ralph K. Davies Medical Center in San Francisco. He is also clinical assistant professor of rehabilitation medicine at Stanford University; principal investigator, Model Head Injury Rehabilitation Program, Santa Clara Valley Medical Center, San Jose, California, funded by the Rehabilitation Services Administration; chairman of the Task Force on Brain Injury Rehabilitation and member of the Task Force on Sexuality and Disability, American Congress of Rehabilitation Medicine. Dr. Berrol serves as medical consultant and member of the board of directors of the Center for Independent Living, Berkeley, California. He obtained his degree in medicine from the California College of Medicine (now the University of California, Irvine).

25 Sexuality and major medical conditions

A PILOT STUDY

Joseph K. Nowinski and Toni Ayres

In September, 1979, we began a research project to study the effects of major medical conditions on sexuality. Our goal in this chapter will be to describe the first year of this continuing project. We will devote some space to issues of experimental design and outcome but will focus on our personal experiences in getting the project approved and accepted by hospital staff and patients.

BACKGROUND
Joe Nowinski

I arrived at the Human Sexuality Program of the University of California School of Medicine in San Francisco in late August of 1979. Trained as a clinical psychologist, I had just finished a 2-year fellowship in sex therapy and research.

As a new assistant professor in the Department of Psychiatry, I was eager to pursue the sort of methodologically rigorous research I had been trained to do. My earlier experience as a sex therapist had taught me that many of the sexual dysfunctions I was asked to treat had their roots in life crises of various sorts. At times the dysfunction an individual or couple complained of seemed to have its beginnings when one or the other suffered a serious illness, was diagnosed as having a medical condition, or had undergone surgery. Previous research in this area was not extensive, and it appeared to be a potentially fruitful area for future investigation.

Toni Ayres

I had just finished co-authoring a chapter on sexuality and medical-surgical nursing.[1] While writing that chapter I became aware of the need for more detailed research in the area of acute and chronic conditions and their effects on sexual health. I had also been discussing, with my graduate students, the fact that current

209

literature rarely differentiated whether sexual dysfunctions occurred as a result of the illness or surgery itself or as an emotional reaction to the condition. I felt that most professional articles provided a particularly dim expectation for future sexual functioning among diabetics and persons with end-stage renal disease; I felt that sexual counseling could possibly reduce the actual numbers of sexual dysfunctions in those populations. In addition, the literature provided information mostly about male patients; there was very little available in regard to females.

At a meeting with Evalyn Gendel, director of the University of California Human Sexuality Program, and Marianne Zalar, director of the Nursing Education in Human Sexuality Project of the University of California School of Nursing, I agreed to collaborate on the task of designing and implementing a pilot study with Evalyn and Marianne's support. I had been teaching graduate courses in sexuality and illness and was enthusiastic about the idea of developing an empirical research project. As it turned out, this enthusiasm, plus a healthy measure of patience and perseverance, proved essential to the eventual success of the project.

GOALS OF THE STUDY

Our initial goal for the pilot study was to use small samples of subjects to obtain information about the sociosexual impact of a number of different medical conditions. Since good instrumentation for such research appeared lacking, a subgoal of the pilot study was to test and revise a structured interview. Second, we hoped to study our patient-subjects over a period of 18 months, which would enable us to study possible changes in their sexuality. Third, we planned to use a common set of questionnaires and the same interview protocol for all our clinical groups, thus permitting us to make comparisons among them.

We put a great deal of thought into the issue of research design. We believed that previous studies were limited in this regard, and we wanted our study to be as methodologically rigorous as possible. We felt that, although costly in terms of time, the use of an interview to supplement self-report inventories would yield data that could not possibly be tapped through the use of simple questionnaires alone. We also felt that it was important to put the same questions to all our subjects; in this way we could compare, for example, the impact of heart disease versus diabetes on frequency or satisfaction of sexual relations. Finally, no longitudinal studies had been reported; therefore we did not know how many people experience "transient" versus "permanent" sexual difficulties following, say, a heart attack.

Both the department of psychiatry of the school of medicine, and the department of family health care of the school of nursing lent their institutional support to the concept of a collaborative research project. Concretely, what this boiled down to was our shared commitment to the goals of the project and our ability to pool what limited resources were available toward these ends. The gap between conceptualizing the project and implementing it proved to be fraught with obstacles of different kinds, including (but not limited to) time, red tape and institutional lethargy, resistance in various forms, finances, and staffing. More than once we were quite discouraged to say the least, and at times things seemed to crawl along so slowly we thought we'd never get any appreciable return for our investment.

SETTING UP

As a first logical step in starting our pilot project, we came to some tentative decisions as to which medical conditions we would concentrate on. We ended up with the following set of five groups:

1. Diabetes mellitus
2. End-stage renal disease
3. Posthysterectomy
4. Postmastectomy
5. Postmyocardial infarction

In this way we were able to include both men and women having acute and chronic surgical and nonsurgical conditions.

Once we had selected our target groups, we began approaching the appropriate departments and units within the university hospital. Through her former students, Toni also had contacts in a number of other hospitals in the San Francisco Bay Area, and we pursued these leads as well. We were interested in building a referral network so that we could recruit subjects from more than one medical setting. We were able to establish a network and were in a position to get substantial numbers of subjects. This, however, created yet another problem: finding and training sufficient numbers of interviewers who had the time and interest and who also met our selection criteria.

We consistently found that as a group, physicians' and nurses' attitudes toward our project differed as did their functions with respect to it. Generally speaking, physicians were more reserved in their support. Although we needed the approval of physicians to approach patients for participation, we also needed the support and cooperation of nursing staffs. Without the help of both groups we would never have gotten off the ground.

Our method of approach was to make contact with both physicians and nursing staff and to ask for an opportunity to present our ideas. These requests were almost always granted, with nursing personnel often in turn requesting in-service consultations.

As individuals, nurses varied in the degree of comfort they experienced when addressing patients' sexual concerns. As a group, however, they were in agreement that the kind of study we were proposing was very much needed to clarify the nature and extent of the sociosexual impact of illness and surgery. However, it was also apparent that many felt either too uncomfortable or not competent to deal with sexual issues. To paraphrase a frequent comment: "I really feel badly for that patient, but I'm not a sex therapist, and I don't know what to say." These in-service consultations provided us with insights into the nature of patients' concerns. We learned, for example, that many patients feared that surgery involving the breasts or genitals would render them sexually repulsive to their partners. Others feared that surgery or illness eventually would lead to marital infidelity, conflict, and or divorce. Seldom did patients express these fears directly to partners; rather, they talked to their physicians or most commonly a nurse. We also discovered that sexual concerns per se were common rather than exceptional. It appeared that patients often worried about their relationships, families, and careers more than they did about their physical health. In short, the advice frequently given to patients—that they put all else out of mind and concentrate on getting better—seems to be a naive approach to dealing with real people.

In exchange for what we learned, we were able to share some of our knowledge of human sexuality and sex therapy. Usually the nurses wanted advice for dealing with specific cases: what to tell Ms. So-and-so who asked such-and-such. We were able to provide moral support for nurses' interest in their patients' emotional and sexual health, encouraged them to continue to be open to discussing sexual concerns, and suggested that they did-not have to be experts in human sexuality or sex therapy to elicit information and make an appropriate referral. Often we pointed out, a sympathetic ear has powerful curative powers itself.

In general, the response of physicians to our proposal was more aloof, formal, and reticent than that of the nursing community. We rarely got the sort of enthusiastic response or encouragement from physicians that we typically received from nurses.

Members of the various medical staffs often expressed fears that questioning patients about their sex lives might somehow bring about or exacerbate sexual or psychological problems. More than one physician expressed a belief that an intensive focus on sexuality could lead to depression or anxiety that could in turn hinder convalescence.

We had no way of reassuring physicians regarding the potential side effects of our study. We have some such data now, but at that point the only information we could offer came mainly from our talks with nurses, who had led us to believe that patients frequently expressed sexual concerns and welcomed an opportunity to discuss them. More problems, in their opinion, were caused by not asking than by asking.

Obviously, the process of setting up took much longer than we'd ever expected it would. It often seemed that we spent all our time in meetings seeking approval. Presentation followed presentation. Always it turned out that there was someone else who needed to be consulted, another procedure to be followed, or another approval to be gotten.

At the same time that we were working our way slowly through the bureaucratic

maze of the medical establishment, we were busy developing our interview protocol and recruiting and training interviewers. Their interest, like our own, seemed
to grow rather than diminish in response to the frustrations of the setting-up process. As time went on a team spirit appeared. The study became more and more of
a personal commitment as opposed to an academic interest for all involved. If this
was true before we began interviewing subjects, it was even more true once we
began to have personal contact with those who volunteered to participate. This
experience of emotional involvement proved unique and personally rewarding,
since we were accustomed to approaching research in a more intellectual, objective
manner.

GOING FURTHER
Devising the interview and training interviewers

Determining the questions to ask patients was difficult only in the sense that
we had to decide which questions to eliminate to keep the interview to a reasonable
length. We didn't want to burden our subjects, but at the same time we did want
to inquire into a range of areas including, but not limited to, subjects' sex lives.

We also became sensitive to physicians' concerns about self-report questionnaires. One particularly common fear was that patients might have adverse emotional reactions (anxiety, depression) in response to detailed questions about their
sexual performance or intimate relationships, especially if there was no one with
whom to discuss their feelings. We therefore decided to forego self-report measures
for the time being in favor of a longer interview.

We'd also discovered that the idea of using experienced nurses to administer
the interview appealed to physicians and relieved some of the reticence we'd encountered. Fortunately, we had such a resource available in the form of graduate
nurses enrolled in Toni's practicum in sexuality and illness. We were able to use
nurses experienced in the care of cardiac patients for interviewing postcoronary
patients, and so forth.

Our prototype interview protocol, the SISQ-A, consisted of 108 questions broken down into eight topic areas:

1. **Demographics.** The SISQ-A begins with questions that provide information
   such as subject's age, marital status and history, number of children, education, and occupation.
2. **Physical health status.** It focuses on alcohol and cigarette use, medications,
   outstanding medical conditions, activity and energy level, diet, and
   so on.
3. **Vocational status.** It contains questions regarding information about income,
   effects of medical condition on income-earning capacity, and job satisfaction.
4. **Psychological status.** It measures conditions such as anxiety, depression,
   alienation, self-esteem, and locus of control.

5. **Relationship status.** It includes questions designed to assess marital satisfaction, feelings of love, intimacy, sexual attraction, plus areas of conflict and strength, and so on.
6. **Sexual relations.** It includes data such as frequency of relations as well as importance of sex and level of satisfaction, interest, and concerns and dysfunctions.
7. **Perceived counseling needs.** It indicates perceived need for short- or long-term counseling, previous counseling experience, and so on.
8. **Summary.** It gives an overall assessment of the impact of a medical-surgical condition on relationships in general and sexuality in particular, plus feedback regarding the interview.

Parts of the SISQ-A contain open-ended questions designed to supplement information collected via questions that use categorical response formats. At the same time, the protocol is sufficiently structured so as to avoid unlimited or free-ranging, and therefore time-consuming, discussion. The bulk of questions are objectively scorable and in a number of cases are grouped so as to form a priori scales.

Recruiting and training

Five graduate nurses who were completing work as clinical specialists or nurse practitioners at the master's level were recruited for training to do the interviews. They came from a variety of clinical specialities such as adult health, women's health, maternity, and gerontological care. All were women, and all had completed an introductory upper division course in human sexuality. All but one had also taken at least one advanced course in human sexuality (Sex Counseling or Sexuality and Illness) and so had an opportunity to acquire factual knowledge about human sexuality and to examine their own attitudes, values, and biases.

The primary selection criterion for interviewers was a demonstrated ability to deal comfortably with discussions of sexuality. These interviewers needed to be equally capable of giving nonjudgmental responses to client material and able to ask the SISQ-A questions in such a manner that the subject felt safe enough to answer honestly.

A second criterion was to be able to personalize the interview so that the interviewer could use the subject's name at the beginning of selected questions, keeping in mind the subject's relationship status and unique history. We were looking for an ability to maintain consistency throughout the interview.

Our third criterion was an ability to gently probe for clarification whenever answers were vague. Determination of the interviewers' ability to meet these various criteria was made by observing the students' role playing. All our interviewers met these criteria by the end of the training program.

There were three main parts to the training of the interviewers: the institutional arrangements, role playing, and direct observation. The institutional arrangements were mainly handled by us as we went through the seemingly endless number of meetings with both physicians and nurses. Whenever possible the nurse interviewers were invited to join in the arrangement process. One nurse interviewer was instrumental at her hospital in obtaining permission for us to jointly conduct research in the dialysis unit.

The interviewers were instructed in the institutional requirements of the University of California for conducting research. This is governed by the Committee on Human Research, which reviews research proposals for risk and informed consent. A special consent form specific to our project was devised. Interviewers were asked to emphasize two aspects of the consent process in particular. One was that whether or not a subject agreed to be interviewed, he or she was to be assured that that decision would in no way affect his or her nursing or medical care. The second point was that the interview could be stopped at any time, and subjects could refuse to answer any question they found objectionable.

Other institutional arrangements included selection of one of the specific medical or surgical conditions to be studied by each nurse interviewer and planning for an optimum interview setting that would be both convenient and private. Some of the interviewers were able to choose subjects from their own units where they worked part-time; others got their subjects from lists of previously hospitalized patients who were returning to a clinic for follow-up. Head nurses in both outpatient clinics and inpatient units were instrumental in referring subjects to our study.

The research protocol consisted of first, locating a potential subject with an appropriate diagnosis; second, contacting the appropriate physician to secure his/ her consent to the interview; and, third, contacting the patient by phone to outline the project and seek agreement to participate. If the patient agreed to be interviewed, arrangements for a time and place were made. Subjects were told to allow at least 1 hour for the interview.

As background preparation for the role-playing phase of training, each nurse interviewer was given a task of doing a literature review of relevant material in the area they would be focusing on, for example, the sexual sequelae of diabetes mellitus. During the role playing, the SISQ-A questionnaire was used as the basic format for the interview. Each of the nurse interviewers was asked to play both the role of the patient and the role of the interviewer. All the interviewers had a chance to interrupt the role playing for clarification, to express concerns, and to seek advice about rephrasing. Many suggestions were made as to how questions could be asked most comfortably, how to proceed as smoothly and efficiently as possible, how to create a "safe," or comfortable environment for the subject, and how to acknowledge responses in a neutral manner. Emphasis was placed on clarifying for the subject the nurse's role as interviewer and not therapist.

The nurses brought up different questions and concerns during the second role-playing session in which each interviewer took the role opposite to that they'd had in the first session. A third session was then scheduled, to help each nurse pick up speed and become more comfortable with the questionnaire. In addition, each was asked to role play introducing herself to the subject, explaining the consent form, and ending the interview. There was also some discussion of how to include a small amount of casual conversation during the introduction so as to help build rapport. Some of the nurses then went home and practiced again using the questionnaire with their partners or friends in the role of patient.

Each of the nurses expected that role playing the interviewer would be most informative to them. To their surprise they found that playing the patient most helped them to develop a degree of sensitivity regarding the interview situation. Although each nurse sounded perfectly confident while role playing the interview, there was anxiety for everyone at the thought of interviewing a real patient. The support of the group was helpful in this respect, as was a feeling that they were some of the first members of their profession to be involved in this sort of research.

Initially, all the nurses feared, to a greater or lesser extent, that subjects might regard the interview as an invasion of privacy. They expressed fears of being turned down or even scolded. They found, however, that nearly all clients contacted readily agreed to be interviewed. Those who refused did so on the basis of the research content. Those who did participate seemed comfortable reporting the personal information about their sexuality. Much to our surprise, what discomfort or embarrassment was encountered was more frequently associated with questions about personal finances than sex.

PRELIMINARY FINDINGS

Early results of the pilot study can be broken down into general or informal findings and more formal or statistical data. On a general level, we have already learned a great deal about the limitations and strengths of the SISQ-A protocol. We now realize it had a distinct bias toward heterosexuality and monogamy. That is, its questions were worded in such a way that it was assumed the subject was heterosexual and in a single sexual relationship. In fact, some of our subjects considered themselves to be homosexuals, and not all of the subjects were monogamous. In some cases, their primary sexual (and emotional) relationships have been extramarital. Questions relating to frequency and satisfaction of sexual relations, therefore, will elicit different responses depending on which relationship they are referenced to.

A second finding was that some questions on the interview were difficult to interpret when applied to certain clinical groups. For example, it may make some sense to ask a postcoronary patient about the quality of his or her sexual relationship prior to the medical condition. It is a very different matter, however, to ask this same question to a patient with diabetes mellitus or end-stage renal disease. In the first case, there is a more or less clear temporal datum; in the other, the issue of "before" versus "after" becomes vague at best.

Contrary to the concern that had caused us a good deal of anxiety, no subjects found the interview objectionable. The feedback we received was universally positive. The great majority of patients welcomed an opportunity to discuss the sorts of issues covered during the interview. Rather than having to press for information, our interviewers more typically had difficulty limiting the amount of free discussion. For this reason, the interviews on occasion ran longer than an hour. Of course, our subject sample was not by any means random, and one might argue that we interviewed only the most highly motivated patients. Regardless, the fact is that we have yet to encounter a single untoward reaction.

Yet another unexpected but very pleasant result of our work so far has been a developing trust and rapport between ourselves and the various participating medical departments and clinics. Some have asked us to consult on selected cases; for example, a woman who had undergone radical pelvic surgery was upset over its implications for her marriage and future sexual life. We believe that the kind of confidence implied by these referrals represents an invaluable asset. Indeed, it might be a good idea for researchers to plan for the professional trust-building phase of a project with as much care as they give to issues of experimental design.

As we write this chapter, the amount of statistical data we have at hand is limited. However, the project is continuing, and we look forward in our second year to adding to the data base. For purposes of this discussion we will concentrate on the two groups for which we have collected the most data: posthysterectomy women and patients with end-stage renal disease. However, the present data are suggestive rather than conclusive, and it should be kept in mind that future results, based on larger subject samples, may vary from those reported here.

Posthysterectomy patients can differ from persons suffering from end-stage renal disease in a host of ways, and differences in their responses to questions may be due to factors other than their medical conditions. In our sample to date we interviewed eight men and two women who were undergoing renal dialysis. Their mean age was 42. The mean age of our eight posthysterectomy patients was a comparable 44. All but two of the renal patients and all of the hysterectomy patients were married. In doing our research we were interested in studying persons whose medical conditions were chronic, as well as some who suffered from more acute conditions. Though women who eventually undergo hysterectomies frequently have histories of prior discomfort, they nevertheless differ from persons who suffer from more insidious conditions such as chronic and progressive renal failure.

One question on the SISQ-A reads, "Indicate your degree of agreement or disagreement with the following statement: Most of what happens to us in life is beyond our control." All eight hysterectomy patients expressed *disagreement* with this statement. Six indicated that they disagreed strongly with the idea that life's consequences are essentially beyond personal control or influence; the remaining two stated that they disagreed somewhat with this statement. In contrast, eight of ten renal patients indicated *agreement* with the statement. Six indicated that they strongly agreed with it, and two indicated that they agreed somewhat with it. Only one renal patient strongly disagreed with the statement.

In other research,[3] Rotter and his students have studied correlates of the belief that consequences are essentially the result of uncontrollable forces or chance, called an "external locus of control." The so-called "external" person, in contrast to those who believe that consequences can be affected by personal effort, tends to lack motivation, is more passive, and feels alienated from the social environment.

In the area of relationships, six of the hysterectomy patients asserted that there was typically very little conflict in their marriages. None of this group indicated a great deal of conflict as typifying their primary relationships. On the other hand, four renal patients did indicate that there was typically a great deal of conflict. Along with this goes our finding that five renal patients, but only one hysterectomy patient, said that they were unsatisfied with the way their relationships had been going.

Yet another section of the SISQ-A focuses on patients' sexual lives. One question asks for an assessment of the impact of the medical condition on frequency of sexual relations. Nine of ten renal patients stated that frequency of relations had decreased as a result of their condition. Only two hysterectomy patients so indicated, with the majority saying that there had been either no change or else an increase in frequency of relations. This difference between the groups may relate to the fact that eight renal patients indicated that the sexual aspect of their relationship was currently *very* important to them. Among the hysterectomy patients, only one checked off the "very important" category in response to this question. Most hysterectomy patients stated that the sexual aspect of their relationship was either *mildly* important or important. Similarly, whereas only one hysterectomy patient said that she was unsatisfied (mildly) with her sexual relationship as it had been, four renal patients indicated strong dissatisfaction with sex.

When asked about specific sexual dysfunctions and difficulties, both groups tended to indicate a substantial number of problems of various sorts. The most commonly cited difficulties were loss of sexual interest, problems getting aroused and or staying aroused, plus difficulty relaxing during sex. Specific performance dysfunctions, for example, anorgasmia or impotence, were less commonly cited. These data seem consistent with recent surveys of couples from the population at large[2] and may not indicate a higher incidence of sexual malaise in our clinical groups. Taken as a whole, however, these studies do suggest that sexual difficulties may be more common than previously thought.

One of the last questions on the SISQ-A asks subjects if they feel that counseling, either brief or long-term, might be helpful to them. Seven out of eight hysterectomy patients replied "no," but eight of the ten renal patients said "yes."

To summarize this brief presentation of results, our preliminary data indicate that of the two groups discussed, renal patients express a good deal more psychologic and sexual discomfort than hysterectomy patients. At the very least the data suggest that further and more detailed inquiry is warranted. Though the differences observed may be due to factors other than the medical conditions per se, such as sex differences, we can hypothesize that these conditions and differences between them do enter the picture to some extent. We hope that continued research with larger subject samples and more groups will help us to sort out some of the factors involved and eventually to design programs that might alleviate some of the problems our patients are encountering.

SUMMARY

As we indicated at the outset of this chapter, this research project is ongoing at the University of California and other participating medical centers. As we enter the second year, we can reflect on what we have learned, some of which we've shared in these pages. We can also use this opportunity to contemplate where we wish to go with the project.

In some ways this next year will find us confronting some of the same issues we've dealt with before. We must, for example, recruit and train a new group of interviewers. We would also like to revise our interview protocol. One option we are exploring is the development of a series of interview protocols to replace the single one used to date. We may end up with an SISQ-MI, for cardiac patients, an SISQ-ESRD for renal patients, and so forth.

In looking back, what strikes us most of all from the personal perspective is the energy and enthusiasm that this project often has inspired in those who chose to get involved. Speaking purely personally, we think that is a very significant result.

Although the goal of the research has been to study effects rather than provide therapy, we have occasionally received such requests. It has been our impression that patients who are experiencing sexual difficulties are inclined to believe that problems are a direct result of the medical condition. This is not necessarily totally true. It has been gratifying to be able to provide help to such couples and individuals.

REFERENCES

1. Ayres, T., and Thornton, C. E.: Sexuality in medical-surgical nursing. In Sitzman, J., editor: Medical-surgical nursing, Los Altos, Calif., Lange Medical Publications (in press).
2. Frank, E., Anderson, C., and Rubenstein, D.: Frequency of sexual dysfunction in "normal" couples, N. Engl. J. Med. f29299:111-115, 1978.
3. Rotter, J.B.: Generalized expectancies for internal versus external control of reinforcement. In Rotter, J.B., Chance, J.E., and Phares, E.J., editors: Applications of a social learning theory of personality, New York, 1972, Holt, Rinehart & Winston.

♂ ABOUT THE AUTHORS ♀

Joseph K. Nowinski, Ph.D., is assistant professor of psychiatry and director of clinical services for the Human Sexuality Program, University of California, San Francisco. He did his graduate work in clinical psychology at Syracuse University and the University of Connecticut, following which he held a National Research Service Award at the State University of New York at Stony Brook, where he specialized in sex therapy and research. His first book, *Becoming Satisfied: A Man's Guide to Sexual Fulfillment*, was published by Prentice-Hall in 1980. In addition to teaching, training, and research, Dr. Nowinski maintains a private practice in San Francisco.

Toni Ayres, R.N., D.A., is a graduate of the School of Nursing of the University of California, San Francisco. Dr. Ayres now lectures to graduate nursing students at the University of California, San Francisco as part of a grant from the National Institute of Mental Health to provide nursing education in human sexuality. A certified sex educator and therapist, she has worked in the field of human sexuality continuously since 1972. She was a founder of both the Sex Advisory and Counseling Unit at the University of California San Francisco and the San Francisco Sex Information switchboard. She has served as director of training for the National Sex Forum, and received her doctor of arts in human sexuality from the Institute for Advanced Study in Human Sexuality.

ISSUES IN SEX EDUCATION AND THE DEVELOPMENT OF SOCIAL SKILLS

26 Sexuality-related services for disabled people

A NEEDS ASSESSMENT*

Sophia Chipouras

The primary goal of the Sex & Disability Project* was to develop a handbook that would help individuals and organizations interested in effective sexuality-related services for disabled people. As one of the initial steps in meeting this goal, the Sex & Disability staff (Debra Cornelius, Susan Daniels, Elaine Makas, and I) conducted five different surveys to find out the sexuality-related service needs and concerns of disabled consumers, counselors, other community service providers, trainers, and policymakers.

These surveys were designed to gather information; they were not intended to be part of a carefully controlled study. The survey results suggest possible trends and attitudes, and they support information obtained from more scientifically valid sources. The consumer, counselor, and community resource surveys were conducted in two states, one on the east coast, the other in the midwest. An attempt was made to collect data from rural, suburban, and urban areas. The remaining two surveys—policymakers and trainers—were conducted on a nationwide basis with some concentration on the two focal states. Survey findings include the following:

1. *Disabled people report that they are not receiving as many sexuality-related services as they need and/or want.* Sex and disability courses, for example, were chosen most often by disabled consumers as a service they would use (48.9%). Yet, only 2.1% of the sampled population indicated that they had actually received this service. Group discussions were also a popular service (47.9%), yet only 14.4% of the survey respondents had participated in such groups. The following are other examples of the discrepancy between services desired and those received:

- Access to audiovisual materials (35.1% would use, 9.3% have received)

*The Sex & Disability Project was funded by the Rehabilitation Services Administration, DHEW Grant No. 12-P-59099/3-01.

- Individual counseling (40.4% would use, 6.2% have received)
- Couples counseling (31.9% would use, 5.2% have received); for a complete breakdown of services desired versus services received, see Fig. 26-1.

2. *The service providers from whom disabled individuals expect to receive sexuality-related services are frequently not providing those services.* Out of a list of 11 potential service providers, disabled people chose the following as most appropriate for the provision of sex education and counseling: (a) physician (64.2%); (b) sex counselor/therapist (54.7%); (c) psychologist (50.5%); and (d) other disabled person (49.5%). Yet when the same respondents were asked who had actually provided sexuality-related services, there was a marked drop in the percentages. Physicians, who were first on the list of expected providers, were cited by only 11.6% of the consumers as actually providing any services of this nature. This gap between expectation and actuality was apparent for all the providers listed.

3. *Most respondents believed that medical or psychologic "experts" are the best qualified providers of sexuality-related services.* The majority of consumers, counselors, and policymakers chose the following providers as the most appropriate persons to offer sex education/counseling: sex counselors/therapists, physicians, and

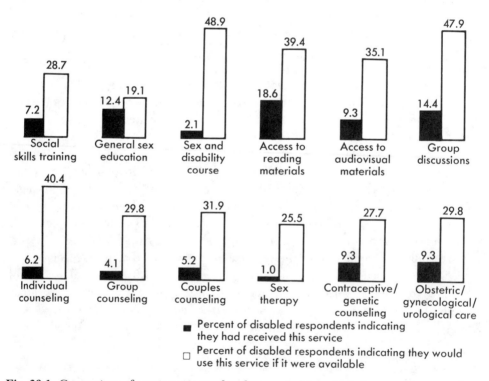

Fig. 26-1. Comparison of services received and requested (number of respondents = 97).

psychologists. This emphasis on "experts" is inconsistent with the sexual issues that are most frequently raised by clients, such as:

- "Is it okay to have an active sex life even though I'm in a wheelchair?"
- "I have trouble meeting people."
- "Where can I get birth control pills?"

Concerns such as these can be discussed and answered by individuals who are not "experts" in the area of sexuality and disability. Often a client is simply seeking permission ("Am I okay?") or information about his or her sexuality. Referral to a sex therapist for these kinds of concerns is obviously inappropriate.

Some sexuality-related services do require specialized training on the part of the provider. Intensive sex therapy and genetic counseling, for instance, call for a high level of specialized training. Not all services, however, fall into this category. Dr. Jack S. Annon[1] has developed a model to determine what level of services an individual can competently provide. This model is divided into four levels: (1) Permission, (2) Limited Information, (3) Specific Suggestion, and (4) Intensive Therapy, or PLISSIT (see Chapter 23). Most people are capable of providing the first and probably the second level without extensive traning. Usually training for these two levels of service delivery involve attitude reassessment and basic information about sexuality and/or disability.

Some survey respondents stated that job title is generally unreliable in determining whether a particular service provider will deal effectively with a client's sexual concerns. One disabled woman wrote the following:

> Unfortunately, no one can always receive a guarantee of a particular service from a person just because he calls him or herself, for example, a teacher, social worker, etc. It is the person behind the title that I would like to know a bit about before I ask for any services of any kind from him. Many times I have found that a teacher (for example) is also a social worker, psychologist, counselor, etc., and other times people merely carry these titles around with them.

4. *Newly disabled people tended to prefer special services, whereas individuals who have been disabled for a long period of time preferred the same services as those offered to the general population.* Also, individuals who have disabilities that directly affect sexual functioning generally opted for separate services. Spinal cord–injured respondents, for example, expressed greater interest in special services (75%) than did the disabled consumers in general (just over 50%).

The Sex & Disability Project staff concluded that although special services should be available to disabled people, community-based services for the general public should be made accessible to disabled people. "It must be up to the individual person to decide whether to use these same services or services designed specifically for disabled people. The decision should not be made for him or her by a provider's unwillingness or by a facility's inaccessibility."[2]

5. *Seventy-two percent of the rehabilitation counselors polled stated that they did not provide sexuality-related services to their clients.* When asked why, the most common response (70%) was, "Clients don't request this service." "Lack of appropriate training" received 51% and "Lack of time" was checked by 22% of the counselors. Initiation of the topic seemed to be a major stumbling block in providing appropriate sex education/counseling services. It is especially interesting to note that most counselors (and other service providers) initiate other topics with little difficulty, for example, vocational plans, physical conditions, activities of daily living, and so on. Yet somehow the subject of sexuality is often viewed as taboo, unless it is brought up by the client. This situation is probably due more to service provider discomfort than to inappropriateness of the topic.

In the handbook *Who Cares?*, the authors emphasize the need to initiate discussion about sexuality.[2] A client may feel uncomfortable bringing up sexual concerns. If the provider never asks, the client may never receive needed services. Whereas if the counselor initiates the topic, he or she can at least refer the client to an appropriate provider.

6. *Counselors overwhelmingly chose "agency staff development workshops" (76%) as the most effective way to receive training in the area of sexuality and disability.* The findings indicate that many counselors (and other service providers as well) would be willing to participate in training workshops on the topic if they were available.

7. *Trainers were asked, "Has your agency/program adequately addressed the training of rehabilitation counselors in human sexuality?" A resounding 89% responded with a "no."* The reasons for this lack were: (a) no administrative support for such training (47%); (b) not our training mission (35%); and (c) inadequate preparation of training staff (24%).

It is fair then to conclude that many service providers and trainers need and want training about sexuality and disability. It is also clear that disabled people are interested in receiving sex education/counseling services. To meet these needs, the provision of sexuality-related services must be considered a higher priority than it has been in the past. Policymakers and service providers need to view sexuality as an integral part of every person's well-being, and services addressing sexual issues should be included (if appropriate) in a client's overall rehabilitation plan.

With the development and distribution of the handbook *Who Cares?*, the Sex & Disability Project staff has attempted to help bridge the gap between needs and actual service delivery. The manual is based on the survey results, literature searches, discussions with professionals and disabled consumers, resource information, and the authors' own ideas. It is hoped that this book can be used by a wide variety of people including parents, counselors, medical personnel, disabled individuals, advocacy groups, spouses, administrators, supervisors, trainers, teachers, students, and other interested people. The handbook includes the following topics related to sexuality and disability: myths, attitudes, and rights; needs assessment; settings; roles of service providers; training; accessibility; and conclusions and recommendations. There are also separate sections addressed to specific readers: disabled consumers, counselors, trainers, and policymakers. The last part of the book is composed of appendices that list related resources such as service programs, training programs, literature reviews, survey summaries, consultants and organizations, books and journals, audiovisual and tactile materials, and bibliographies.*

---

*Anyone interested in ordering a copy of *Who Cares?* should contact: RRRI, 1828 L Street, N.W., Suite 704, Washington, D.C. 20036, 202/676-6377. The cost is $10.00 payable to George Washington University.

REFERENCES

1. Annon, J.S.: Behavioral treatment of sexual problems, vols. 1 and 2, New York, 1976, Harper & Row Publishers, Inc.

2. Chipouras, S., Cornelius, D., Daniels, S.M., and Makas, E.: Who cares? a handbook on sex education and counseling services for disabled people, Washington, D.C., 1979 (unpublished manuscript).

♀ ABOUT THE AUTHOR ♀

Sophia Chipouras, M.A., is a family therapist who received her master's degree in rehabilitation counseling from George Washington University. She was research coordinator and associate director of the Sex & Disability Project in Washington, D.C. and co-authored *Who Cares? A Handbook on Sex Education and Counseling Services for Disabled People.* Ms. Chipouras is currently conducting family and individual therapy in the Drug and Alcohol Program of Prince William Mental Health Center, Manassas, Virginia. She also works with psychodrama groups in the northern Virginia area.

27 Sex education for disabled children and adolescents*

Carla E. Thornton

Children and adolescents who are physically or mentally disabled have very much the same concerns about sexuality as do other children. They must learn to cope with generally the same biological changes as other children, as well as with the new sexual feelings and desires that come in early adolescence. However, individual disabilities can complicate these tasks of growing up. Quality family life education can benefit disabled children in this process.

With young children, one of the primary needs is for social skills training. Without adequate social skills, it is incredibly difficult to function independently, to gain employment, and, of concern in this chapter, to develop social and sexual relationships.

In the past disabled youth were most often isolated from able-bodied peers. Both schools and families were extremely overprotective, and youth who were disabled were often given very low expectations for their functioning. There is hope that with the passage of Public Law 94-142 (federal legislation that mandates free appropriate public education in the least restrictive environment for disabled youth) disabled youth who are mainstreamed will receive adequate feedback about expectations of them. Disabled children are often "observed" and rarely get the chance to observe others. Since most people develop social skills by watching other people and how they handle situations, lack of these opportunities can hinder the development of social skills.

An additional concern is that disabled youth are frequently neither taught nor expected to behave appropriately. When a 12-year-old adolescent who has Down's syndrome hugs everyone, it is not only socially inappropriate, but it is also potentially dangerous to the child, who could be sexually exploited in such a situation. They also need opportunities to role play ordinary social situations. It is surprising how many physically disabled adolescents do not know how to use the telephone

*Preparation of this article was supported by Department of Education Grant No. G007601869.

correctly. They will assume that the person on the other end automatically knows who is calling. Some other areas that should be addressed for preschool disabled children include social skills development, identification of body parts, discussion of roles in families and relationships, and exercises in positive self-image.

SELF-ESTEEM

Many of the students who I worked with had problems with positive self-esteem. There may also be problems in having a realistic assessment of one's own capabilities. I remember one student who had been isolated in a special school for many years and was the smartest student in the class. When he came to a regular high school, he wanted to become a neurosurgeon. It was a real shock for him to discover that he was not the smartest student in the high school and that being a neurosurgeon was not a viable option for him. When planning their futures, disabled youth need to know the realities that exist for them.

It is very important to self-esteem that young disabled children be exposed to older children and adults who are disabled, since they will serve as positive role models. Generally, it has been a recent phenomenon that disabled people have become teachers in special schools or special classrooms. We need many more disabled people teaching and working in these schools and in other settings to allow young people to see that there are disabled adults in this world who do indeed function successfully and have full lives.

DEVELOPMENTAL TASKS

Some of the tasks of adolescence include developing identity, developing independence, assuming responsibilities, preparing for relationships, and developing values and ethical systems. Disabilities can complicate the completion of these tasks.

In developing our identity, we generally use feedback from others. In many respects, if the feedback is unrealistic, or if a student is isolated in a special school or a special program, he or she may not get realistic feedback or enough feedback. Adolescence is a time when differences are negatively viewed by peers, and self-image and self-esteem can suffer. Sixteen-year-olds commonly feel that they should be a certain shape, a certain height, and wear certain clothes because being different in any way may lead to social isolation.

LEARNING ABOUT REJECTION

Another issue that children who are disabled need to learn to deal with is rejection. There are many varieties of rejection. Indeed, one can be rejected because one is disabled, but also because of having the "wrong" color of eyes, hair, or clothing. You can also be rejected because of obnoxious behavior. Every student needs to know that there are disabled people as well as able-bodied people who are obnoxious. Role-playing situations of rejection can be very positive and instructive by helping students to discriminate between behaviors that result in social rejection and by teaching them that rejection is something everyone faces at some time or other. One of the teachers I've worked with recently wrote that it is her belief that loneliness is the worst disability of all; adolescence is a time that can be very lonely.

INDEPENDENCE

Disabled youth need to develop both economic and emotional independence from their families. Being independent includes being able to get places and do things with others. It can be very distressing to plan to go to a musical concert, and then discover there are 16 stairs going up to the place. Another problem results from overprotection: often students who are disabled are not allowed or expected to participate in activities that other adolescents participate in. Transportation can be a large hindrance in developing independence. It is not likely that an adolescent who is physically disabled is going to have a car at age 16, although many of his or her able-bodied peers may. Public transportation is virtually nonexistent for persons in a wheelchair. Even the school bus situation is not sufficient. Often the schedule for the bus precludes any participation in extracurricular activities.

Often disabled students do not receive much peer support for developing independence. If none of them are starting the struggle to become independent, they are not able to provide support for each other. When we started talking about independence in one family life class, it was surprising how little the students had done in this area and how easy it was to encourage them to start to become more independent. One student eventually decided that an electric wheelchair would be most useful to her and that it would help in her independence. It took a 6-month battle with her parents to get an electric wheelchair. This was the first time she had a real conflict with her parents, and she was 18 years old. If one has never been given any responsibilities or been expected to be responsible, assuming responsibilities can be difficult. Again, this is a result of overprotection. All disabled children can be given responsibilities and can be expected to participate in family activities in a responsible way.

Preparing for relationships and developing a set of values often can be complicated by the myths that most of the public believes: disabled people are not sexual, and disabled people do not have intimate relationships. In 1974 I interviewed physically disabled high school students to determine if there was a need for a special family life class. They all had taken the regular family life class offered at our school. It was a course covering anatomy, physiology, venereal disease, and pregnancy but included nothing on values, feelings, or decision making. These students were really enthusiastic in their response to the idea of having a special class for them. The primary reason was that in the regular family life class there would be one or two disabled students, and all the other students would be able-bodied. The disabled students had questions that they did not feel comfortable asking in a regular family life class, such as the following:

- Because I am disabled, does that mean that my sperm are defective?
- Will I be able to have sex?
- Will I be able to have or to father babies?
- Would my child be born with the same problem I have?
- How have adults who are disabled learned to handle questions and harrass-ment from others who look at you like you are a freak?
- How can I handle these kinds of things?
- Am I physically capable?
- Could I really fall in love some day?

That last question raised a whole new possibility for one of my students.

They also had questions like any other students have. Their questions were not only about sexuality but also about how to deal with the stigma that disabled adolescents often experience.

Disabled youth definitely need sexuality information and need the opportunity to explore their feelings about the information that they receive. One of the primary concepts disabled youth should know is that all of us share similar needs, feelings, and desires. Disabled or not, we all make individual adjustments to our needs.

Another point that is very important for disabled youth to know is that the male-superior position in intercourse is not the only mode of sexual expression. There are many ways to be sexually active, to express oneself sexually. There are certainly other positions for genital intercourse and other options to sexual pleasure, such as cuddling, massage, and oral/genital activity. I found that oral/genital activity was something that can sound repulsive to an adolescent. When one is teaching a family life class, it is very important that oral/genital sex be included gently, and there should be plenty of time allowed for getting all the "oh, yucks!" out of the way.

Another important piece of information for disabled youth is that nongenital orgasms are quite possible. Orgasms can happen through fantasy, dreams, and stimulation of other areas of the body that often are not considered sexual areas. Youth really need to know that they can have satisfactory or better social/sexual relationships; this is an area in which disabled role models can have a positive impact on the students. Disabled youth need to have discussions about myths and misinformation. They need to start working on decision making. As for all other people, it is important for them to explore conflict, independence, stigma, and rights and responsibilities together with values and life-styles.

In a discussion of the sociosexual concerns of children and adolescents who are disabled, the concerns of their parents must also be considered. Parents frequently have concerns in three different areas; one is attitudinal. Often parents believe the myth that disabled people are not sexual, and therefore their child cannot be sexual. It's not uncommon for a parent to ask, "Why teach them about something they won't ever be able to do?"

Another common attitude held by parents is that their child will only be hurt if he or she should get involved in a relationship. We all have been hurt in a relationship, and this is one of the risks we all take. If the rest of the world can take the risk, disabled youth should also be allowed that option.

One concern of parents is often due to a lack of awareness about the facts of the potential sociosexual functioning of their child. I've found, in leading parent groups, that often a parent will say something like: "My daughter is ten and has spina bifida. I don't know whether she can get married, or have kids, or have pleasurable sexual activity." Simply spending 5 minutes with a parent and giving him or her a little basic information can make it possible for the parent to go home and start talking to the child. It doesn't take a lot of time to provide a parent with that kind of information.

Occasionally parents have language problems. The parent may speak primarily one language, for instance, Tagalog, and the child may speak primarily English. They may, indeed, wish to talk to their child but may not have the English words to use. The provision of reading materials or discussion of areas of concern for the parent can make it possible for the parent to better understand the language and initiate discussions with his or her child.

Another concern for parents is in the area of values and morals. At the first parents' meeting in preparation for the commencement of a family life education class, the other teacher and I made the curriculum and all the teaching materials that we'd be using in the course available for parents to review. The parents very dutifully read through the entire curriculum and one of the fathers said, "I see you have masturbation in here, and I want to know how you are going to handle it because I know that masturbation causes senility." Dr. Robert Geiger (who was attending the meeting to answer any questions the parents might have and to provide moral support for the novice teachers) was unusually quiet. I finally said that until recent times even medical students were taught that masturbation was a horrible thing and caused a variety of physical and emotional problems, but now we know that masturbation cannot physically hurt you. One of the other parents spoke up and said that he was a Buddhist and Buddha had said many thousands of years ago that masturbation was all right. Dr. Geiger finally spoke up and said, "Sure, he sat under that tree all by himself for 7 years." This definitely dissolved the tension in that meeting.

The parents were also assured that the teachers were not interested in examining only one value system but believed that all the students needed to have reliable information about masturbation. It is not the teacher's right or responsibility to impose a singular value system.

In 1979, the United Nations Year of The Child, many rights of children were examined and affirmed. Sexuality of all children, disabled and able-bodied, is one area that also must be addressed and provided with more attention to ensure that the complete rights of children and youth will be respected.

RECOMMENDED READINGS

1. Buscaglia, L.: The disabled and their parents: a counseling challenge, Thorofare, N.J., 1975, Charles B. Slack, Inc.
2. Edwards, J.: Sara and Allen: the right to choose, Portland, Ore., 1976, Edwards Communications.
3. Gordon, S.: Living fully: a guide for young people with a handicap, their parents, their teachers, and professionals, North Scituate, Mass., 1973, Duxbury Press.
4. Gordon, S.: The sexual adolescent: communicating with teenagers about sex, North Scituate, Mass., 1973, Duxbury Press.
5. Johnson, W.: Sex education and counseling of special groups: the mentally and physically handicapped, ill and elderly, Springfield, Ill., 1975, Charles C Thomas, Publisher.
6. Robinault, I.P.: Sex, society and the disabled: a developmental inquiry into roles, reactions, and responsibilities, New York, 1978, Harper & Row, Publishers, Inc.

28 Sexual abuse of disabled persons and prevention alternatives

SEATTLE RAPE RELIEF DEVELOPMENTAL DISABILITIES PROJECT*

Ellen Ryerson

The Seattle Rape Relief Developmental Disabilities Project in Seattle, Washington, has been addressing the problem of sexual abuse of both physically and mentally handicapped children and adults. This article, therefore, will consider some negative and exploitative aspects of sexuality as opposed to positive sexuality. It is difficult for many of us to admit that these problems exist, but there is increasing public awareness that they do. Fortunately, there are some positive beginning steps to addressing these issues that indicate this need not be a neglected area of health education and care.

This article will both describe some of the dynamics involved in sexual abuse of handicapped persons and also consider the special education program concerning sexual abuse created by the Developmental Disabilities Project. Parent participation, which is a vital part of this program, will also be reviewed.

First, it is important to clarify what is meant by sexual abuse and how common this problem is among the disabled population. Our project has been in existence for 3 years. During the first 2½ years, our data indicated that we assisted over 300 victims of sexual abuse who were either physically and or mentally handicapped. These included children, adolescents, and adults. We estimate that only 20% of all handicapped persons who have been sexually abused report these incidents to anyone, and therefore there are hundreds of disabled people in our community for whom we have no data. This 20% figure is partially based on FBI statistics, which state that only 20% of all adult rape cases are reported to social service agencies or police.

If we assume that these 300 persons represent only 20% of all actual victims in

*1825 S. Jackson, Suite 102, Seattle, Wash., 98144, (206)-325-5531

the Seattle area during this $2\frac{1}{2}$ year period, then there may have been 1500 disabled persons who were victims of sexual abuse just in the Seattle–King County area alone. There is no reason to believe the incidence rate is very different in other parts of the country. Sexual exploitation is a pervasive problem that we all need to be concerned with.

Legally, sexual exploitation refers to rape, incest, and indecent liberty, which is more commonly known as child molestation. I would like to define each of these offenses and explain further why we assume such a low reporting rate among handicapped persons who have been victims of these crimes.

Rape refers to sexual intercourse when the offender used physical force or when the victim did not consent to the act. Some states, such as Washington, have an expanded definition of rape. Under this definition, forced intercourse includes oral, anal, or vaginal penetration with a penis or with an object, such as a finger or pencil. Under this law boys and men are considered to be potential victims of rape.*

Some states have included in the rape statute an "informed consent" clause. A person can be deemed by the court incapable of giving informed consent to the act of intercourse, either because of a physical disability, for example, because a person cannot talk or cannot physically resist, or because of a mental disability, whereby the person has no understanding of sexual intercourse or possible consequences. A person who has intercourse with a disabled individual deemed incapable of giving informed consent can be charged with rape under this law. These issues are decided on an individual case basis, and the clause is intended to protect persons who either did not understand the sexual activity or were forced into sexual activity that they were physically unable to resist.

A second sexual offense, incest, is sexual intercourse between family members, usually a grandfather, foster father, stepfather, uncle, or brother with a female such as a daughter, foster daughter, or niece. Indecent liberty, sometimes termed "child molestation," is sexual fondling of the private body areas other than sexual intercourse. These are both extremely common offenses against disabled persons.

Review of data from the project's first year revealed that an alarming 99% of the sexual offenders were people well known to the handicapped victim. Only 1% were strangers. These offenders commonly had considerable access to handicapped individuals. Incest and child molestation are compulsive behaviors, and it would seem that some offenders seek means of gaining access to handicapped persons, often through employment roles. Offenders included neighbors, relatives, bus drivers, work supervisors, special education personnel, and residential facility staff. It is important to consider that sexual offenders are individuals of all ages, races, and

---

*Statistics indicate that men who rape other men are not usually homosexuals and may have female sexual partners. These rapists choose to perpetrate their violence on other men.

social and economic backgrounds. These are only a few examples of the many types of persons who have committed sexual offenses.

Considering these data, the educational emphasis in many public schools on "dangerous strangers" and "the dangers of accepting candy from strangers" is not the only area of self-protection that needs attention. Our focus needs to be education of youth about inappropriate touching by all kinds of adults, including relatives. We also need to concern ourselves with thorough screening of service providers who educate and care for disabled youth.

The fact that sexual offenders are frequently caregivers or relatives of handicapped persons, coupled with the dynamics involved in these sexual offenses, explains the low reporting rate among this population.

Incidents involving sexual exploitation by a family member or caregiver create a very distorted situation for the handicapped individual. Often the offender will convince the victim that sexual activity between two family members is normal and acceptable. The offender may define the sexual activity as "special" or "secret." For children, secrets are sacred. Children, and often retarded adults, have never been taught to distinguish appropriate affectionate behavior from sexually exploitive behavior and therefore can easily be taught such misconceptions.

The offender has additional control in these situations because youth are taught in general to obey authority figures, particularly relatives and caregivers. Some physically handicapped children are additionally vulnerable because of their limited self-care abilities. These youth are accustomed to being handled for their basic physical care and may not discriminate fondling done for the pleasure of the caregiver or relative as exploitive. Sexual abuse of this nature is rarely reported, but I believe it is probably quite frequent.

In more extreme cases victims are threatened into compliance by the offender. The offender may threaten to deprive the child or adolescent of such basic needs as meals or social activities, or may threaten to tell other "authorities" in the family that she or he has been involved in some imaginary wrongdoing.

Even the victim, should he or she want to report these incidents, lacks information about appropriate persons or resources to contact. Who can be trusted with this knowledge? Who will believe that this has occurred? Some youth also have fears about consequences for the offender or the family if it is reported. Is he or she to blame if negative consequences occur? It is clearly difficult for a handicapped individual to gain assistance when faced with such confusing and threatening issues. Because many individuals do not report offenses, victimization sometimes begins between 2 and 5 years of age and continues for a period of 5 to 15 years. These dynamics are no different in sexual abuse cases involving nonhandicapped children or adolescents. The one difference is the tendency for mentally handicapped persons to be victimized through adulthood because they often continue to live in environments where they are dependent on relatives or caregivers.

PARENTAL CONCERNS

Parents who have attended informational meetings about the Developmental Disabilities Project have expressed a number of concerns and fears regarding potential sexual abuse of their children. If their child is mentally handicapped, parents often fear that he or she is not capable of discriminating between positive and exploitative touching, and that the possibility of sexual exploitation is extremely high. Parents of physically handicapped youth fear that their children are unable to defend themselves or run away from a child molester or rapist. I find it interesting that parents often become particularly concerned about sexual abuse as their children reach adolescence and begin to overtly express interest in their sexuality and intimate relationships. Parents often do not realize that their children were just as vulnerable, or perhaps more vulnerable, to sexual abuse as young children.

Parents are not only concerned about their daughters' safety, but their sons' safety as well. Their concerns are well-founded, because our project has assisted a number of mentally disabled men and boys who were raped by other males.

Parents have expressed fear, but also a sense of hopelessness, concerning their child's inability to protect himself or herself because of a disability. I think that part of this sense of hopelessness results from focusing on the disability of the child rather than on the child's abilities to learn self-protective skills. Parents need to be knowledgeable about high-risk situations regarding their children where molestation or rape may occur. They also need to know the specific self-protective practices that both mentally and physically handicapped children can learn to avoid at least some high-risk situations.

I am concerned about the handicapped child's vulnerability and also with parents' own vulnerability, which results from their inadequate information about self-protection. People in general in our society are often not socialized to protect themselves. We place ourselves in very vulnerable situations to be polite or because we trust in the good intentions of others. In many situations we may not even think of the possibility of assault or sexual abuse. The parents who allow strangers into their homes to use the telephone are vulnerable to assault themselves and also model inappropriate self-protection skills for their children.

In summary, all these areas of concern and uncertainty have lead parents to be motivated to obtain information about sexual abuse and self-protection.

THE DEVELOPMENTAL DISABILITIES PROJECT'S TRAINING AND EDUCATION PROGRAM

To address the issue of sexual abuse, our project has developed an information and education program for handicapped students, special education personnel, and parents. This program includes a special education curriculum concerning sexual abuse for use with students ages 6 through 18 and mentally retarded adults. These materials are designed for use with moderate to borderline mentally retarded students and can be easily adapted for hearing or visually impaired and orthopedically handicapped students. The project offers training for special education personnel to increase their awareness and understanding of sexual abuse and to familiarize them with effective teaching techniques for presenting curriculum concepts.

Prior to personnel training or student exposure to the curriculum, an effort is made to provide an overview of this program with parents of the students who will be receiving this information. The project has assisted school personnel with these presentations locally, but special educators in other areas of the country have integrated this program without direct assistance from the project. Our intention is to increase parental knowledge about this problem and also to integrate parental perspectives and ideas into this educational effort.

Before and after our presentation sessions, parents complete an attitude survey that includes items such as the following:

Curriculum materials used in the classroom to teach my child about sexual exploitation would be: excellent; acceptable; not acceptable.
Education concerning positive sexuality prior to education about sexual exploitation is: very needed; somewhat needed; not needed.

Comparative results of this survey indicate that parents either enter the session feeling supportive of this kind of education and leave with essentially the same attitudes, or they arrive with concerns and doubts about the program and indicate a much more positive, comfortable attitude after the session.

The curriculum on sexual exploitation is lengthy, but discussion of one exemplary slide story will provide a general sense of its content. Each slide story includes a series of slides accompanied by a written script with key discussion questions for use by the instructor.

One such story, entitled "Uncle Harry," concerns a molestation incident that an uncle initiates with his niece. The adolescent's visit with her uncle is sanctioned by the residential facility staff where she lives; they encourage activity outside of the residential group environment as a positive growth experience. Uncle Harry takes his niece to an enjoyable lunch. It is important for students to recognize how this uncle is viewed by his niece. He is an authority figure and a loving relative who provides many positive experiences for her. He makes visits away from the group home possible and provides individual attention that may meet important needs for her. He pays for her lunch, which raises issues concerning the favors he provides and her indebtedness to him.

After lunch, Uncle Harry takes his niece to his home where the fondling occurs. The pictures portray the Uncle unbuttoning the niece's blouse and placing his hand under her blouse. The intention here is to visualize the inappropriate actions as clearly as possible for students with learning handicaps. Fortunately, this material has been deemed acceptable by numerous school systems.

The niece's facial expression conveys her confusion about the uncle's actions. She may very well have been sheltered from information regarding sexuality in general and consequently has no knowledge with which to assess his intentions. She is defenseless not because of her mental handicap, but because of her lack of information about sexuality and sexual abuse. Whatever distorted explanation this sexual offender provides will most likely be accepted by her. She has no reason to assume this behavior is wrong and, therefore, to seek help. At this point in the story, students would be asked: "Is it okay for Uncle Harry to do this? What might the niece try to do to protect herself?" Students who have received some education might respond: "I would say no, don't touch me that way." "I would tell my counselor (or mother or teacher)."

With nonviolent sexual offenders, this assertive action may stop the behavior. Students are not encouraged to use this approach if they are threatened or physically forced. The major goal of the story, however, is to encourage students to report these incidents to an authority figure immediately. This is what occurs during the conclusion of the story. The niece is taken home with no apparent harm done. The housemother does not know that anything has happened until the niece reports the day's occurrences. Students are told that Uncle Harry has a problem and needs special help or counseling; he should not be allowed to see his niece alone while he is receiving this help. Every effort is made not to condemn the relative, but to point out that sometimes adults do things which are not acceptable. Also emphasized is the fact that it is not the niece's fault that this unfortunate incident occurred.

This story is one of 12 included in the curriculum, which also contains pictures, cassette tapes, and short stories regarding a number of sexual abuse situations.

Although all this material is taught by special education teachers, nurses, and counselors in a classroom setting, parents also play an essential role in this education. Most important is parental support and reinforcement of this program. This means not only support of education concerning sexual exploitation but also of basic positive human sexuality education. I feel this latter education is essential prerequisite material. Although we have no data to support my contention, I believe that students who do not receive instruction concerning acceptable sexual options prior to learning about sexual abuse are at risk of perceiving all touching, or at least all sexual touching, in a negative light.

I am concerned by the occasional parent who interprets this education to be a method of avoiding issues concerning their handicapped child's sexuality by assuming that the child can simply be taught "don't let anyone touch you or you are in danger." During parent meetings, I point out the need for prerequisite information concerning friendship, intimate relationships, marriage, and other aspects of positive human sexuality. I also emphasize the need for basic instruction concerning anatomy and appropriate terminology for parts of the body.

Many handicapped children have been competent witnesses in court trials because of their ability to discuss their bodies articulately. Very detailed questions may be asked during a trial, for example, "Where did the man put his finger? Did he put it inside your vagina?" The detailed testimony of deaf, blind, and mentally retarded children has resulted in a number of successful convictions in the Seattle–King County area.*

A second critical role played by parents in this program is that of a supplemental teacher to augment classroom instruction. Self-protection skill training must be done in a consistent manner between school and home. If the teacher demonstrates specific strategies to prevent a salesman from entering the home, whereas in reality the mother lets him in and offers him coffee, then clearly we are confusing the child and losing the campaign to teach self-protective skills. To clarify the instructional objectives of our program, parents are provided with two brochures. One brochure outlines sexual abuse in legal and statistical terms. The second brochure describes in a detailed manner the curriculum level at which their child is being taught.

Through mutual parent-teacher involvement, I believe there will be an optimal opportunity for handicapped children to learn self-protection against sexual abuse and therefore to more adequately enjoy the right of a positive experience with their sexuality.

---

*The Developmental Disabilities Project provides counseling, medical and legal advocacy for disabled persons, as do many rape crisis centers throughout the country.

♀ ABOUT THE AUTHOR ♀

Ellen Ryerson, M.S.W., is a social worker and has been director of the Seattle Rape Relief Developmental Disabilities Project since 1977. She had provided counseling as well as legal and medical advocacy for numerous mentally and physically handicapped children, adolescents, and adults who were victims of sexual abuse. Ms. Ryerson has developed a number of model approaches to educating handicapped individuals, parents, and professionals about sexual abuse and self-protective techniques. She facilitated the development of several special education curricula that are gradually being adopted by special education programs throughout the nation. She has also developed training and informational materials for parents and professionals regarding identification of victims and use of curricula in teaching handicapped students. During the past 3 years Ms. Ryerson has trained over 200 individuals.

29 Social skills: the process of learning to take risks*

Robert S. Badame

Social skills as a concept is difficult to teach and is still more difficult to experience. Frequently it is confused with learning "social graces," a much simpler "how to" approach toward socialization. It is as though if we smile and act nice enough, somehow people will love and accept us. Our painful experiences growing up teach that this is not the case. Indeed, the world can sometimes be cruel, unloving, and uncaring. This does not mean happiness or self-fulfillment does not exist in the world, but that the individuals needing to develop social skills have lost or never developed the ability to believe that they themselves are worthy and deserving of it.

How can an individual facilitating social skill development cultivate a sense of self-worth in another person? How do we come to understand, as Ayn Rand expressed in her treatise on selfishness, that "an individual has a right to expect the very best for himself. This does not mean one will always get his needs met, only that the desire to want them is good, positive and appropriate."[7] The corollary further developed by Rand is that only when an individual *has* or experiences the very best that life has to offer can he or she then offer the world the best of themselves. The key to social *skills* from this vantage point, then, is the understanding within oneself that "I am worth something, I matter, I am important. I can reasonably expect some people, in attempting to get my needs met, to accept me. I believe that there are people who will recognize, appreciate, and cherish me. I not only seek and desire love, I am worthy of it, and expect it."

If this understanding of self constitutes the basis of social skills, then clearly it differs from the development of social graces or amenities. The cultivation of social graces alone contributes little toward a sense of self-worth. It is a little like a beautiful, shiny, new automobile with all the latest gadgetry and comforts—and no gasoline. It looks nice, feels comfortable to sit in, but for all practical purposes

*The preparation of this chapter was supported in part by Department of Education Grant No. G007601869.

might as well be a planter. It is essentially useless. How do we provide the fuel? We do this by cultivating the ability to take risks, and the concepts of and approaches to this will be developed further in this chapter.

One might ideally say that a sense of self-worth should be developed in childhood. To do this requires the opportunity for experiencing social risk taking, to acquire the necessary information needed to develop a sense of self-worth. It is reasonable to assume then, that the ability to take social risks is also most developed primarily in childhood. The problem is that for the person lacking a sense of self-esteem, what did or did not transpire in the past cannot be changed and matters little in the present. All too frequently the present for these individuals consists of a world of isolation, fear, mistrust, and anger.

The individual needing social skills often feels little connection with the world. Indeed, the person feels a sense of separateness from other people. For the disabled individual, whether the disability is congenital or acquired later in life, this perception is particularly real. The disabled person *is* seen as different by the world at large, and not infrequently, this sense of appearing different has a negative "stigma" attached to it.[3]

Acknowledging this difference to oneself has the potential of being turned around to be seen as a part of one's uniqueness. For example, exercises involving role playing and modeling of behavior can be employed.[2] The uniqueness and desirability of the disabled individual can thereby be presented as a privilege to be experienced. Having a classroom game for children in which the prize or reward is the "privilege" of using a wheelchair or wearing a blindfold or earplug for an hour or class period can help facilitate this goal. As a method in mainstreaming disabled children and adolescents in a classroom environment, this technique can be both instructive and fun.

Any individual can rightly feel afraid of the world, afraid of allowing risk involvement with others at any but the most remote and superficial level. A fear of relationships can be further exaggerated by the belief that if one did take a risk and reach out, he or she would be rejected because of being undesirable and having nothing to offer. This attitude can cultivate withdrawal from virtually all human contact. Fear can also breed mistrust. Why should I trust you if my expectation is to be rejected? Ultimately this mistrust becomes an inner statement that says (when anyone attempts a social approach toward us), "What does he/she want from me?" This attitude will virtually assure the person who approaches us the feeling of being rebuffed and the approachee of remaining alone, afraid, and skeptical.[8] He or she has effectively fulfilled his or her own prophecy of rejection. A sense of hopelessness, defeat, despair, and, very likely, anger and even rage results. It is within anger and rage, often directed at ourselves through a sense of impotence at being unable to get our needs met and a sense of injustice, that another method of cultivating social skills can be approached. The educator, therapist, or teacher-trainer potentially has a wedge, a lever, if you will, to initiate interventions intended to allow the individual with limited social skills the opportunity to risk developing new behavior. Using highly structured exercises involving the expressing of anger through "hostility rituals," as developed by George Bach, can be useful.[1]

Anger can be channeled and discharged if the teacher, therapist, parent, or facilitator has some understanding of fair fighting techniques. Beating on pillows and pillow fights (they work fine with people in wheelchairs, too) are useful. Time-limited periods of expressing resentment need to be allowed and encouraged.

One may ask why is it necessary to employ techniques where there is the potential use of anger and resistance. The answer is that individuals lacking social skills are often characterized by noninvolvement. "Waiting around" for life to happen to you typically generates anxiety, boredom, passivity, and fatigue.[11] The reality, of course, is that we cannot avoid starting social encounters unless we live in a vacuum. Thus through the use of anger we possibly can energize an individual, so the potential exists to persuade, manipulate, support, or push them into taking some actions that involve risk.

Not too surprisingly, many people lacking social skills show what we call a martyr complex: "Why am I chosen to suffer?" We can make a constructive game of the martyr role by asking a group of people, for example: "How does one become a good martyr?" By asking people to role play a good "poor me" kind of person, a whole set of rules and guidelines emerges.[4] It is interesting to note that teachers or instructors who have tried this technique report getting their most insightful comments from precisely the individuals who display the use of martyr behavior in their daily life.

Another method of using this process is through the use of progressive exercises in risk taking. For example, in a group setting a leader, teacher, or facilitator can direct half the group to go around the room collecting rejections, that is, asking the other half for some small trifle or favor such as a dime for a phone call or getting a cup of coffee. The person asked this is to simply respond negatively to the request—no explanation, no compromising, just a simple "no."[10]

What would you expect as a reaction from participants to an exercise like this? Children or adults can and do react by being negative toward exercises that involve action. They frequently express hurt and anger over this small rejection. The leader may have to cajole or even direct people into an interaction involving rejection and risk taking. It can be pointed out to the participants that the *risk is small,* and that only by experimenting with taking small risks with rejection can they develop the feeling of confidence necessary to take larger risks. Anger, hurt, and a sense of defeat can be used to an individual's benefit when presented in a controlled, safe situation.

Body language and its use is another important concept. For disabled individuals there can be a lack of understanding in how to modify behavior so that it becomes more acceptable in the population at large. How do you facilitate social interaction using appropriate body language if you use a wheelchair, for example? For starters, it would help if eye contact were on the same physical level. In a role-playing situation then, it becomes the responsibility of the individuals in wheelchairs to ask nondisabled, standing persons to come down to their level of eye contact. To do this nondisabled persons almost invariably sit and make contact with persons in wheelchairs. A tacit bond between individuals in wheelchairs and sitting persons has been established. This exercise can provide material for discussion between the participants observing the role play. How, for example, would this feel, having people interact from different height levels?[9]

Setting limits on behavior is another important concept in social skills development. When *not* to interrupt, for example, is an important social skill. Some socially unskilled persons have not learned the appropriate cues of pausing to wait for someone to complete a thought or learning how to "listen" to what's being said without thinking ahead to a response. For example, with a deaf individual, a set of socially appropriate cues can be established *with* eye contact. A person using sign language can finish a sentence and make direct eye contact with the receiver, the prearranged meaning being "your turn."

For a blind individual, it can be important to learn to face a speaker with the face and not the ear. If you have no example of what eye contact is, you must rely on responses derived from voice, personality, touch, conversation, and personal interest. The lack of awareness of the importance of teaching social cues is underscored in a study conducted by Eugene Lorenzo, San Diego State University, concerning dating opportunities with blind individuals.[5] From questions submitted to a student sample, several social perceptions emerged. One is that the consensus of blind individuals shows that blind females have better dating opportunities with both sighted and unsighted individuals. The overall tabulation suggests that blind females have about twice the dating opportunity as do blind males. The explanation offered for this is that blind males face certain customs that they find difficult to follow, such as calling for a young woman at her home, seeing her home after the date, and providing transportation (from not being able to drive a car). In our culture it has been the custom for the male to play the assertive role in dating. His social virility, physical mobility, and self-image seem directly correlated to his ability to actively assume this role. The blind males would seem to have ample opportunity to *not* develop social skills. Conversely, women are perceived as assuming a more passive role in dating situations, and it is therefore supposedly easier for them to wait and have a male initiate a social contact.[5]

Related to the concept of learning to set limits is the concept of power and control. People strive for attention; this is natural and to be expected. However, when the need for attention-seeking behavior becomes intrusive, individuals using this behavior may have to be shown that their actions will get them the opposite of the attention they seek, namely, nonattention. This does not mean ignoring the behavior, but rather showing individuals that by becoming intrusive, they will get the opposite of what they expect. Jerry Patterson, in his work at the University of Oregon with recalcitrant and hyperactive children, has developed a series of exercises and techniques calculated to "extinguish" the behavior.[6] This is accomplished by having children stop what they are doing and go to a neutral environment (i.e. hallway, bathroom or empty room) for a specified period of time, usually 3 to 5 minutes. This "freezing" of the action is called "time out." It is important that a child understand that "time out" is the result of the behavior. It is time limited to not encourage the exercise to be seen as punishment. Individuals being controlled are not stripped of dignity; they have a right to be angry and express their anger. They must still take the consequences for their previous behavior, however. It is important to understand in using this technique that strong and frequently angry feelings can develop in the child. Equally important in the administration of this technique is the use of praise and encouragement when the appropriate response *is* displayed.[6]

This chapter began and shall close with the concept of risk taking as a foundation to the development of social skills. Someone once said that there are only two things people fear: rejection and acceptance. To be able to accept some rejection is a first and primary step to acceptance of oneself as a total and unique person. The reality is that everyone experiences rejection at some time in life. By learning how to use rejection and channel anger as a learning process, we possess a vehicle that potentially offers the individual in need of social skills a sense of personal strength, purpose, and direction.

REFERENCES

1. Bach, G., and Goldberg, H.: Creative aggression—the art of assertive living, New York, 1974, Avon Books.
2. Dunn, M., Lloyd, E.E., and Phelps, G.H.: Sexual assertiveness in spinal cord injury, Sex. Disabil. **2**:293-300, 1979.
3. Goffman, E.: Stigma—notes on the management of spoiled identity, Englewood Cliffs, N.J., 1963, Prentice-Hall, Inc.
4. Greenberg, D.: How to make yourself miserable, New York, 1966, Random House, Inc.
5. Lorenzo, E.: Interactions of the blind with sighted concerning sex curiosity, dating and intermarriage, San Diego State University, 1976 (Unpublished manuscript).
6. Patterson, G.R.: Families—applications of social learning to family life, Champaign, Ill., 1973, Research Press.
7. Rand, A.: On the virtue of selfishness, New York, 1957, Simon & Schuster, Inc.
8. Shapiro, D.: Neurotic styles, New York, 1965, Basic Books, Inc., Publishers.
9. Simon, H., and Kirschenbaum, M.: Values clarification: a handbook of practical strategies for teachers and students, New York, 1972, Hart Publishing Co., Inc.
10. Zilbergeld, B., and Rinklieb, C.: Social skills training as an adjunct to sex therapy, J. Sex Marital Ther. **5**(4):340-350, 1979.
11. Zimbardo, P.G.: Shyness, Menlo Park, Calif., 1977, Addison-Wesley Publishing Co.

♂ ABOUT THE AUTHOR ♂

Robert S. Badame, Ph.D., is a licensed marriage, family, and child counselor and a psychologist. He was trained at the California School for Professional Psychology and at the Human Sexuality Program, Department of Psychiatry, University of California, San Francisco. He has supervised sex therapy interns and has developed a curriculum to train special education teachers in the teaching of social skills at the Sex and Disability Unit, University of California, San Francisco.

30 Sexual assertiveness in spinal cord injury*

Michael Dunn, E. Elaine Lloyd, and Graham H. Phelps

W/M quadriplegic, 31 years old, seeks woman
for kinky sex. Call John 473-2961.

Although not a technique that is recommended for all, this ad, which appeared in the *L.A. Free Press*, does illustrate several major issues relating to assertiveness, sexuality, and spinal cord injury (SCI), namely (1) meeting eligible partners is difficult (perhaps more so when physically handicapped); (2) asking for what one wants in a direct manner usually leads to a positive outcome (as did this ad); and (3) when some sexual options are denied, other options may need to be explored.

This chapter will discuss the following aspects of sexual assertiveness[9] and SCI: (1) What is it? (2) Who needs it? (3) What can it do for you? (4) How do you get it? (5) Trying it!

WHAT IS IT?

The literature on assertiveness training[7] discusses the concept of assertiveness in terms of behavioral skills, anxiety, and cognition. We thus define sexual assertiveness as the acknowledgement of yourself as a sexual being and the utilization, with little anxiety, of a set of behavioral skills to obtain sexual satisfaction for yourself and your partner. In SCI or other physical handicaps the techniques used to achieve these goals may be different, but it is felt that with appropriate exploration of alternatives and expression of feelings (both physical and emotional), a reasonably satisfactory sexual adaptation can be made even by the most severely handicapped quadriplegic. For example, sexual assertiveness in the SCI individual may take the form of new ways of meeting people, flirting, seduction, dealing with external appliances, clothes removal, and exploration of different erogenous zones.

It should be emphasized that sexual assertiveness also involves (1) learning to receive pleasure as well as give it; (2) giving others permission to be sexually assertive; and (3) taking responsibility for your own sexual pleasure. Many sexually active

*From Dunn, M., Lloyd, E.E., and Phelps, G.H.: Sex. Disabil. **2:**293-300, 1979. Reprinted with permission, Human Sciences Press.

SCI people get to the point at which they find that they can satisfy their partner but go no further in the exploration of their own sexual pleasure. Understanding of sexual assertiveness in terms of one's own responsibility to one's self[1,11] may help these individuals progress in the sexual adaptation to their injury.

WHO NEEDS IT?

Those SCI persons and/or their partners dissatisfied with the sexual component of their lives need to learn to be sexually assertive. Those SCI persons who view themselves as asexual or not entitled to be a sexual person may also benefit. Dissatisfaction with the sexual component of their lives might be the result of a variety of reasons such as

1. A total absence of any sexual activity with a partner since injury
2. Current sexual activity not pleasurable enough
3. Sexual inexperience before injury and therefore reluctance to initiate sexual activity
4. No current sexual component to life-style but desire to change this

For some SCI persons injured at an early age, the question might be "What is sexual pleasure?" For others, it may be responding to the mythology present in our culture such as "People in wheelchairs can't have sex;" "If you can't get it up, no woman will have sex with you;" or "Disabled people are not supposed to be interested in sex, or a relationship with someone of the opposite sex, or marriage or children of their own." When friends and family operate with this mythology in mind (usually out of ignorance), they refrain from using language of a sexual nature, making references to future sex-linked behavior such as "When you have kids of your own, you'll understand," or they abandon casual flirting for behavior that is not sexual in nature out of fear of frustrating the SCI person. Conversely, friends and acquaintances may behave in a sexually exaggerated manner such as telling in great detail every conquest, making inappropriate physical advances, or only relating via dirty jokes and/or locker room humor. Such individuals, who are insecure in their own sexuality and build themselves up at the expense of someone they see as asexual, must be recognized and dealt with assertively.

WHAT CAN IT DO FOR YOU?

As one becomes more sexually assertive, there is an increase in the satisfaction of the sexual component of one's life. This may take the form of actual satisfying sexual activity with a partner or may simply be a change in attitude to viewing oneself as a sexual versus asexual person. This change in attitude is accompanied by the confidence necessary to take steps to experience pleasurable sex. The confidence comes from having thought through or rehearsed the sexual activity desired and what will have to be asked of a partner in terms of assistance, for example, asking to be undressed, as well as how a partner will be given verbal and nonverbal feedback during and after the sexual experience.

In the nonsexual areas of one's life and relationships, the clarity and directness used while communicating during sex is carried over. The more skillful a communicator one becomes, the more interpersonal relationships are enhanced.

An additional gain from enhancing relationships in general because of increased communication skills is the increase in self-esteem and improvement in body image. The SCI person must go through adaptations to body image that are facilitated or hindered by changes in sensation. Many SCI persons will be touched as part of the care regimen, but they will not have the opportunity to receive touch from a body-pleasure point of view, particularly if functional limitations preclude self-exploration for intact or new erogenous zones. When one becomes sexually assertive and engages in sexually pleasurable activities, there is the opportunity to expand on the knowledge of one's body, such as areas of hypersensitivity, perhaps even discovering areas that were thought to be insensitive. Such knowledge, gained through mutual exploration and accompanied by giving and receiving feedback, cannot help but improve body image.

As body image improves, so do feeling of self-esteem. The sexually assertive person is constantly giving and receiving feedback. When you receive feedback that what you are doing sexually feels good to a partner and have the chance to be close and experience each other in a way that is not possible in the usual social sense of interacting, self-esteem is increased.

When an SCI person becomes sexually assertive, he or she also may become desirable to potential partners. The desirability comes about because sexually assertive persons immediately begin cueing in potential partners to the fact that they consider themselves sexual persons, that they consider sexual satisfaction as a natural part of life, and that sex might be a part of a mutually satisfying relationship. This early cueing does not allow any chance for mythology to take over and retard a potential relationship, particularly when the partner may be totally inexperienced with physically limited persons. The SCI person can "ooze sex appeal" every bit as much as an able-bodied person.[10]

The sexually assertive SCI person also has worked through the steps necessary to put a partner at ease about preparing for sexual activity to prevent possibly embarrassing situations. A female SCI person can alert her partner before undressing that she has a Foley catheter in place, that it is easier for her not to have it removed for sex, and unless her partner finds it distracting or uncomfortable, that she does not find that it interferes with her enjoyment of sex (in fact it may increase it). Or a male SCI person can explain his urinary collection system before his partner discovers it. It is the unexpected that often causes a situation to be embarrassing when otherwise, with a little forewarning, the same situation might be used to illustrate a point, for example, "This is what the leg bag looks like that I was telling you about."

Cultural prohibitions can also be overcome with sexual assertiveness. Prohibitions against anal intercourse and oral sex have to be thought through when SCI individuals make a decision to be sexually assertive. The prohibitions are weighed in the light of what that prohibition means to them today, given the fact that they may have to exercise their sexuality in different ways because of the physical limitations of the injury.[3]

HOW DO YOU GET IT?

To assertively fulfill one's needs for sexual expression, the SCI person must become aware of the variety of personal and community resources available.

Knowledge gained through previous or attempted sexual encounters provides a baseline by which the individual can identify standards or levels of fulfillment that are satisfactory or need to be changed. Curiosity or inquisitiveness about sexuality (one's own or that of others) can serve to enhance personal fulfillment through direct as well as vicarious experience. Of paramount importance is the need for the individual to recognize that social skills are necessary[4,5] and are acquired through experience.

Resources that exist outside of oneself need to be recognized. Community-based resources available for contacts and/or sexual expression exist in the form of special interest centers such as center(s) for independent living, rap groups, churches, SCI centers, sexual attitude reassessment seminars, bars, and community or junior colleges. Sex-oriented media and other commercial operations are also options. It is important for individuals to give themselves permission to explore the availability of prostitutes, massage parlors, and surrogates. These services may not fulfill emotional needs but may help SCI persons to learn more about their bodies and serve as a first step to sexually experiencing a partner.

TRYING IT

For the individual who has decided to seek sexual fulfillment, three phases of specialized activities must be recognized: (1) the approach, (2) the delivery, and (3) the follow-through.

The approach. After one has made a decision to be a sexual person, the trick is getting up the nerve to make a correct approach. It should be strongly emphasized that it is more important to make any approach, even if it is unsuccessful, than it is to have that "perfect opening." Therefore it is recommended that a simple "Hello, my name is _____. May I join you?" is usually sufficient. Compliments, comments about the location, open-ended questions, or positive personal statements are possible ways of continuing the conversation. All these are problems for the nonhandicapped as well, but the SCI person must deal with the following additional problems:

1. *Making eye contact.* Typically, eye contact is a good index of interest, but the wheelchair user may have to differentiate sexual interest from curiosity about the handicap (although a number of our patients report that they sometimes use

the curiosity of others to make an acquaintance). No studies on this topic exist that we are aware of, but we would expect that eye contact from curiosity would be more quickly broken by the nonhandicapped person.

2. *Managing the topic of the wheelchair and the injury.* Most information of this nature is best given briefly, simply, and matter-of-factly with a change of topic as soon as it is felt that the other person is comfortable. Information given in small doses is less likely to bore or shock the listener and will also convey the impression that the disability is only a small aspect of one's life.

3. *Initiating physical contact.* Many cues about whether the other is interested are gained from casual physical contact. Pulling away, coming closer, or returning a squeeze all indicate different things. The person in the wheelchair must find techniques to communicate in this way, such as making eye contact and saying "that feels nice" to a caress or initiating physical contact by touch or verbal request.

4. *Clearing up sexual misinformation.* Dealing with the sexual stereotypes mentioned earlier may require the SCI person to work sexuality into the conversation at an opportune time. When a potential partner expresses surprise that a paraplegic is living by himself, a reply might be, "Yeah, it is really no problem for me, but it just shows there are a lot of things that people don't know about SCI, like sex for instance." These are good opportunities, as the relationship develops, to let the partner know about such topics as hypersensitive areas, longer lasting erections, multiple orgasms, "internal" sensations, and increased consideration for the partner. Not only are misconceptions cleared up, but this kind of talk may serve an arousal function as well. This may facilitate the "one-night stand" as well as the developing relationship.

5. *Finding a location.* Location for sexual advances is less of a problem for the nonhandicapped than for the SCI person. However, creativity can aid biology here. If the wheelchair interferes with casual touching or physical closeness, transferring onto the front seats of cars, couches, swimming pools, and therapy mats all make physical contact a lot easier.

The delivery. Many people feel that somehow "Nature" is supposed to take over after a couple is finally in bed. While possibly true for procreation purposes, for the SCI person, married or single, it is often unrealistic. This section will attempt to explore how sexual assertion can facilitate sexual pleasure in the act itself.

1. *Know thyself.* For the sexually nonassertive or inexperienced individual, self-exploration through masturbation and other stimulation techniques is highly recommended. Contemporary sexual education has gone beyond masturbation phobia in the nonhandicapped, but it is still a taboo topic in most rehabilitation hospitals. We feel that re-exploration of the body as it is now (unassisted *and* assisted) constitutes an important way of finding out where secondary erogenous zones, hypersensitive areas, and internal sensations are located. For the development of these "internal" sensations referred to by our sexually experienced patients, self-exploration

is an important starting point. Some patients will say, "Why bother. I can't feel there," to which we reply, "Well, it takes a lot of practicing and paying attention to your body to become aware of new or different sensations, similar to those you may have achieved about your bladder or bowel."

2. *Clothes removal.* High-level quadriplegics may have difficulty removing their own and/or their partner's clothes and therefore avoid potential sexual relationships. Assertively asking the partner to take off clothes item by item may be very arousing for both partners and thus a good way of initiating sexual relations.

3. *Communication.* Sexual communications are accomplished in a variety of ways. Verbalizations expressing invitations, pleasure, excitement, instructions, etc., and their negatives may be part of most sexual encounters. Less obvious, and sometimes unacknowledged, are the more subtle forms of sexual communication; that is, body language, eye contact, touching, body noises, and odors. The sexually assertive SCI individual must reassure a new partner that he or she is not being hurt, must acknowledge pleasurable stimulation, must let the partner know that nonejaculation does not mean lack of fulfillment, and must occasionally ask to be stimulated while being passive to get in touch with his/her body.[2]

4. *Changes in marital sex.* Couples often develop sexual patterns after long relationships that require little verbal communication. A spinal cord injury may require them to begin talking about matters such as when, where, and how, which they may not have discussed since early in their marriage. One or both of the partners must assertively start asking these questions while reassuring the partner at the same time. A wife, who prior to her husband's injury was passive in initiating and/or physically participating in sex, may need a great deal of encouragement from her husband to be more active, for example, inserting penis in vagina. Both will be experiencing changes in their sexual expression from the comfortable familiar.

5. *Permission giving.* Telling your partner "Please tell me if that feels good" and/or "I'd really like for you to tell me what you like" helps to encourage and support the partner to become more assertive, thus facilitating communication.

6. *Positions.* By the male assertively initiating a position change, culturally influenced personal preferences such as the missionary position may be reconciled with the physical necessity for the female superior position.

7. *Props and aids.* Sexually assertive SCI persons and their partners may want to explore various devices such as vibrators and dildos to find out if they contribute to sexual pleasure.

8. *Fantasy.* The active use of fantasy is sometimes reported by the SCI persons as a frequent supplement to tactile stimulation. The fantasy may be sexually explicit or, not uncommonly, the fantasy may be a recollection of a previous experience where a sense of well-being and pleasure was obtained. Sharing of the fantasy may facilitate sexual pleasure.[12]

Follow-through. The SCI person must evaluate initial sexual encounters carefully. For some the experience of increased emotionality,[8] changed body sensa-tions, and/or expectations may facilitate or hinder the feedback process and/or in-terfere with sexual pleasure. For these reasons, repeated sexual encounters are highly recommended. Ritualization such as scheduling a regular time for sex or arranging future dates will help to overcome factors interfering with desired sexual pleasure.

CONCLUSION

This chapter has reviewed the concept of sexual assertiveness in SCI persons and attempted to show that (1) assertiveness is a necessary precondition to satisfac-tory adaptation in spinal cord injury; (2) sexual assertiveness may enhance commu-nication, self-esteem, body awareness, desirability, and so on; and (3) differences in technique (as suggested in this chapter) may be necessary for the SCI individual— in fact, these differences may enhance sexual pleasure rather than detract from it.

We believe that the following quote applies to SCI individuals as well[6]:

> It is all wrong that gentlemen have a world of fair ones to select from, while ladies can only choose between two, three, or half a dozen stupid admirers, who may offer themselves. There is no weighty reason that it should be so, and the female sex is recreant to its own rights and happiness if it does not assume the right to choose and propose.*

---

*Foote, E.B., New York, 1896, privately printed manuscript.

REFERENCES

1. Alberti, R.E., and Emmons, M.L.: Your per-fect right, ed. 2, San Luis Obispo, Calif., 1974, Impact Press.
2. Bach, G.R., and Deutsch, R. M.: Pairing, New York, 1970, Avon Books.
3. Barbach, L.G.: For yourself: the fulfillment of female sexuality, New York, 1975, Doubleday Publishing Co.
4. Dunn, M., VanHorn, E., and Herman, S.H.: *Social skills and the SCI patient*, videotape available from National Audiovisual Center, Washington, D.C., order no. NAC 004-179, 1977.
5. Dunn, M., VanHorn, E., and Herman, S.H.: Social skills and SCI: a comparison of three training procedures (Unpublished manuscript, 1978).
6. Foote, E.B.: Medical common sense applied to the causes, prevention and cure of chronic diseases and unhappiness in marriage, New York, 1896 (Privately printed manuscript).
7. Heimberg, R.G., Montgomery, D., Maen, C.H., and Heimberg, J.H.: Assertion train-ing: a review of the literature, Behav. Ther. 8:952-971, 1977.
8. Hohmann, G.W.: Some effects of spinal cord lesions on experienced emotional feelings, Psychophysiology 3:143-156, 1966.
9. Mayers, K.S.: Sexual and social concerns of the disabled: a group counseling approach, Sex. Disabil. 1:100-111, 1978.
10. Newmann, R.J.: Sexuality and the spinal cord injured: high drama or improvisational the-atre? Sex. Disabil. 1:93-99, 1978.
11. Smith, M.J.: When I say no I feel guilty, New York, 1975, Dial Press.
12. Zilbergeld, B.: Male sexuality: a guide to sex-ual fulfillment, Boston, 1978, Little, Brown & Co.

♂ **ABOUT THE AUTHORS** ♀

Michael Dunn, Ph.D., is a licensed clinical psychologist and is currently staff psychologist working at the Spinal Cord Injury Service, Veterans Administration Medical Center, Palo Alto, California. He has been a paraplegic for 11 years and has worked on the spinal cord–injury services at three V.A. hospitals for the past 10 years, where he has obtained extensive experience in sex counseling and social skills training.

E. Elaine Lloyd, R.N., M.S., is a clinical nurse specialist at the Spinal Cord Injury Service, Veterans Administration Medical Center, Palo Alto, California.

Graham H. Phelps, M.S.W., is an outpatient social worker at the Spinal Cord Injury Service, Veterans Administration Medical Center, Palo Alto, California.

31 Sexuality and the disabled: implications for the sex education of medical students*

Douglas H. Wallace

Attitudes toward sexual expression by the physically handicapped have tended to be characterized by restraint and uneasy tolerance of an "unusual behavior." Such attitudes have negatively influenced the delivery of sexual health care to the physically disabled. It must be noted, however, that the basic concept of sexual health care, as an integral component of total health care, is a relatively recent phenomenon.[6]

In response to the developing awareness of need, sex education courses for medical students have in the past 15 years moved in status from virtual nonexistence to a position of priority.[15] Furthermore, understanding of sexual problems and their management is now seen as one of the more important areas in which a nonpsychiatrist physician should possess information and skills.[4,14] At least one state (California) has passed legislation making such training a prerequisite for licensure. The recognition of the need for training has resulted in a proliferation of courses and a considerable diversity of approaches.

Sexuality education courses for medical students vary as to (1) their status within the school's curriculum—required vs elective, year of offering, concentrated vs dispersed; (2) the objectives of the course—knowledge acquisition or attitude change or both; (3) format—didactic, experiential, or some combination of the two; (4) content—the patient populations and issues presented; and (5) the mode of presentation—lecture, panelists, multimedia presentations.[5,11] Common to each course have been the complex objectives of increasing the students' knowledge of human sexuality and concomitantly their ability to relate to their patients' sexual concerns in a supportive, nonjudgmental manner. With less frequency and self-awareness, most courses have also sought to move the sexual attitudes of the students toward a position more consonant with a humanistic orientation toward medicine.[7]

*From Wallace, D.H.: Sex. Disabil. 3:17-25, 1980. Reprinted with permission from Human Sciences Press. The research and preparation of this chapter was supported in part by National Institute of Mental Health Grant No. MH29633.

These objectives, if achieved, would appear to foreshadow improvements in the delivery of sexual health care to the physically disabled, individuals with chronic illnesses, and other health care consumers. Analysis of course evaluation data obtained from medical students taking a required course in human sexuality at the University of California San Francisco School of Medicine (UCSF) raises a question concerning whether current medical school curricula are preparing students to become effective health care providers. A discussion of this thesis, and the central role that the topic of sex and disability and presentations by individuals who are themselves disabled play in this assessment, will follow a brief description of the UCSF course and the students' evaluations of it.

The human sexuality course at UCSF is a required 30-hour course presented in one weekend for all preclinical students and is generally taken during the spring of the second year. Spouses or partners of the students are invited to attend the course. A modified Sexual Attitude Reassessment (SAR) is used during the first segment of the course to focus on personal reactions to varied sexual life-styles and activities.[11,15] Content areas presented include sexual socialization, alternative lifestyles, etiology and maintainers of common sexual dysfunctions, medical conditions and sexual expression, and sex and the physically disabled. Practical aspects of sex-

Table 31-1. Medical student evaluation of a required course in human sexuality*

Course segment	Personal value		Adequacy of presentation	
	Mean	S.D.†	Mean	S.D.†
Sexual attitude reassessment	3.14	1.41	2.52	1.24
Female sexual response cycle	2.19	1.08	2.80	1.40
Female panel	1.80	1.06	1.99	1.06
Treatment of female "dysfunctions"	2.02	1.93	1.89	1.23
Male sexual response cycle	2.18	1.08	2.17	1.02
Male panel	1.87	1.07	2.05	0.92
Treatment of male "dysfunctions"	2.17	0.98	2.89	1.07
Medical panelists				
Obstetrics—gynecology	1.99	1.02	2.04	1.10
Pediatrics	1.61	0.79	1.89	0.98
Urology	2.00	1.02	1.67	0.88
Geriatrics	2.05	0.92	2.16	1.01
Internal	2.56	1.20	2.32	1.06
Family practice	2.22	1.05	2.46	1.14
Sex and disability	1.61	0.78	2.12	0.98
Disability panel	1.39	0.68	1.85	0.93
Sexuality counseling	1.95	1.00	2.08	1.01

*Males: N = 91; females: N = 75; total: N = 166. Scale end points: 1 = very valuable/adequate; 6 = not valuable/adequate.
†S.D. = standard deviation.

uality counseling, such as sexual problem history taking, are presented using a role play format. Group discussions are conducted immediately following each major block of didactic presentations.

Table 31-1 presents the students' evaluations of the course segments on the dimensions of "value" and "adequacy." A glance at the results indicates that the SAR segment (explicit films) was seen as less valuable than were other segments of the course, whereas the segments relating to sex and disability were seen as valuable or more valuable than other presentations, including the presentations by practicing physicians on the medical panel. Significant pre-post changes in sexual attitudes (toward a more "tolerant-open" position) were obtained. Responses to items inquiring about "personal" and "professional" benefits were positive. Discussion of possible sources and implications of these results will be considered in the following discussion section.

The *Sex Role Inventory (SRI)*,[1] which assesses sterotypical masculinity and fem-

Table 31-2. Sex differences on dimensions of stereotypical masculinity and femininity*

Gender	SRI* scale	Mean	S.D.†	t†	df†	p†
Male	Masculine	5.115	.673	.539		ns
	vs					
Female	Feminine	5.065	.508			
Male	Feminine	4.769	.507	.680		ns
	vs					
Female	Masculine	4.839	.706			
Male	Masculine	5.115	.673	2.520	164	.013
	vs					
Female	Masculine	4.839	.706			
Male	Feminine	4.769	.507	3.630	164	.001
	vs					
Female	Feminine	5.065	.508			
Male	Masculine	5.115	.673	4.179	102	.01
	vs					
Male	Feminine	4.769	.507			
Female	Feminine	5.065	.508	2.036	60	.05
	vs					
Female	Masculine	4.839	.706			
Male	Androgyny	− .967‡	1.724	5.620	159	.001
	vs					
Female	Androgyny	.609	1.734			

Sex Role Inventory (SRI) end points: 1 = not true of me; 6 = always true of me.
†S.D. = standard deviation; t = "t" score; df = degrees of freedom; and *p* = probability.
‡Minus sign indicates that the score is in the direction of stereotypical masculinity.

Table 31-3. Sex differences on selected adjectives from the *Sex Role Inventory**

Adjectives	Male		Female		t†	p<†
	Mean	S.D.†	Mean	S.D.		
Feminine	2.29	1.00	5.27	0.98	13.20	.001
Analytical	5.89	1.11	5.37	1.07	2.12	.039
Truthful	5.59	0.86	6.00	0.85	2.61	.011
Compassionate	5.29	0.92	5.73	0.69	2.26	.026
Masculine	5.50	0.82	3.00	1.26	11.01	.001
Tender	4.81	1.08	5.37	0.99	2.30	.024
Unsystematic	2.94	1.54	3.63	1.07	2.13	.032
Does not use harsh language	3.76	1.70	4.70	1.56	2.50	.014

*Sex Role Inventory scale end points: 1 = not true of me; 6 = always true of me.
†S.D. = standard deviation; t = "t" score; p< = probability less than.

Table 31-4. Sex differences on selected items from the *Somatosensory Index of Affection**

Item	Males		Females		t†	p†	df†
	Mean	S.D.†	Mean	S.D.			
Nudity within the family has a harmful influence on children	4.93	1.24	5.40	0.89	2.02	.05	82
Hard physical punishment is good for children who disobey a lot	5.27	1.09	5.63	0.62	1.96	.05	82
Responsible premarital sex is not agreeable to me	5.38	1.34	5.83	0.47	2.22	.03	82
Physical punishment and pain help build a strong moral character	5.16	0.99	5.63	0.72	2.28	.03	82
Sexual pleasures help build a weak moral character	5.56	0.78	5.80	0.48	1.71	.10	82
Capital punishment should be permitted by society	4.36	1.79	5.10	1.16	2.30	.02	82
I tend to be conservative in my political points of view	4.04	1.48	5.03	1.13	3.20	.01	82
I view physical punishment and pain as more moral than sexual pleasure (a factor scale)	−0.152	0.644	0.232	0.534	2.79	.007	

*Index of Affection items are rated on a six-point scale; end points: 1 = strong agreement, 6 = strong disagreement.
†S.D. = standard deviation; t = "t" score; p = probability; df = degrees of freedom.

ininity and a computed score for androgyny, and the *Somatosensory Index of Affection*,[8] which assesses the level of deprivation of physically expressed affection during early childhood and some adult behavioral correlates, were also administered to the students (N = 164; 102 males and 62 females). The pattern of sex differences that emerged from analysis of the data (see Table 31-2) indicated that the female medical students are more "androgynous" than the male students, and that they are significantly more sterotypically "masculine" than the males are stereotypically "feminine." The difference between the "masculine" and "feminine" scales, while statistically significant for both sexes, is larger for the males (larger w^2 value), indicating that the males are more stereotypically "masculine" than the females are "feminine" (see Table 31-3). These results support the thesis advanced by Remen[9] regarding the separation of the masculine and feminine principles in the practice of modern medicine. The polarity of these principles is translated into different role behaviors, largely along gender lines. The "male" doctor diagnoses, performs surgery, prescribes medicine, and issues orders, whereas the "female" nurse either does not participate or acts on instructions from the doctor. The higher score on the androgyny variable for the female students indicates that they have achieved a higher level of integration of the two principles than have the males.

Analyses of the *Index of Affection* questionnaire, a 52-item factor analytic derived instrument, are supportive of the stereotypical nature of the males' responses to the SRI. Males, significantly more than females, state that they believe that physical punishment builds character, favor capital punishment, disagree with premarital sex, believe that family nudity is harmful to children, and believe physical punishment is beneficial to the development of children (see Table 31-4). Though the mean values for the males on each of these items is in the "positive" or "humanistic" direction, they are nonetheless indicative of the masculine principle in that collectively, they represent a denial of the value of physical pleasure. This observation is supported by the finding that the males agree significantly more than the females with the factor scale "physical punishment and pain are more moral than sexual pleasure."

DISCUSSION

The question of "why" such results were obtained, for example, why the course segments on sex and disability were accorded such importance, is of more than academic interest, for a consideration of plausible explanations might provide some ideas concerning curriculum modifications. Whereas several explanations might be advanced regarding the positive evaluations of the sex and disability segments, two of the more plausible are (1) the students' heightened sensitivity to the topical area, whether from an increased sense of vulnerability or from anxiety, and (2) a possible confusion of the concepts "physical disability" or "disadvantage" and "chronic medical condition". The two explanations are not mutually exclusive, and, indeed, the four members of the disability panel (themselves disabled) gave witness to the fact that they are sexual beings, capable of giving and receiving expressions of sexuality, and that they did not see themselves as being "patients" with chronic sexual disabilities. Social comparison processes (students with panelists) undoubtedly served to facilitate the arousal of feelings of increased vulnerability. But concomitantly, the didactic presentations of information on sexuality among the "disabled" and the first person accounts by the panelists disconfirmed the students' tendency to perceive the disabled as being "feminine" (e.g., dependent, passive) and in need of "masculine" medicine (e.g., prescription, authority), particularly with respect to their sexuality. The students learned that there is no necessary relationship between a physical disadvantage and the individual's sexual adjustment. I suspect that such a realization would eventuate into a reaffirmation of the students' own sexuality.

Taken with the findings of others[2,3,10] that suggest that medical students tend to increase in cynical and decrease in humanitarian attitudes during their medical schooling, the results obtained would appear to have several implications for the delivery of sexual health care by physicians currently being trained. Problems of self-selection or entrance selection procedures aside, it appears unlikely that current training programs are providing medical students with either the context or the processes with which to develop a repertoire of sex role enactments that will meet the expectations and/or needs of the health care consumer—expectations that some research has indicated as tending toward androgyny; that is, the consumer tends to desire a compassionate, supportive, yet decisive physician who is highly competent.[12] Some preliminary evidence obtained in studies with nurse practitioners has indicated that competency is positively related to androgyny.[13]

More specifically, I believe that these findings give direct implications for the spectrum of health care services being provided the physically disabled in particular and other health care consumers in general. For unless the physician can begin to perceive the disabled person as an individual who happens to have certain physical limitations rather than as a patient defined by the same limitations, the physician is likely to continue to view the person as being nonsexual: "Patients are not supposed to have sexual feelings or desires." This faulty labeling will affect the doctor-client relationship in several ways, one being a tendency toward the nondelivery of sexual health care on the grounds that "it's not needed or important."

Relating the previously mentioned results and discussion to the conduct of medical student sex education courses, I believe that courses currently being offered should be revised to reflect an expanded conceptualization of sexuality, including, but not limited to, a consideration of sex role behaviors and their implications for sexual expression, and for the integration of the masculine and feminine principles in the delivery of health care. More consideration needs to be given to the sex role scripts held by students, particularly those which serve to devalue or block certain inputs. Perhaps additional attention to the modeling of behaviors that reflect the integration of the two principles would be effective in promoting humanistic sexual education. Such modeling could be obtained from instructors and practicing physicians and, as discussed earlier, from representatives of various types of sexual health care consumers. As demonstrated in the present instance, the presentations on and by the physically disabled assisted the students toward the development of positive definitions of sexual health and provided the students with some useful ideas on how to relate such definitions to health care services provided to the physically disabled.

In summary, the evaluational data discussed indicate that the presentations on sexuality and the disabled by persons who themselves are disabled have an importance that transcends the mere presentation of information. The students are confronted with the need to alter their preconceptions regarding sexuality and its expression as well as their ideas regarding the relationship between sexual expression and physical/medical conditions. The ensuing reassessment of their belief and attitudes regarding sexuality must be regarded as being of considerable importance. For if the principle objective of human sexuality courses is the facilitation of the delivery of adequate sexual health care, it does little good to package a high level of knowledge into a professional vehicle that can only express itself in ways which are likely to be seen as being countertherapeutic by increasing numbers of sexual health care consumers who may happen to be physically disabled.

REFERENCES

1. Bem, S.: The measurement of psychological androgyny, J. Consult. Clin. Psychol. **42:**155-162, 1974.
2. Eron, L.: The effect of medical education on attitudes: a follow-up study, J. Med. Educ. **50:**25-33, 1958.
3. Gordon, L., and Mensh, I.: Values of medical students at different levels of training, J. Educ. Psychol. **53:**48-51, 1962.
4. Johnson, W., and Snibbe, J.: The selection of a psychiatric curriculum for medical students: results of a survey, Am. J. Psychiatry **132:**513-516, 1975.
5. Karlen, A., and Lief, H., editors: Sex education in medicine, New York, 1976, John Wiley & Sons.
6. Long, R.: Sexual health care, SIECUS Rep. **3:**1, 1974.
7. Pellegrino, E.: Educating the humanist physician, J.A.M.A. **227:**1288-1294, 1974.
8. Prescott, J., and Wallace, D.: Developing sociobiology and the origins of aggressive behavior. Delivered to XXI International Congress of Psychology, Paris, July 18-25, 1976.
9. Remen, N.: The masculine principle, the feminine principle and humanistic medicine, San Francisco, 1975, The Institute for the Study of Humanistic Medicine.
10. Rezler, A.: Attitude changes during medical school: a review of the literature, J. Med. Educ. **49:**1023-1030, 1974.
11. Rosenzweig, N., editor: Sex education of the professional, New York, 1978, Grune & Stratton, Inc.
12. Ware, J., Wright, W., Snyder, M., and Chu, G.: Consumer perceptions of health care services: implications for academic medicine, J. Med. Educ. **50:**839-848, 1975.
13. White, M.: Personal communication, November 16, 1977.
14. Woods, S.: Sex and the uptight doctor, Med. Opinion, **1:**13-46, 1972.
15. World Health Organization (WHO) position paper: The teaching of human sexuality in schools for health professionals, Geneva, 1974, World Health Organization.

SUGGESTED READINGS

Coombs, R.: Sex education for physicians: is it adequate? J. Consult. Clin. Psychol. **17:**272-277, 1968.

Garrard, J., Vaitkus, A., and Chilgren, R.: Evaluation of a course in human sexuality, J. Med. Educ. **47:**772-778, 1972.

Golden, J., and Liston, E.: Medical sex education: the world of illusion and the practical realities, J. Med. Educ. **47:**761-771, 1972.

Marcotte, D., and Kilpatrick, D.: Preliminary evaluation of a sex education course, J. Med. Educ. **49:**703-705, 1974.

Marcotte, D., and Kilpatrick, D.: Persistence, planning, patience, and prevention: aspects of sex education in medicine, J. Sex Marital Ther. **2:**47-52, 1976.

Strahan, R.: Remarks on Bem's measurement of psychological androgyny: alternative methods and supplementary analysis, J. Consult. Clin. Psychol. **43:**568-571, 1975.

♂ ABOUT THE AUTHOR ♂

Douglas H. Wallace, Ph.D., attended Wayne State University and received his doctorate in social psychology in 1971. For the past 7 years he has served as director of program research and evaluation for the Human Sexuality Program, Department of Psychiatry, University of California, San Francisco. During this time, he has focused on the development of a sex counseling outcome data base. His current research interests include the cross-cultural comparison of adolescent sexual development and sex role enactment and the influence of somatic processes on personality.

ISSUES IN SEX THERAPY AND COUNSELING

32 Consumer-based sex education

A DIFFERENT LOOK AT THE PEER COUNSELOR*

Susan E. Knight

The scene takes place in a counseling room at the Sex and Disability Unit of the Human Sexuality Program in San Francisco. Three people are seated, talking with each other. Two of these people, a man with a quadriplegic spinal cord injury and a woman with cerebral palsy, are the "counselors." A man in a wheelchair who has been paralyzed from the waist down for the past 5 years is the "client." The three people are gathered for the first time to decide if what the client wants in the way of information and feedback is what these counselors can provide. As the scene opens, the client has just finished talking about how difficult it has been for him to develop relationships with women since his injury. He has described his frustration and dismay at not being taken seriously by women he finds attractive. The counselor in a wheelchair begins to talk about some of his own experiences of feeling isolated and scared. He also speaks briefly of some of the ways he asserts himself with women now, and how they work sometimes, and how sometimes they do not. While he is relating this, the woman in our drama begins to have misgivings. She has heard him share this information before, and even though it is valuable, she believes he is setting himself up for the client to discount. By the counselor sharing his own experience so early in the session, the client has a perfect opportunity to respond: "But, that's not me." Instead, the client is smiling and saying: "You know, I've said these same things to a lot of people, and they've all tried to cheer me up. You're telling me what you do . . . well, I just can't say you don't know what you're talking about. If you can meet women, maybe I can, too."

I was the female counselor in the scenario. What impressed me in the scene was the realization that the man who had come to us for assistance was so simply and eloquently able to sum up one of the major goals of the Sex and Disability Unit. This goal—enabling a number of disabled people to provide accurate sex informa-

*The preparation of this article was supported in part by National Institute of Mental Health Grant No. MH 14346. An earlier version of this chapter was published in Disabled U.S.A. 3:11-13, 1979.

269

tion in an empathetic manner to other disabled people—is at the core of our phi-losophy. This idea of consumer-based sex education, though not a new one, had a particular evolution I would like to describe. I think this process might be of help to people doing similar work in the future.

I met Dr. Robert Geiger in 1972 when I was in college at the University of California, Davis doing an independent research project on sex and disability, funded by the National Sex Forum, San Francisco. He was lecturing to medical students at the University of California, San Francisco (U.C.S.F.) about the effects of spinal cord injury on sexuality. We were both "one of a kind" in those days when sex and disability was a nonentity, except in the hearts and minds of many disabled people who were aware that the rest of society didn't see us as sexual beings. When we met, Bob was spending much of his free time at various rehabilitation centers, spreading the word that disabled people are sexual and getting a lot of strange looks from people in the medical profession.

Bob and I spent a lot of time discussing the potential impact of a sex and disabil-ity education movement on not only disabled people but on the helping professions as well. Very early in our debates Bob introduced me to the concept of the "ringer." He basically believed that anything he said to a group or audience about sex and spinal cord injury needed to be presented in relation to the experience of disabled people themselves, particularly if there were any people with disabilities in the audience. What he had developed was an amazingly effective educational tool. After speaking to a group for a prescribed period of time and then answering questions, he would take a question and address it to a spinal cord–injured person in the audience. This approach not only gave participants some firsthand informa-tion, but also raised the status of disabled participants from being specimens under study to colleagues with information and experiences to share.

Even before I met Bob, I was interested in finding out more about the sexual and social information needs of people like myself with cerebral palsy and other congenital and early onset disabilities. Even though the development of information on sex and spinal cord injury was in its infancy in the early 1970s, both through Bob's work as well as that done at the Program in Human Sexuality at the Univer-sity of Minnesota and a few other places throughout the country, there was a be-ginning awareness among the helping professions that a person who becomes dis-abled as an adult will frequently have sexual concerns and a need for information during and following rehabilitation. On the other hand, the experience of many people with lifelong disabilities is one of being treated as asexual all their lives, and little attention had been given to this. Bob and I felt that both of these groups had a right to have their sexual and social needs addressed.

In the fall of 1973, through funding made possible by the national office and San Francisco affiliate of United Cerebral Palsy Association, Inc., to the Human Sexuality Program at the University of California, we were able to begin to assess the needs of people with cerebral palsy. Through flyers and press releases distributed throughout the San Francisco Bay Area, we asked adults to meet with us and to describe what it had been like for them growing up with cerebral palsy. How did other people relate to them socially and sexually? How did they feel about themselves as social and sexual people? What ideas were they told by their families when they were small about their potential to have both sexual and social relationships, raise families, and so on? What information do they now have about sex, and how did they find it? The results of this counseling study are published elsewhere.[1] What I think is important to this discussion is that, in gathering information, we sought out the "experts" themselves, the people with the particular disability and life experiences. In fact, I repeatedly said, "The reason we are asking you to speak with us is because we don't have the information. By you and others telling us about your individual experiences, we hope to develop programs that will assist not only you but all of us with congenital disabilities."

One of the major points made by many people with all types of disabilities is the need to inform health professionals that disabled people are sexual. Not only our program, but others throughout the country, have used panels of disabled persons sharing their own experiences so that health professionals can begin to see disabled persons as people rather than "patients." One of the most exciting experiences I still encounter in educational sessions is having an able-bodied participant come up to me and say, "You know, until I heard you and these other people speak, I thought I'd kill myself if I ever ended up in a wheelchair. But hearing all of you say that life goes on and that it can still be worthwhile and even fun (much less sexy!) makes me feel better. I don't have to worry so much about the future, and maybe being disabled isn't such a tragedy after all."

There is life and often love after disability, and that brings up the question, "Who really needs the disabled sex educator?" Is it mostly the disabled person? I think a disabled "peer" counselor can add a unique degree of credibility and specific information due to his or her personal experience. However, I know able-bodied people, who because of their personal empathy and professional skill, are also excellent sex and disability educators. It seems that a disabled person can benefit from contact with either of these. I personally feel that the people who *really* need the disabled educator and counselor are able-bodied; the able-bodied helping professional, the family member of the disabled person, and the person on the street all need clear, correct information on sex and disability from disabled persons who exemplify and exhibit the social skill and comfort with sexual issues that is so lacking in most persons, regardless of physical abilities. Whether giving a lecture, counseling or consulting, or just engaging in a casual conversation, the disabled person who is competent, sensual, and emotionally self-aware does much to demonstrate that disabled people are sexual. This image should not be misconstrued as the "super gimp" who works an 80-hour week and would rather be dead than admit that he or she feels scared and/or helpless at times. Instead, we need people who know both their strengths and weaknesses and who have some degree of comfort with each. Only by being human will others begin to see us that way.

After the 3 years of the sexuality and cerebral palsy project, Bob and I and disabled colleagues who had worked with us in conferences and workshops decided that our next step toward gaining sexual and social rights would be to train people to provide sociosexual education and counseling. We wanted to reach two specific groups: (1) disabled and able-bodied persons who have significant personal and/or professional relationships with them who could become educators and counselors and (2) teachers and parents of disabled children who could begin to provide accurate and effective sex education and social skills development in the classroom and at home. Believing the first group could have an effect on the able-bodied and disabled adult population, whereas the second could provide children with the information and encouragement that might facilitate a more fulfilling and enjoyable adolescence and adulthood, we wrote two grant proposals, which were funded.

The Training Project in Sex and Disability funded by the Division of Manpower and Training Programs National Institute of Mental Health, trained 28 people from 1976 to 1979 to become educators and/or counselors (depending on their individual skill level) in sex and disability. This halftime, 1-year training program gave these people exposure to specific information about sexuality, social skills development, and various disabilities and medical conditions. Additionally, 70% of the trainees were themselves disabled, and each person worked during training in either a community agency serving the disabled or in a hospital setting. They gained experience doing in-service training and community education with a wide variety of professional and consumer groups. One of the major findings from their community work was the realization that disabled persons with sexual and social concerns do not, for the most part, need "psychotherapy" to deal with these issues. Instead, education and information sharing in an empathetic manner either individually or in a group often supplies the support many of us need to make our lives more fullfilling. By exploring their own feelings about disability and their own life concerns during the training process, these people have been able to assist both disabled and able-bodied persons in finding their own solutions to their questions about sex and disability.

I would like to address what these people are like and what some of their current interests are following the training, as well as one experience that received very high ratings during the training program.

Fifty-two percent of the people we trained had no experience providing counseling or education prior to being in training; 42% had some experience in one of these two areas. So, overall these people as a group had little or no professional experience prior to getting into the training. When we looked at those people after the training, some of them 4 years later, over 90% were either employed or in school obtaining graduate training in counseling. Over the years people have asked me, "When you've got someone who is not a professional, who has not been through the professional mill and doesn't necessarily agree with the three-piece suit model, how are they going to interact with the medical profession? Are they going to be appropriate in a medical setting, are they going to be seen as valid givers of education and counseling?" I have talked to numerous people who finished the training and who say one of the things they got from the training was the desire to go ahead and get the credentials that are needed so they can make a greater impact on society and the medical profession. For some of these people, this was the first time that they considered the fact that they might be able to have a real career for themselves.

The training was evaluated very highly by the participants. Two of the highest rated parts were two courses that the program conducted, one called the Health Aspects of Human Sexuality, a 3-day general sexuality course, and a course called Principles of Sex Counseling, a 2-weekend course providing an overview of sexual dysfunction counseling. These courses gave the people in the training opportunity to talk with other professionals in the sexuality and counseling fields. People also felt very positive about their group interaction. Being able to share with other people in their training group was very important to them as was hearing the personal experiences of people who came in to lecture. Also highly rated was being able to do client counseling in our clinic. I think what this points out was that it was the person-to-person aspects of the training that were the most important for these people.

The highest rated part of the training was an experience that was not mandatory but voluntary for our trainees. For those who were interested, we arranged to go to a massage workshop at a place called "Getting In Touch," which is in the Santa Cruz Mountains. Historically, the Human Sexuality Program has offered trainees in its various programs the option to be part of this experience.

When Mary Rodocker, David Bullard, and I started talking about the things that we wanted to include in the training, we all felt that this was an option that we wanted to make available to our people. We had reservations about how it was going to work, especially on a physical level. The facilities at "Getting In Touch" were minimally accessible. There was a hot tub that had steps leading up to it, and we didn't know how some people would be able to get up on a massage table.

Because we had a lot of concerns about mobility, we wanted to make sure that we offered this to people at a time when they felt that they could be assertive with other people in the training group about getting assistance and being able to offer assistance to others. What we found was that when it was brought up, many people dealt with the issue of independence for themselves. Some of the people in the training were in wheelchairs and were accustomed to using hired attendants to provide all their physical care. An issue that came up for the people who decided to attend this workshop was that many people in the group didn't want attendants involved because the attendants were not part of the training group, and the people wanted the experience to be for the people in the training only. They felt that attendants, even though they were close to the person that they were working for, were not part of the group. This brought up another issue of whether people with mobility limitations felt comfortable asking for physical help from their fellow trainees and staff. The other big issue that came up for many people was body image: "Am I willing to go through an experience of touching with people that I know this well?" "How do I feel about my body, do I feel it's okay for other people to see my body?" One of the people in the training, Terry Brickley,[2] who is also a journalist, wrote the following about going to "Getting In Touch":

An interesting thought hit me the other day while sitting in an outdoor hot tub with 11 friends. My thought was that everyone looked the same—peaceful, relaxed, a slight grin on most faces. A true feeling of closeness seemed to be the general mood shared by all of us. Sameness is not usually one of my needs but sometimes it would be nice not to have to hassle the unconscious, stigmatizing and stereotyping that often happens to people who appear different. What brought all this up is that about a dozen of my friends, both able-bodied and not so able-bodied, went to a place called "Getting In Touch." We went there because we care about ourselves and each other and this fine place provides an environment that allowed us to see ourselves and each other in a new way. Six of us were in wheelchairs and it's safe to say that our bodies don't quite live up to TV, Madison Avenue, *Vogue* or *Playboy* concepts of the body beautiful. And I think that it's true also of the others who didn't have to be carried, manhandled and lowered into the tub. I don't use plumbing (a catheter and leg-bag) so I don't know how some of my friends felt to be that exposed and perhaps that vulnerable in such a social setting. There were big bodies, little bodies, straight bodies, not-so-straight bodies; there were enough new things exposed to each of us that I'm sure the old locker room concern of penis size or breast size was the least of anyone's worry. In fact, once we made the initial commitment of getting into the tub, the only concern that I felt was that the day would end much too soon. Sitting in the hot tub relaxed more than our bodies, the self-induced anxieties and apprehensions we had been building up over the preceding days relaxed, too. Later, as we went into the large and comfortable lodge-type room, I guess some anxiety returned briefly because we were about to embark upon a massage sharing, if we chose to. The word "massage" may convey different images to different people. What we all shared within the confines of our physical ability was a moment in time where it was okay to be caring, to be intimate without being sexual, to be sensuous without being threatened. We weren't there to give or receive a therapeutic rubdown or a Paris-fingertip special. We were there to experience our own joy in touching and being touched by another human being. When one thinks of the word "touch" usually the hands come to mind. But consider one woman who can't lift her hands far from her lap. Her touch was done with her chin, lips and cheeks. Many of us with limited or no feeling in our hands are very conscious of the way we touch someone else and even more conscious of what we think the other person is feeling. How neat it was to find that a back or leg doesn't have the same perceptions as a brain. This was a day, a brief instant, where we could give ourselves permission to just be, to put our body image away and just appreciate what it could give and receive.*

From July 1979 to June 1982 we are implementing an intensive short-term training in sex and disability (also funded by the National Institute of Mental Health) for persons connected with agencies throughout the western United States. The goal of this project is for trainees to function within their home communities as sex educators/counselors for physically disabled persons and for various members of the health care team, both during and following the training period. At least half of the people trained will themselves be disabled. At the conclusion of the training, a resource and referral network will exist in each area to continue these services.

Our second group, teachers and parents, have been reached by conducting "Family Life Education Training" workshops for 300 people throughout the country through a grant from the Bureau of Education for the Handicapped, H.E.W. (now the Department of Education). Much of the teaching and small group facilitation in these courses has been provided by disabled teaching staffs. These staffs have done much to assist workshop participants, most of whom are able-bodied and often only deal with young disabled people, in seeing that disabled people can grow up and form satisfying social and sexual relationships.

Also during 1979 to 1982, this project will give priority to teachers and parents of students who are either hearing or visually impaired. Whereas these groups of students are distinctly different from each other and from persons with physical disabilities in the problems they face with their particular sensory impairment, they are similar in the experience of lacking social and sexual education during school years. It is our hope, by providing accurate information and encouragement to teachers and parents using teaching staff who are themselves deaf or blind, that participants will gain a positive outlook about the social and sexual potential of their students.

What I have described is how one group, the Human Sexuality Program in San Francisco, has approached the topic of sex and disability. By engaging the people most affected, disabled people ourselves, we hope to have a lasting effect both on ourselves and on the society in which we live. I believe it is our humanness and our ability to love that can bridge the gap called "difference."

---

*Brickley, T.: Santa Cruz Sentinel, March 28, 1977, p. 4.

REFERENCES

1. Geiger, R., and Knight, S.: Sexuality of people with cerebral palsy. Med. Aspects Hum. Sex. 9:70-79, 1975.

2. Brickley, T.: Handicapsules, Santa Cruz Sentinel, March 28, 1977, p. 4.

♀ ABOUT THE AUTHOR ♀

Susan E. Knight, M.S.W., is director of the Sex and Disability Unit, Human Sexuality Program, Department of Psychiatry, University of California, San Francisco. She is also a member of a number of national advisory committees serving persons with disabilities, such as the Professional Services Committee, United Cerebral Palsy Associations, Inc., and the Advisory Council, Allied Health Disabled Child Find and Advocacy Project of the American Society of Allied Health Professions. She has done counseling, training, and program development in the area of sexuality and disability for the past 8 years and has authored several publications relating to this work. In 1979 and 1980, she was co-chairperson for the First and Second Annual National Symposia on Sexuality and Disability. She herself has cerebral palsy. Her undergraduate degree in community education and counseling was received from the University of California, Davis, and her master's degree in Social Welfare was received from San Francisco State University.

33 Basic issues in sexual counseling of persons with physical disabilities*

Mary M. Rodocker and David G. Bullard

As part of the program at the Sex and Disability Unit of the University of California, San Francisco, counseling services have been provided to over 100 individuals and couples over the past 3 years. In addition, 28 disabled and nondisabled persons were trained in year-long programs that included supervised experience in a variety of rehabilitation and habilitation agencies. Based in part on these experiences, we would like to address some basic issues that we regard as significant in providing sexual education and counseling services to persons with physical disabilities, their families, their partners, and in consulting with health care providers.

The process of becoming comfortable with one's own sexuality before working with clients has been previously described in the literature. Working with disabled clients requires the additional step of exploring one's feelings and attitudes about disability, perhaps by seeking out disabled friends of whom to ask questions and share feelings. We consider these steps crucial in the training of sex educators and counselors.

Of equal importance in counseling is providing validation that each of us is a unique sexual being. Although the word "validation" itself may have been overused, we continue to be impressed with the potential for healing when a person's difficult life experiences are shared with and understood by another. We attempt to convey the spirit of the word "validation" by emphasizing the importance of listening to our clients and asking them to describe their own experiences and feelings. Listening to a person describe his or her sexual concerns conveys a message of acknowledgment that the person is indeed a sexual being. Reassurance that it is natural and understandable at times to feel anxious about one's sexuality is also validating. This basic skill of providing validation and reassurance can be taught to potential counselors regardless of their level of professional training.

*The preparation of this article was supported in part by National Institute of Mental Health Grant No. MH15811.

Some health care professionals feel secure talking with a disabled person about sexuality only after having had a thorough medical understanding of that person's disability from reading textbook descriptions of the disability and its ramifications for sexual functioning. Without negating the value of acquiring information about various disabilities or medical conditions as they relate to sexuality, we feel that such reading must be done cautiously, critically, and without generalizing the information to any particular individual. We are each uniquely sexual, and a physical disability may or may not affect a person's sexuality or may affect it quite differently than the literature would lead one to believe. There is often a tendency to make assumptions about sexual functioning based on textbook or journal information that may discourage a particular person from exploring and experimenting to discover what he or she is able to enjoy sexually. Clearly, diagnosis does not dictate sexual functioning.

Most of the disabled clients we have seen do not ask complicated questions about the physiology of their disability when in sexual counseling. They often know more about their bodies than health professionals do and can answer some of their *counselor's* questions. In our experience, disabled clients also do not usually inquire about the mechanics of sex, how to's for pleasuring that may leave the counselor feeling inadequate in his or her imaginative abilities. Usually they do ask for validation of feelings: "Will I ever find someone who will consider me attractive?" or "Is it really possible to be a sexual person if I can't feel my genitals?" Disabled counselors who are skilled in providing validation, reassurance, and encouragement for sexual exploration are often seen by such clients as role models who have dealt positively with such questions in their own lives. In considering sexuality and disability, problems that exist more often reflect attitudinal barriers set up by our culture and accepted by both disabled and nondisabled persons rather than actual physical limitations on sexual functioning. Many health professionals already have the basic skills needed to provide positive assistance to their disabled clients who have sexual concerns. With limited additional information about common myths, attitudes, or unrealistic expectations about sexuality or disability, they can be helpful to clients by listening rather than telling, by encouraging them to explore their sexual and sensual sensations, and by helping them discuss their discoveries. The addition of some simple suggestions, geared to a client's particular situation, is often very effective. These steps of validation, providing information, and offering simple suggestions can be taught in many settings and have widespread usefulness in dealing with a variety of sexual concerns.[1] Knowing when to acknowledge one's limitation regarding information and/or ability to deal with a particular problem and recognizing when to refer to someone with greater expertise are also important.

The following examples of counseling situations highlight some of the previously discussed principles and other issues that we believe to be important. (Although we have changed the names and some of the identifying characteristics of the persons involved, the concepts remain the same.)

One of us and a co-counselor met with a man with an ileostomy who wanted sexual counseling. He was 35 years old and had apparently never spoken to anyone other than his physician about the ostomy. He had been sexual with a couple of women but had never mentioned it to them either; instead, he kept a bandage wrapped around his abdomen during sexual activities. The ostomy was a secret that made it very difficult for him to relax and enjoy being sexual with a partner.

We guess that most people at one time or another have felt something negative about themselves and sought to keep those feelings a secret from others. It can be a very powerful and positive experience to finally entrust the information and feelings to someone and still be accepted. In this counseling situation the client eventually learned that the co-counselor also had an ileostomy. This enabled him to explore these issues even more openly; talking about his feelings about the ileostomy and having them validated was an important first step in his becoming more comfortable and accepting of himself. Having a co-counselor with a similar condition that was not a secret provided him with a role model, which helped him explore these issues. The counseling certainly didn't solve all his problems, but it was an important start for him in dealing with his body image and its effect on his sexuality.

Quite frequently, people who have been in some form of counseling or psychotherapy report that sexuality was never really discussed. One young woman with a congenital hip deformity came to our clinic after several years of psychotherapy. She was anxious and felt very uncomfortable talking about her "problem": she hadn't been able to have intercourse and felt quite badly; in her own eyes she was a failure and believed that it wasn't possible to be truly sexual without being able to have intercourse. When we spoke with her about other kinds of sexual pleasure, she reported that she had experienced and enjoyed manual and oral stimulation and was orgasmic. When we questioned her assumption that only intercourse "qualified" as the "real thing," she began to cry and said that she had never considered otherwise. We spoke with her about women who are able to have intercourse yet aren't orgasmic, and how they also sometimes feel that they are lacking sexually. Even though our culture stresses that "sex *is* intercourse," we don't have to abide by such narrow definitions of sexuality. She returned one more time to report that she felt tremendously relieved that she wasn't so strange (validation and reassurance) and that her disability didn't make her so different from other women.

The skills of intensive sex counseling obviously require extensive training. However, in our experience, simple suggestions can also have a positive impact on people with sexual concerns as, for example, in the following situation.

A couple that we saw reported that they had not had intercourse for 10 years, since the man had had a surgical procedure for cancer. The woman had had a physical disability since birth, and they described having an active and enjoyable sex life with frequent intercourse prior to the man's surgery. When the couple consulted the physician involved regarding the man's lack of erections following the treatment for cancer, the reply was, "Well, you should just be grateful you're alive."

That was the only time the couple had discussed their concern with a professional person. Now at our clinic they were understandably hesitant to discuss their worry. Obviously at ease with each other, they described their relationship as "good in every way" except for their frustration about sex. Even that was not a major concern because they had adjusted to limiting their relationship. When asked why they had decided to come for counseling at this particular time, the man described having attended a workshop on sexuality and disability in which one of our former trainees had given a talk (role modeling). The positive messages they heard in that workshop—that there are many ways to enjoy being sexual—prompted them to come and explore further their own possibilities. After listening to the man talk about and then discount his morning erections, we suggested that they go home and try some exercises such as taking a bath together, and that they not attempt intercourse for the next week, even if he happened to get an erection. Three days later, we received a telephone call from the couple reporting their successful attempt at intercourse: "Guess what? We ignored your orders, and it was great!"

Another couple who had congenital physical disabilities complained in counseling that they had one position for sexual intercourse that worked well for them but that it wasn't the *right* position. We asked, "What do you mean, not the *right* one?" They then described a position in which the man had entry from behind the woman; for physical reasons, it wasn't convenient or comfortable for them to have the man on top. We told them that many couples come in for counseling to explore how to have other positions because they were tired of the classical man on top one; we also mentioned that it sounded as if they had an enjoyable way to pleasure each other with intercourse that worked well for them (validation). They looked at each other and said, "You mean, that's an O.K. way to do it?" Our response was that many people thought that the way this couple had intercourse was a *great* position!

Since they had come a long distance, we asked if there were other issues they wanted to discuss. For example, as sex counselors, we often find that people who have concerns about sex eventually stop touching each other—whether sexually or nonsexually. They replied, however, that they had been trying to get married for several years, and now that they finally were married, no one could keep them apart! They were certainly right about that; in our office they had shown that they enjoyed touching and cuddling, so that certainly wasn't a problem area for them.

They then told us that they had only been married 3 months. We let them know that many people take a lot longer than 3 months to get used to each other sexually (validation and reassurance). That was news to them, and they felt better after hearing that. One concern did appear briefly when the woman said that she knew more than her husband about sex and had to teach him. Before we could validate anything, he supported himself by saying: "Look, I didn't have the opportunity to go out on dates in high school and to have other social experiences because I was out earning money to be able to live independently. It's taken me awhile but I'm a good learner now at the age of 30!" We asked her if it was really so bad, "teaching" him about her sexual likes and dislikes. She giggled that, in a way, she really enjoyed it. Later, feedback from the person who had referred them to us from their home community—where they hadn't talked to anyone about the specifics of their concerns—was as follows: "You know, they came back and we asked them how the counseling session went and they said, 'Well, we met two really nice people, but you know, *we* know as much about sex as *they* do!'" We think that letting people be their *own* sex experts is another key issue. None of us can be experts about anyone's sexuality but our own, but we can help people develop a better sense of what they want and like.

We want to assure you that we do not always have success stories. Sometimes a client's situation appears impossible. One client who was living in a board and care facility wanted to become sexually active. She spent her time in counseling being frustrated and angry. In her view, to even choose her own clothes was a threat to the people who were managing the facility. She had been institutionalized for several years prior to board and care home placement and was afraid to risk being sent back to such a setting if she became sexually active. Solutions for her were not easy to come by.

In conclusion, we would like to offer the following observations:

1. Validation, reassurance, provision of information, and offering of simple suggestions are useful approaches in counseling disabled clients with sexual concerns.

2. The sexual problems that exist for disabled clients are more often related to culturally established attitudinal barriers rather than physical limitations.

3. Although there is much we have yet to discover about sexuality and disability, we can be of real service to clients by encouraging them to fully explore their sexual and sensual potential. The mind is one's greatest erogenous zone, and sexual pleasure is restricted only by the imagination.

4. Many disabled clients continue to struggle with complex issues of sexual freedom as experienced in institutions such as hospitals, board and care facilities, and nursing homes. We need to devote a great deal more attention to these neglected areas.

REFERENCE

1. Annon, J.: The behavioral treatment of sexual problems. Vol. I. Brief therapy, New York, 1976, Harper & Row Publishers, Inc.

RECOMMENDED READINGS

Hale-Harbough, J., Norman, A., Bogle, J., and Shaul, S.: Within reach: providing family planning services to physically disabled women, New York, 1978, Human Sciences Press.

Mooney, T., Cole, T., and Chilgren, R.: Sexual options for paraplegics and quadriplegics, Boston, 1975, Little, Brown & Co.

Shaul, S., Bogle, J., Hale-Harbough, J., and Norman, A.: Toward intimacy: family planning and sexuality concerns of physically disabled women, New York, 1978, Human Sciences Press.

♀ ABOUT THE AUTHORS ♂

Mary M. Rodocker, R.N., M.S., is project coordinator of intensive training in sexuality and disability and is director of the sex and disability clinic at the Human Sexuality Program, Department of Psychiatry, University of California, San Francisco. She also maintains a private practice in marriage and family counseling in San Francisco.

David G. Bullard, Ph.D., is an assistant clinical professor of medical psychology (psychiatry) and project director of intensive training in sexuality and disability at the Human Sexuality Program, Department of Psychiatry, University of California, San Francisco. He also has a private practice in clinical psychology and marriage and family counseling in San Francisco. Dr. Bullard is a consulting editor to the journal, *Sexuality and Disability,* and was co-chairperson for the First and Second Annual National Symposia on Sexuality and Disability.

34 Sex therapy and end-stage renal disease

A CASE STUDY

Toni Ayres and Joseph K. Nowinski

A participant in a study evaluting the effects of major medical conditions on sexuality (see Chapter 25) disclosed in the research interview that he had erectile dysfunction. The following is a report of his subsequent treatment in sex therapy. (The actual names have been changed for confidentiality.)

Norman was 58 years old and suffered from end-stage renal disease. He had been on home dialysis treatment for 3 years and was retired from his job as a bus driver. Norman was referred to us as a research subject partly because he had complained to the head nurse of the dialysis unit that he could no longer "do it" with his wife. One of the trained graduate nurses interviewed Norman, and Toni observed. Many times during the interview he made reference to his erection difficulties. We told him, however, that he would have to complete the entire interview before we could focus the discussion on his sexual dysfunction per se.

During the research interview we learned that for approximately 1 year Norman had noticed gradual difficulty maintaining an erection during intercourse. Over the last year he became progressively more discouraged about his sex life. He believed, and kept telling his wife, that his difficulties were due to the dialysis treatments. He also expressed strong fears that his wife would leave him if she didn't get enough sex (meaning intercourse).

After the formal interview was completed, some time was devoted to discussing Norman's erection problem in an effort to determine if the difficulty had an organic or a psychologic basis. During the interview, he stated that he didn't masturbate at all, which precluded our getting further information about his erectile capacities from a description of his masturbation pattern. Norman did say that he would often wake up in the morning with an erection and that he occasionally had wet dreams.

We didn't believe that Norman's morning erections were due to a full bladder, since he suffered from renal failure. We told him that his morning erections and wet dreams suggested that the problem was psychologically based, rather than a by-product of dialysis. Therefore if he so chose, he could be seen by a sex counselor who would attempt to alleviate his erection difficulties through behavioral techniques. We should add that had we felt that the erection problem was the result of organic factors, we would still have offered a counseling referral. In that case, counseling could have focused on helping Norman develop a fulfilling sexual relationship that didn't depend on erections or he could learn about penile implants (prostheses).

Norman was not totally relieved to hear that his difficulties were, in our opinion, "psychologic." He had been attributing them to the dialysis, and it seemed to us he was distinctly ambivalent about changing his mind at that point. Still, he did seem to want to discuss the issue further with his wife and a counselor.

Further counseling with Norman and Dorothy began a week after the interview. They were seen once a week for 5 weeks by Toni. In the initial session both partners were seen together for the first half hour, and then Toni spent some time talking with Dorothy alone. During the second session a more in-depth history was taken from Norman alone. For the last three sessions both partners were present at all times.

During the first session, Norman and Dorothy shared their previous experiences in trying to get help for their problem. They had been originally referred by the hospital to a therapist who, though generally well-qualified, had not had specific training in sex therapy. He met with them together for 50 minutes and then offered the opinion that they should each be referred to separate therapists. Dorothy went to her assigned therapist, who informed her after one interview that she would need years of psychotherapy and analysis. There was no further mention of the erection problems that had motivated Norman and Dorothy to seek help in the first place. Understandably, both were frustrated and confused and stopped attending sessions soon after they'd started. Unfortunately they also concluded at least for the time being, that there was no help for them. This may have partially explained Norman's mixed reaction to our diagnosis. It must have taken more than a little courage for him to seek help a second time.

Dorothy's way of coping with the erection problem was to ignore it as much as possible and hope it would spontaneously improve. She stoically asserted that she wouldn't miss intercourse if she didn't have it any more, adding that she believed intercourse was "80% so that the man can have an orgasm." In the past, however, both she and Norman had enjoyed manual and oral stimulation of each other. Dorothy described herself as somewhat "old-fashioned," and said she was not at all aggressive sexually. She was regularly orgasmic with manual and oral stimulation but rarely with intercourse. She had given up on stimulating Norman because "it didn't work." According to her, they had last had sex 3 weeks previously. Norman had had a partial erection, and was able to ejaculate, but Dorothy described the encounter as unsatisfactory to both of them.

Dorothy claimed that her husband had an extremely low sex drive after he was first diagnosed as having renal failure and began the dialysis treatments. His life seemed to become centered around the treatments and his dialysis schedule. After a while his interest in sex began to reappear, but only until he was switched from hospital to home dialysis. Then he became preoccupied again with "the machine," and his desire for sex waned. Later, it once again started to develop, but the erection problems began. Dorothy now believed that she was no longer attractive to Norman, which was her explanation for his lack of interest and performance difficulties.

As Dorothy began to describe a typical week in their lives, it became obvious that one contributing factor to their sexual difficulties probably had to do with their schedules. Dorothy worked from 8:00 a.m. to 5:00 p.m. daily as a secretary. Norman dialysed Monday, Wednesday, and Friday nights. When Dorothy got home from work on those evenings, she would help Norman get set up on the machine and then would fix dinner. Soon after eating, Norman would fall asleep on the couch with the dialysis machine still running. He would wake up early the next morning, frequently with an erection and would then approach Dorothy for sex. She, meanwhile, needed to get up at 5:30 a.m. to be at work on time. She had always preferred sex in the evening, after the household chores were done, and she had some time to relax. But for a long time now it was Norman's pattern to be asleep by early evening. Norman, she knew, resented that she didn't respond to his early morning sexual initiatives. By the same token, she resented his falling asleep so early and leaving sex for when she felt tired and pressured.

Additional stress in this relationship was caused by the fact that Dorothy's elderly mother lived with them, and neither Dorothy nor Norman were currently getting along with her. They also felt that they had very little privacy on weekends, which was when they potentially had the most time together. Norman had always been an edgy person anyway, they agreed, and the situation with his mother-in-law was only making matters worse for him. In fact, Norman said he felt so tense that at times his teeth would ache from clenching his jaws. Progressive relaxation training was then started, using a combination of breathing exercises and guided relaxation fantasy. He did well with the breathing and enjoyed focusing his mind on a relaxing fantasy. This training was repeated twice in later sessions.

Norman and Dorothy were asked not to attempt to have sexual intercourse, though they were encouraged to engage in spontaneous sex play. Norman was also asked to begin masturbating, using his morning erections in a stop-start fashion. Emphasis was placed on both husband and wife discussing the time issue, with focus on finding a mutually agreeable weekend time away from home on their boat.

Time was spent in the therapy sessions explaining the concept of performance anxiety and how self-conscious worry can undermine sexual arousal and performance. Norman was told that he was "straining" to get an erection rather than allowing it to happen. Rather than attempting to force his sexual response, he was told he needed to devote more time to learning something about his needs for stimulation and to learn to relax again during lovemaking.

In the third session Norman reported that he wasn't doing the masturbation exercise that had been assigned, ostensibly because "it didn't work." In the previous session, however, he'd said that he often "rubbed" his penis and got erections while he was on the dialysis machine. We concluded that it may have been the term "masturbation" that he objected to, and we decided not to press the issue of self-pleasuring at that time.

A major portion of the counseling time with Norman and Dorothy was devoted to the task of developing effective communication within the context of their sexual relationship. They had never really discussed or shared much information about their personal preferences for things like touching or kissing. They were assigned half-hour, sensate-focus pleasuring exercises, with a focus on giving verbal feedback to each other.

Between the third and fourth session, Dorothy and Norman were able to spend some time on their boat. Dorothy initiated a pleasuring session when Norman laid down to take a nap. Although they had been asked to refrain from attempting intercourse, Norman proceeded to get a "100%" erection, and the lovemaking ended in a mutually satisfying experience of sexual intercourse.

Through this first successful experience, Norman began to appreciate the importance of a relaxed situation and a nonpressured attitude. In addition, he reported being very turned on by Dorothy's taking the initiative. He was becoming more aware of how he'd been trying to force himself to get an erection and how worried and self-conscious he usually was during lovemaking. Toni noted that he was smiling spontaneously a good deal during this therapy session.

The half hour of mutual caressing with feedback was reassigned, again with the caution against attempting intercourse. By the next therapy session, however, Norman and Dorothy had had two more sexual encounters that included intercourse. Norman estimated that he'd had a firm erection for approximately 15 minutes. Dorothy said she was somewhat embarrassed by the fact that they couldn't stick to the homework as assigned, that is, the intercourse ban. She felt, though, that these had been successful sexual encounters and that Norman really was functioning much better. At that point, she and Norman both wanted to terminate therapy, but said they would call again if problems developed.

35 Sex therapy and organogenic erectile dysfunction*

David G. Bullard and Jean M. Stoklosa

As more information about the physiology of erectile response becomes available and new techniques such as surgical implantation of penile prostheses are developed, refined, and utilized,[14,18,22] questions about the etiology of and treatment decisions for erectile dysfunction become increasingly complex.

A review of the recent literature regarding the assessment and treatment of erectile dysfunction discloses several trends:

1. Medical and surgical approaches and interventions (in contrast to the psychological interventions of the "New Sex Therapy") are gaining widespread attention.[9,13,19]
2. The generalization that 90% of all erectile dysfunction is psychogenic is being reconsidered by some investigators as an overestimation.[9,13]
3. A more sophisticated conceptualization of organic erectile dysfunction is emerging.[17]

This chapter will briefly review the literature addressing these issues, specifically noting nocturnal penile tumescence (NPT) monitoring for the differential diagnosis of organogenic versus psychogenic erectile dysfunction and treatment with the penile prosthesis. The uses of sexual therapy in differential diagnosis and treatment will then be outlined.

NOCTURNAL PENILE TUMESCENCE (NPT) MONITORING

Karacan and Salis[9] caution against making the assumption that the presence of a disease or medical condition is the cause of any particular person's sexual dysfunction. In the absence of objective data for diagnosis, they state:

> For virtually no condition has there been a solid demonstration of a cause-effect relationship between specific pathophysiology and erectile impairment . . . a posi-

*The preparation of this chapter was supported in part by National Institute of Mental Health Grant No. MH15811.

tive diagnosis of organogenic impotence is at best a presumptive, unconfirmed diagnosis and a negative diagnosis may well be in error because of a failure to identify relevant organic pathology.

These authors suggest that a diagnosis of psychogenic erectile dysfunction by default (in the absence of medical conditions implicated in impotence) is questionable. They proceed to discuss the findings of 15 years of research in NPT monitoring, which they find to be a reliable measure of physiologic erectile capability in the waking state. This group has also used penile pulse volume measurements and angiograms to identify arterial occlusions that have responded to bypass surgery. They believe that their studies have supported the following:

1. Potent men have patterns of NPT in the normal range.
2. Impotent men, in whom the probability of organogenic impotence is high due to medical information and evaulation, have deficits in NPT.
3. Impotent men with impaired NPT benefit from the correction of contributory physiologic deficits and do not respond well to behavioral (sex therapy) or psychiatric treatment of impotence.
4. Impotent men with low probability of organogenic impotence show normal NPT.
5. Impotent men with normal NPT respond well to behavioral or psychiatric treatment of impotence.
6. Psychologic factors do not influence NPT significantly.
7. NPT is relatively insensitive to perturbations of rapid eye movement (REM) sleep and to level and recency of sexual activity.[9]

Fisher et al.[4,5] have questioned whether the research data available at present truly substantiate points 6 and 7 of the list. These data, as cited by Wasserman et al.,[25] more conservatively estimate that NPT measurement used in conjunction with a thorough clinical evaluation can be helpful in distinguishing organic and psychogenic erectile dysfunction in approximately 80% of these cases. They conclude that further research is warranted to determine whether some men with psychogenic impotence also have impaired NPT.

In related work, Hosking et al.[8] compared NPT in 30 diabetic patients complaining of erectile failure (15 were completely and 15 partially dysfunctional), with NPT in 11 healthy men with no erectile complaints. In contrast to the widely quoted correlation that approximately 50% of diabetic men have erection failure[3] and the assumption that this represents an organic etiology, only 6 of the 30 diabetic men showed NPT deficits. These authors concluded that the incidence of organic erectile impairment in diabetic men has been overestimated. These data also support the clinical contention of Renshaw[15] that a majority of diabetic men complaining of impotence respond favorably to brief sex therapy. Such clinical findings question the commonly accepted explanations of neurophysiologic influence on sexual functioning in diabetes.

In the study of NPT, four additional issues remain unclear at present:

1. NPT studies do not appear to identify those men who may be able to attain erections with increased stimulation beyond that which is commonly assumed to be sufficient. Clinical evidence suggests that some men are able to obtain erections with the use of vibrators, for example, but are unable to do so with manual or oral stimulation alone.

2. Some men who show NPT deficits during the autonomic activation of REM sleep might be able to attain erections with stimulation during a waking state of deep muscle relaxation.

3. Identification of pathophysiology in one series of NPT studies over three successive nights may represent a transitory cause of dysfunction (such as temporary effects of medication) rather than a "permanent" one.

4. The cost for such monitoring (involving three nights in a hospital or laboratory setting) and the resultant need for the patient to be examined by a team of professionals (consisting at one center of a urologist, sleep researcher, psychiatrist, and psychologist[19]) may prohibit the use of this technique with some patients. Barry et al.[1] have suggested the use of postage stamps around the base of the penis as a simple, low-cost alternative to NPT that can be performed by the patient at home. This technique should obviously be more thoroughly explored and validated, although Wasserman et al.[25] report that adequate NPT evaluation requires measuring increases in both the base and the tip of the penis, simultaneous monitoring of sleep stages, and direct observation of a maximum erection to see whether it is adequate for penetration. The portable NPT equipment being developed for "at home" use and the stamp technique of Barry et al.[1] would have obvious drawbacks in these areas.

THE PENILE PROSTHESIS

Sotile[23] has critically reviewed the literature concerning both the rodlike and the hydraulic penile prosthesis. He concluded that further research is needed:

1. To assess subjective as well as objective (functional) results of the implant.
2. To present more extensive follow-up data.
3. To delineate significant prognostic factors for successful adjustment to this treatment.

Scott et al.[19] have reported the results of 5 years of clinical experience with the inflatable prosthesis. Although 234 of 245 men were able "to use the device to their satisfaction," no partner data or further explicit subjective or objective outcome criteria or follow-up data were presented. The incidence and management of complications with the rodlike prosthesis have been reported.[12,20] Kramarsky-Binkhorst[11] has studied 31 female partners of men with the prosthesis and concluded that the partner should be included in both pre- and postoperative counseling.

One important issue concerns the reported use of the prosthesis with psychogenically impotent men. Several investigators explicitly require that a course of sex therapy without response be done prior to the insertion of the prosthesis.[21] Others mention psychiatric assessment or psychodiagnostic testing as part of the screening process with no inclusion of sex therapy.[9,19]

Although objective measurement of erectile capacity such as with NPT studies, phalloarteriography, and penile pulse volume show promise, brief sex therapy would seem to have considerable use as a noninvasive technique for differential diagnosis and for the treatment of erectile dysfunction. Schiavi[16] pointed out the importance of an assessment of the relative balance of organogenic and psychogenic factors (rather than a diagnosis of "*either* organogenic *or* psychogenic etiology"). A "threshold" concept may clarify that sex therapy approaches to reduce stress and anxiety in the patient and his partner can be helpful in even predominantly organogenic erectile dysfunction. The following section will describe the contributions sex therapy can make in the evaluation and treatment of such cases.

CASE REPORT 1

♂ Mr. T., aged 62, complained of a 3-year history of erectile failure. He had no morning erections but had occasional weak erections of short duration with manual stimulation. Six years prior to his visit, he had been in an automobile accident and sustained numerous injuries that eventually necessitated his confinement in a nursing home and separation from his wife. While there he developed progressive weakness, incontinence, and seizures, ultimately diagnosed as caused by a frontal meningioma. This was removed, and with subsequent improvement in his symptoms Mr. T. returned home.

When seen by a urology service for his complaints of erectile failure, it was thought that his problems were most probably secondary to central nervous system damage, and he was offered a prosthesis. Because Mr. T. wished to explore other options available to him, he and his wife were referred to a sex therapy team for further evaluation and counseling. After three sessions, during which the effects of prolonged illness on sexuality were discussed and suggestions for senate focus/nondemand pleasuring were given, Mr. T. was able to attain erections that were firm enough for intercourse and satisfactory to both him and his wife.

In this example, sex therapy was successful and kept the client from being exposed to what would have been unnecessary surgical risk with uncertain psychological outcomes.

A CLINICAL PERSPECTIVE ON PROSTHESIS SURGERY

An important question to be asked when considering surgical implantation of a penile prosthesis is, "What results do the client and his partner (if he is in a relationship) expect from the operation?" If a person undergoes this operation with the expectation that it will solve all his problems, sexual and nonsexual, he will most likely be disappointed. Therefore it is essential to treat sexual dysfunctions within the context of an individual's own personal and interpersonal experience and expectations. Another case report may illustrate the importance of attempting to explore with prosthesis candidates and their partners the nature of their expectations about the operation.

CASE REPORT 2

♂ Mr. L., a 55-year-old diabetic, had a history of increasing difficulty obtaining and maintaining erections for the past 4 years. The relationship of his diabetes to his erectile functioning was unclear. He occasionally attained morning erections and erections with self-stimulation. He himself had requested a prosthesis to deal with his erectile failure. In addition to his sexual problems, Mr. L. admitted to being depressed. He had recently moved, disliked his job and new home, and hinted at marital problems as well.

The recommendation of the sex therapy team who saw Mr. L. was that he should have further assessment with his wife to discuss their sexual and relationship concerns and that he should consider counseling for his depression before any surgical intervention. Mr. L. chose not to follow either of these recommendations and elected instead to have a prosthetic implant. Subsequent to the surgery, he remained depressed, was dissatisfied with the implant, and was strongly considering having it removed.

The foregoing example points out the danger of attempting to correct a sexual impairment as if it existed in a vacuum. To a great extent, our treatment efforts are directed at increasing the range of options through which interpersonal needs can be met as well as increasing the alternatives from which a person may choose to feel fulfilled sexually. Expectations and pressure resulting from the belief that an erect penis is the sine qua non for male sexual expression are often themselves the prime psychologic sources of erectile difficulty. Thus the client's dogged attempts to produce an erection may become the problem itself. The unrelenting focus on the penis is likely to maintain rather than resolve sexual dissatisfaction. Many persons also have difficulty in expressing their sexual needs and desires to their partners in an open and nondefensive manner. Commonly, heterosexual males with erectile dysfunction have assumed that their partners preferred penile-vaginal intercourse, only to be informed much later that other forms of stimulation were equally, if not more, enjoyable.

It is crucial to explore with the client and his partner (if available), their expectations of what improved sexual functioning will and will not change in their lives. Too often the recognition that disruptive life experiences can adversely affect sexual functioning leads people to believe the reverse statement: that a "functional" penis can guarantee a better relationship and self-image or that it will serve as a panacea for depression or other emotional or life problems. Other important motivational factors may not be noticed, despite thorough psychologic/psychiatric evaluation. Such an example is provided by Stewart and Gerson,[24] who reported that a woman who had married her husband after the onset of erectile dysfunction began divorce proceedings 72 hours after he returned home with a prosthesis.

Every person with a sexual complaint who desires treatment should be allowed access to information and counseling procedures that have often been found to dispel or alleviate those complaints in others. If necessary, a treatment regimen can be offered that includes interventions to correct the specific dysfunction and training in communication. We have found the latter to be critical in facilitating the cooperation between couples that must exist for them to do the useful retraining exercises. Men without partners can role play similar communication exercises with the therapist or others.[27] Improved communication should actually prevent transitory sexual difficulties (which most people experience at one time or another) from crystalizing into sexual problems requiring professional treatment.

TREATMENT OVERVIEW

A brief outline of the treatment of erectile dysfunction in men assumed to be organically impaired would be as follows:

1. Ascertain whether erections occur in any situation, for example, when there is no need to perform with an erection. This would be determined by instituting a regimen of sex counseling, including the prescription of exploratory home exercises involving self-stimulation or stimulation by the partner, and communication exercises.

2. If little or no erection resulted, and if a complete physiologic examination (including NPT studies) suggested impairment of innervation or of vascular responses necessary for erection, give the client the opportunity in therapy to consider forms of stimulation and sexual expression that do not require an erect penis. Also make available information about the main types of penile prostheses.

3. Then suggest the client explore this new range of sexuality while allowing for the possibility that the erectile response would improve over time. If erections do not return, the client might discover that the increased sexual options satisfy both his own and his partner's needs and desires without the use of a prosthetic implant.

4. If a client declined to participate in the above steps or, if after completing them, he preferred a prosthesis, recommend that he and his partner obtain preoperative counseling to assess their expectations of the prosthesis surgery and to determine the likelihood that these expectations will be met. If they decide to proceed with the prosthetic implant, postoperative counseling can be offered to help them adapt to the surgically produced change. Examples of the importance of sex counseling for clients who have already obtained penile prostheses are provided by Stewart and Gerson,[24] and by Divita and Olsson.[2]

In summary, in the evaluation and treatment of erectile dysfunction with suspected organogenic etiology, it is crucial for sex therapists and physicians offering surgical treatment for erectile difficulties to work together to provide solutions most likely to ensure the total well-being of each individual client.

REFERENCES

1. Barry, J.M., Blank, B., and Boiliau, M.: Nocturnal penile tumescence monitoring with stamps, Urology **15**:2, 1980.
2. Divita, E.C., and Olsson, P.A.: The use of sex therapy in a patient with a penile prosthesis, J. Sex Marital Ther. **1**:305-311, 1975.
3. Ellenberg, M.: Sexual function in diabetic patients. In Bradley, W.E., editor: Aspects of diabetic autonomic neuropathy, Ann. Intern. Med. **92**(2pt2):331-333, 1980.
4. Fisher, C., Schiavi, R.C., Edward, A., et al.: Quantitative differences in nocturnal penile tumescence (NPT) between impotence of psychogenic and organic origin, Sleep Res. **6**:49, 1977.
5. Fisher, C., Schiavi, R.C., Edwards, A., et al.: Evaluation of nocturnal penile tumescence in the differential diagnosis of sexual impotence, Arch. Gen. Psychiatry **36**:431-437, 1979.
6. Fisher, C., Schiavi, R.C., Lear, H., et al.: The assessment of nocturnal REM erection in the differential diagnosis of sexual impotence, J. Sex Marital Ther. **1**:277-289, 1975.
7. Geiger, R.C.: Sexual implications for spinal cord injury. In Cull, J.G., and Hardy, R.E., editors: Physical medicine and rehabilitation approaches in spinal cord injury, Springfield, Ill., 1977, Charles C Thomas, Publisher.
8. Hosking, D.J., Bennet, T., Hampton, J.R., Evans, D.F., et al.: Diabetic impotence: studies of nocturnal erection during REM sleep, Br. Med. J. **2**:1394-1396, 1979.
9. Karacan, I., and Salis, P.J.: Diagnosis and treatment of erectile impotence, Psychiatric Clin. North Am. **3**(1):97-111, 1980.
10. Karacan, I., Williams, R.L., Thornby, J.I., et al.: Sleep-related penile tumescence as a function of age, Am. J. Psychiatry **132**:932-937, 1975.
11. Kramarsky-Binkhorst, S.: Female partner perception of Small-Carrion implant, Urology **12**(5):545-548, 1978.
12. Kramer, S., Anderson, E.E., Bredael, J.J., and Paulson, D.F.: Complications of Small-Carrion penile prosthesis, Urology **13**(1):49-51, 1979.
13. Magee, M.C.: Psychogenic impotence: a critical review, Urology **15**(5):435-442, 1980.
14. Pearman, R.O.: Insertion of a silastic penile prosthesis for the treatment of organic sexual impotence, J. Urol. **107**:802-806, 1972.
15. Renshaw, D.: Impotence in diabetes. In LoPiccolo, J., and LoPiccolo, L., editors: Handbook of sex therapy, New York, 1978, Plenum Publishing Corp.
16. Schiavi, R.C.: Psychological treatment of erectile disorders in diabetic patients, Ann. Intern. Med. **92**(2pt2):337-339, 1980.
17. Schiavi, R.C., and Schreiner-Engel, P.: Physiologic aspects of sexual function and dysfunction, Psychiatric Clin. North Am. **3**(1):81-95, 1980.
18. Scott, F.B., Bradley, W.E., and Timm, G.W.: Management of erectile impotence: use of the implantable inflatable prosthesis, Urology **2**:80-82, 1973.
19. Scott, F.B., Byrd, G.J., Karacan, I., Olsson, P., et al.: Erectile impotence treated with an implantable, inflatable prosthesis: five years of clinical experience, J.A.M.A., **241**(24):2609-2612, 1979.
20. Shelling, R.H., and Maxted, W.C.: Major complications of silicone penile prosthesis: predisposing clinical situations, Urology **15**(2):131-133, 1980.
21. Small, M.P.: Small-Carrion penile prosthesis: a new implant for management of impotence, Mayo Clin. Proc. **51**:336, 1976.
22. Small, M.P., Carrion, H.M., and Gordon, J.A.: Small-Carrion penile prosthesis: new implant for management of impotence, Urology **4**:479-486, 1975.
23. Sotile, W.M.: The penile prosthesis: a review, J. Sex Marital Ther. **5**(2):90-102, 1979.
24. Stewart, T.D., and Gerson, S.N.: Penile prosthesis: psychological factors, Urology **7**:400-403, 1976.
25. Wasserman, M.D., Pollak, C.P., Spielman, A. J., and Weitzman, E.D.: The differential diagnosis of impotence: the measurement of nocturnal penile tumescence, J.A.M.A. **243**(20):2038-2042, 1980.
26. Zilbergeld, B.: Male sexuality, Boston, 1978, Little, Brown & Co.

♀ **ABOUT THE AUTHOR** ♀

Jean M. Stoklosa, R.N., M.S., is Clinical Nurse Specialist, Nursing Service, at the Veterans Administration Medical Center, San Francisco. She has published several articles on sexual health care and has presented numerous workshops and lectures for health professionals on this topic.

FAMILY PLANNING

36 Issues in family planning and physical disability*

Susan E. Knight

Since the advent of the current family planning movement, conscious control of fertility has been seen as both a panacea and a Pandora's box. The ability to plan family size has given many people greater control over their standard of living, but there is no "perfect" contraceptive method. Most problems with the various contraceptive methods are related to either ease of use or impact on the individual's state of health. The Pill was once heralded for its ease of use and reliability and is sometimes credited for the "sexual revolution" because it has changed sex from a reproductive function to an experience of pleasure for its own sake. However, the Pill is now seen as having negative effects on the health of a substantial number of women. On the other hand, the diaphragm, which has been seen as having few medical side effects, is felt by many people to have a negative impact on the enjoyment of the sex act itself. The diaphragm that "failed" to prevent pregnancy because it was left in the bedside stand still presents the same problems today as it did 20 years ago.

For the person with a disability, these undesirable aspects of contraception are compounded by yet another: the belief that because of being disabled we are inherently "different," and therefore our family planning concerns and methods are unique and separate from those of people who are not disabled. Common prejudices toward disabled persons include: "You don't need gynecologic care because you are not sexually active or sexual;" "You can't have a normal pregnancy and delivery because you are in a wheelchair;" "You shouldn't or can't have children because you are disabled;" and "What do you mean you might have V.D.? You're disabled." The underlying message of these assumptions is that the person with a disability is not totally human; that we do not have the same rights and access to

*The preparation of this chapter was supported in part by National Institute of Mental Health Grant No. MH 14346. The author also wishes to acknowledge the assistance of Mary M. Rodocker, R.N., M.S., and Jennifer H. Wear, M.D..

such diverse sex-related experiences as sexual activity, need for gynecologic care, parenting, and exposure to venereal disease. Both the person with a disability and the health care provider need to be aware of such assumptions within themselves and others to combat their negative effects. It is important to acknowledge that it is not only able-bodied persons who carry these assumptions; disabled people grow up in the same society as those who are not disabled. We are exposed to the same myths and misinformation as everyone else and therefore may believe that family planning is not our concern.

There are three important principles that both disabled and able-bodied family planning health care providers and consumers need to be aware of. When dealing with family planning as it relates to persons with a disability, one must address the following: (1) one must be able to extrapolate from existing information about family planning for use with the individual with a disability; (2) the person with or without a disability has a right to choose the most appropriate method of family planning for his or her individual needs; and (3) there are communication issues between the health care provider and the disabled person and between the disabled person and his or her partner because of differences in physical mobility.

When looking at existing information about contraception, we find that it is usually concerned with those who are either able-bodied and considered to be "in good health" or those who have significant medical conditions such as heart disease or diabetes. What we lack is information on persons who have orthopedic and neurologic disabilities but who are also "in good health." It is often assumed that the person with a disability is ill, that an impairment of the physical structure creates an inherent weakness of one's state of health. This is often not the case. What is important to ask when dealing with the family planning concerns of a person with a disability is, "Besides this person's *apparent* disability, are there any medical problems that contraindicate use of a particular contraceptive method, change fertility, affect pregnancy and/or delivery, or interfere with the ability to raise children?"

Because we lack information on the family planning needs of the physically disabled, we must take what we know in general and apply it to the individual with whom we are concerned. For example, it is often thought that women who use wheelchairs should not take birth control pills. The rationale for this has been that women in wheelchairs have circulation problems and therefore have greater incidences of thrombophlebitis. Oral contraceptives may increase this risk. It is true that many women in wheelchairs, especially where paralysis is a factor, do have decreased circulation. However, this is not always the case. Each woman's circulatory system needs to be assessed individually. Other factors should also be considered, as is done with able-bodied women, such as age, frequency of sexual intercourse, past medical history, and the women's attitudes about both pregnancy and the Pill. For women using a wheelchair who do have circulation problems, the diaphragm is seen as a possible alternative. Current evidence indicates an increase in bladder infections among women using diaphragms, possibly due to the device's placement, which may result in temporary trauma to the urethra and bladder. Spinal cord–injured persons using catheters have increased risk of bladder infections, and so the diaphragm may cause additional problems for a woman who is catheterized. Again, we must look at the individual and determine the extent to which a chronic medical concern such as serious and/or frequent bladder infections poses a problem.

Our ability to extrapolate must become extremely refined and sophisticated when we address an area such as the effect of diminished uterine sensation on pregnancy, delivery, and contraceptive choice. Women who lack uterine sensation may be poor candidates for the intrauterine device (IUD) because they may be unaware of pain from pelvic inflammatory disease which is a possible side effect of this particular method.[2] It has also been suggested that some women with high spinal cord lesions who do not have uterine sensation may need to be hospitalized prior to the beginning of labor to ensure its immediate discovery. The assumption here is that someone else, that is, a medical person, will be closely observing and will note the first stages of labor.

It is interesting that several women with high spinal cord injuries have reported that a lack of sensation is *not* a lack of awareness. They describe perceiving menstrual cramping, pain from pelvic infection, and/or labor contractions through sensations such as chills, pressure in other parts of their bodies, or sweating above the level of their spinal cord lesion rather than uterine sensations. I believe that all these women are aware of their bodies. They have explored themselves both sexually and sensually and understand what their body is trying to tell them. This does not mean that all persons with limited sensation would be aware of such "clues" from their bodies, especially if they had not explored their body reactions for themselves. But for women who have a good awareness of their body function despite a lack of specific uterine sensation, early hospitalization for delivery and the exclusion of the IUD as a possible contraceptive choice may not be appropriate.

The right to choose the most desired birth control method for oneself is a controversial issue. Many physicians believe that, in addition to warning an individual that a particular method may become harmful, they have a responsibility to avoid prescribing such a method even when the individual or a couple desires using it. Does a person or a couple have a right to choose a method that may become physically harmful for them? There is no easy answer to this question. It is important to note that some people would rather risk potential health problems than unwanted pregnancy. I have personally met spinal cord–injured women with circulatory problems who use oral contraceptives and who are fully aware of the increased risk of thrombophlebitis. They have found physicians who are willing to prescribe the medication. It is not my intention to convey the belief that all physicans should prescribe all medication desired by all people. Instead, it is important for the physician who feels that he or she cannot in clear conscience prescribe a medication to know that this is the clients *personal* decision, rather than "no physician in his or her right mind would prescribe this for you." Although this, indeed, may be the case for individuals with existing medical concerns such as past history of cancer, diabetes, or heart disease, it may not be so for individuals who have *not yet* developed a possible side effect such as thrombophlebitis. That person is taking a risk, not exacerbating an existing condition. Again, the question of individual choice is a difficult one, one that concerns *both* the health care provider and the individual consumer.

The third issue, that of communication and family planning, is a universal one. The ability of health care providers and consumers to communicate with each other in a way to ensure the choice and use of the most appropriate contraceptive method is important for able-bodied and disabled people alike. The example of the diaphragm left in the bedside stand is an example of a breakdown in communication. If health care personnel can explore with the individual or the couple their feelings about how any given method will affect their sexual expression, then the chances of finding a successful method are greatly increased.

It behooves disabled consumers to strive to understand their own bodies as much as possible and to seek health care providers who view them as individuals. Unfortunately, the disabled person who succeeds in developing a good relationship with health care providers and gains quality care and information must often first "educate" the care provider. The woman who informs the staff about the position that is most feasible for her during a pelvic exam and the man who says, "But I *can* use condoms, my partner has better hand dexterity than I," are people who will educate that "lack of mobility isn't always a problem" and who will facilitate open communication and exchange of information.

The health care provider has responsibility to communicate as well. Not all family planning personnel *must* work with disabled people. Some will learn that their discomfort and/or prejudices toward persons with disabilities may render them ineffective in providing service to those individuals. In this case the provider is responsible for recognizing the problem as a personal one and not one to be projected on the disabled person. It would then be important to communicate to the individual what other resources, persons, information, and agencies are available to them. We do not have to be comfortable to be effective, but we are responsible for finding resources that are appropriate and helpful to the individual. Both health care providers and disabled persons can benefit from two resource booklets, *Toward Intimacy: Family Planning and Sexuality Concerns of Physically Disabled Women* and *Within Reach: Providing Family Planning Services to Disabled Women.*[1,2]

Another area that needs to be addressed is communication between disabled persons and their sexual partner(s) and/or their attendants. It is not uncommon for women to feel that they are totally responsible for contraception. Comments like

"He never asked me if I was on the Pill" or "I always have to remember to put in the diaphragm" are common dissatisfactions of women in our society. Because an able-bodied woman usually has good hand dexterity and mobility, it is possible for her to take sole responsibility for contraception, even if she would prefer otherwise. Some disabled women do not have the hand dexterity and/or mobility to allow this "independence" in contraceptive use. Many significantly disabled women need their partner or attendant to remove the Pill from its package, insert the diaphragm or contraceptive foam, or check the IUD string. Although I know of no studies about whether disabled people are "better" contraceptors than able-bodied persons, I think this would be interesting to learn. Could the need for assistance in use of birth control create the climate that makes communication not only necessary but also a positive part of the sexual relationship? If two people can openly discuss the easiest and more desirable way for them to use a diaphragm, might this also assist them in beginning to talk about other sexual topics as well, such as what kind of sexual pleasure each of them desires?

A PERSONAL EXPERIENCE

In writing this chapter on contraception, I have found myself looking at my own experience with contraception as a disabled woman. I have mild cerebral palsy that affects mobility and coordination on the right side of my body. Like many college-age women in the late 1960s, my first contraceptive method was the birth control pill. Because I have good use of my left hand, opening the package was no problem for me, thus I was "independent" in the use of oral contraceptives.

In my midtwenties, again like many of my peers, I began to examine whether the Pill was the best method for me to use. By 1975 there was greater knowledge about the Pill's potentially harmful side effects, and I decided to use the diaphragm. My first attempts to use a diaphragm were unsuccessful because I have complete use of only one hand.

A nurse practitioner who was trying to help me solve this dilemma gave me an introducer for the diaphragm that effectively allows anyone to insert a diaphragm with one hand, as long as they can get the diaphragm onto this apparatus. She also prescribed a "flat spring" diaphragm, which is the only kind that will fit on an introducer.

Once I had this diaphragm and introducer "in hand," so to speak, I was again "independent" in my use of contraception. Whereas I inserted the diaphragm myself, it was often easiest to ask my partner to help me put the diaphragm on the introducer and put the contraceptive cream in the diaphragm before I inserted it. This never seemed to create any problems.

When I was 28 years old, I had some corrective surgery that put me in a long leg cast for 6 weeks. Because of my greatly decreased mobility, I was no longer able to insert the diaphragm myself. Instead, I would fill the diaphragm with the cream, and my partner would insert it. He could insert it without the introducer, so that became an unnecessary piece of equipment for us. For the first time in my experience, inserting the diaphragm became a part of lovemaking rather than a chore. This pattern of ours continued once my cast was removed and my mobility returned.

What I realize now is that because I couldn't be "independent" in that situation, we were able to share this experience and find a solution so that it became a part of our caring for each other rather than an "unnatural" intervention. The communication that we developed served us well in our sexual relationship, the use of contraception, and the other areas of our being together as well. Because many disabled persons *must* communicate with their partners about sexual possibilities and restrictions, this opens up avenues for communication in other areas of the relationship that, unfortunately, many people who are totally physically independent may never experience. I am sad about that because what most people seek in intimate relationships is "interdependence," an all too elusive goal for many. I hope we can all learn that part of being caring is to be able to share and that we can be loved for this, not just for what we can give or can be given.

REFERENCES

1. Hale-Harbongh, J., Norman, A., Bogle, J., and Shaul, S.: Within reach: providing family planning services to physically disabled women, New York, 1978, Human Sciences Press.

2. Shaul, S., Bogle, J., Hale-Harbough, J., and Norman, A.: Toward intimacy: family planning and sexuality concerns of physically disabled women, New York, 1978, Human Sciences Press.

Resource list of agencies involved in sexuality and disability

Although we do not endorse the services of any particular individual or agency, the key personnel listed below may assist the reader in locating sexuality and disability education and counseling services in the areas indicated.

The following list is representative only. A number of other excellent resources are listed in *Who cares? A handbook on sex education and counseling services for disabled people* (available from R.R.R.I., George Washington University, 1828 L. Street, N.W., Suite 704, Washington, D.C. 20036; telephone: [202] 676-6377).

EASTERN UNITED STATES
District of Columbia

Regional Rehabilitation Research Institute
George Washington University
1828 L. St., N.W.
Suite 704
Washington, D.C. 20036
(202) 676-6377
Contact: Debra A. Cornelius, M.A.

Max Fitz-Gerald, M.A., Della Fitz-Gerald, M.A., and James Achtzehn, M.A.
Gallaudet College
7th and Florida Ave., N.E.
Washington, D.C. 20002
(202) 651-5801/651-5400

New York

Coalition on Sexuality and Disability
122 East 23rd St.
New York, N.Y. 10010
(212) 677-7400
Contact: Simi Kelley

Department of Rehabilitation Counseling
New York University
21-29 W. Fourth St.
New York, N.Y. 10003
(212) 598-3242
Contact: Nancy Esibill, Ph.D.

Sexuality Film Project
Institute of Rehabilitation Medicine
New York University Medical Center
400 East 34th St.
New York, N.Y. 10016
(212) 679-3200
Contact: Joan Bardach, Ph.D.

United Cerebral Palsy Association, Inc.
66 E. 34th St.
New York, N.Y.
Contact: Tony Bruno

United Cerebral Palsy of New York City
122 E. 23rd St.
New York, N.Y. 10010
(212) 677-7400
Contact: Giovanna Nigro, M.A.

Institute for Family Research and Education
760 Ostrom Ave.
Syracuse, N.Y. 13210
(315) 423-4584
Contact: Sol Gordon, Ph.D.

Pennsylvania

Moss Rehabititation Hospital
12th and Tabor Rd.
Philadelphia, Pa. 19141
(215) 329-5715
Contact: Dorothea Glass, M.D.

Planned Parenthood
1220 Sansom Street
Philadelphia, Pa. 19107
(215) 574-9200
Contact: Winnifred Kempton, A.C.S.W.

MIDWESTERN UNITED STATES
Illinois

The American Association of Sex Educators, Counselors, and Therapists
One E. Wacker Dr.
Suite 2700
Chicago, Ill. 60601
(312) 222-1717
Contact: William Granzig, Ph.D.

The Rehabilitation Institute of Chicago
345 E. Superior St.
Chicago, Ill. 60611
(312) 649-6179
Contact: Don Olson, M.D.

Indiana

Indiana Rehabilitation Institute
600 Grant St., Room SP223
Gary, Ind. 46402
(219) 886-4566
Contact: Robert J. Neumann, M.A.

Institute for Sex Research
416 Morrison Hall
Indiana University
Bloomington, Ind. 47401
(812) 337-7686
Contact: Paul Gebhard, Ph.D.

Department of Urology
Indiana University Medical Center
Indianapolis, Ind. 46207
(317) 264-7338
Contact: John P. Donohue, M.D.

Michigan

Rehabilitation Institute
261 E. Mack Ave.
Detroit, Mich. 48201
(313) 494-9707
Contact: James Cole, M.S.W./Melanee Fishwick, M.A.

Department of Physical Medicine and Rehabilitation and The National Task Force on Sexuality and Disability, American Congress of Rehabilitation Medicine
University of Michigan Medical School
Ann Arbor, Mich. 48104
(313) 764-7163
Contact: Theodore M. Cole, M.D./Sandra S. Cole C.S.E., C.S.C.

Minnesota

Program in Human Sexuality
University of Minnesota Medical School
2630 University Ave., S.E.
Minneapolis, Minn. 55414
(612) 376-7520
Contact: Sharon Satterfield, M.D.

Ohio

Spinal Cord Injury Service
Veterans Administration Hospital
10701 East Blvd.
Cleveland, Ohio 44106
(216) 791-3800
Contact: M.G. Eisenberg, Ph.D.

SOUTHERN UNITED STATES
Alabama

Division of Continuing Education
University of Alabama
P.O. Box 2967
University, Ala. 35486
(205) 348-6266
Contact: Mary Catherine Beasley, Ph.D.

Florida

Collier County Medical Health Clinic
6075 Golden Gate Parkway
Naples, Fla. 33942
(813) 455-1031
Contact: Michael F.X. Geraghty

Mental Retardation Program
College of Education
University of South Florida
Building FAO 170
Tampa, Fla. 33620
(813) 974-2100, ext. 279
Contact: Bernard Lax, Ph.D.

Georgia

Center for Rehabilitation Medicine
Emory University
1441 Clifton Rd., N.E.
Atlanta, Ga. 30322
(404) 329-5513
Contact: Lawrence D. Baker, M.D.

Louisiana

Department of Rehabilitation Counseling
Louisiana State University Medical Center
School of Allied Health Professionals
100 South Derbigny
New Orleans, La. 70112
(504) 568-6535
Contact: Susan M. Daniels, Ph.D. (editor,
Sexuality and Disability)

Mississippi

**Department of Health, Physical Education
and Recreation**
University of Southern Mississippi
Hattiesburg, Miss. 39401
(601) 266- 4321
Contact: Walter Yarrow, Ph.D.

Virginia

Sophia Chipouras, M.A.
Route 2, Box 5BB
The Plains, Va. 22171
(703) 253-5665

**ROCKY MOUNTAIN AND
SOUTHWESTERN UNITED STATES**
Arizona

Planned Parenthood
1301 South Seventh Ave.
Phoenix, Ariz. 85007
(602) 258-4299
Contact: Carol Weston

**Arizona State School for the Deaf and the
Blind**
P.O. Box 5545
Tucson, Ariz. 85703
(602) 882-5282
Contact: Howard R. Busby, M.S./Marilyn
Kallman, M.Ed.

Planned Parenthood
127 South Fifth Ave.
Tucson, Ariz. 85701
(602) 624-7477
Contact: Sherry Sedgwick, M.Ed.

Psychology Department
University of Arizona
Tucson, Ariz. 85721
(602) 792-1450
Contact: George W. Hohmann, Ph.D.

Kenneth Lane, M.Ed. and Kathryn Nessel,
M.Ed. Private Counseling practice
Tucson, Ariz.
(602) 299-6795

Colorado

Craig Hospital
Family and Patient Service Department
3425 Clarkson
Englewood, Colo. 80110
(303) 761-3040
Contact: Jack Dahlberg, M.A.

New Mexico

Stanley Caplan, Ed.D.
700 Cutler, N.E.
Suite E-19
Albuquerque, N.M. 87110
(505) 883-5214

Texas

The Texas Institute for Rehabilitation and Research (TIRR)
P.O. Box 20095
Houston, Tex. 77025
(713) 797-1440
Contact: Joyce T. Salhoot, M.S.W.

Department of Psychiatry
Health Science Center
University of Texas
San Antonio, Tex. 78284
(512) 691-6215
Contact: James M. Turnbull, M.D.

WESTERN UNITED STATES
California

Sex and Disability Unit
Human Sexuality Program
Department of Psychiatry
University of California, San Francisco
814 Mission St., Second Floor
San Francisco, Calif. 94103
(415) 666-1066
Contact: Mary M. Rodocker, M.S.

Sexual Dysfunction Clinic
Center for the Health Sciences
University of California, Los Angeles
760 Westwood Plaza
Los Angeles, Calif. 90024
(213) 825-0243
Contact: Anna Heinrich, Ph.D./Susan Price, Ph.D.

Spinal Cord Injury Service
Santa Clara Valley Medical Center
751 South Bascom
Santa Clara, Calif. 95128
(408) 279-5116
Contact: Dan Mayclin, Ph.D.

Deaf Counseling, Advocacy, and Referral Agency
1320 Webster St.
Oakland, Calif. 94612
(415) 465-9554
Contact: Karen Crosby

Spinal Cord Injury Service
Veterans Administration Hospital
3801 Miranda Ave.
Palo Alto, Calif. 94304
(415) 493-5000, ext. 5874
Contact: Michael Dunn, Ph.D.

Robert Lenz, M.A.
1499 E. 22nd St.
Merced, Calif, 95340
(209) 383-2543

Center for Marital and Sexual Studies
5199 E. Pacific Coast Highway
Long Beach, Calif. 90814
(213) 597-4425
Contact: James Remsberg

Planned Parenthood
14120 Magnolia
Sherman Oaks, Calif. 91403
(213) 990-4300
Contact: Barbara Waxman

Oregon

Handicap Information Program
Portland State University
Portland, Ore. 97201
(503) 229-4422
Contact: Nina M. Lowry/Cindy Callis

Washington

Bogle, Matsuda and Shaul, Inc.
Management, Health and Education Consultants
4134 12th Ave., South
Seattle, Wash. 98108
(206) 525-3165
Contact: Jane Bogle, M.P.A./Susan Shaul, Ph.D.

Department of Rehabilitation Medicine
University of Washington Medical School
Seattle, Wash. 98195
(206) 543-8660
Contact: Jo Ann Brockway, Ph.D.

AUSTRALIA

Lesley Meredith
Nursing Administration
Royal Prince Alfred Hospital
Missenden Rd. Camperdown
N.S.W. 2050, Australia

CANADA
Alberta

Division of Occupational Therapies
School of Rehabilitation Medicines
University of Alberta
Edmonton, Alberta, Canada
T6G 2G4
Contact: Benita Fifield

British Columbia

Department of Psychiatry
Vancouver General Hospital
700 West 10th Ave.
Vancouver, B.C., Canada
V5Z 1M9
Contact: George Szasz, M.D.

GREAT BRITAIN

Committee on Sexual Problems of the Disabled
49 Victoria St.
London, SW1 H OUE
England
Contact: T.G. Gibbs

ISRAEL

Israel Society for Rehabilitation of the Disabled
10 Ibn Gvirol St.
Tel Aviv, Israel
Contact: Emanuel Chigier, M.D.

JAPAN

Genichi Nozue, M.D., Ph.D.
2-11-10 Kita-Aoyama
Minato-Ku, Tokyo, Japan 107

SWEDEN

Swedish Central Committee for Rehabilitation
Fack, S-161, 25 Bromma 1, Sweden
Contact: Inger Nordqvist

SWITZERLAND

Willy Pasini, M.D.
32 Bis Bd de La Cluse
1205 Geneva, Switzerland

APPENDIX II

A selective bibliography on sexuality and disability

BIBLIOGRAPHIES

Athelstan, G.: Psychological, sexual, social and vocational aspects of spinal cord injury: a selected bibliography, Minnesota Medical Rehabilitation Research and Training Center, No. 2, 1976.

Eisenberg, M.: Sex and disability: a selected bibliography, Rehabil. Psychol. (In press.)

Panieczko, S., Cornelius, D., and Frank, W.: Selected annotated bibliography on sexuality and disability 1975-1977, Washington, D.C. Regional Rehabilitation Research Institute on Attitudinal, Legal, and Leisure Barriers, George Washington University, unpublished manuscript, 1978.

Sha 'ked, A.: Human sexuality in physical and mental illness and disabilities: an annotated bibliography, Bloomington, Ind., 1978, Indiana University Press.

ADDITIONAL READINGS

Abse, D., Nash, E., and Louden, L.: Marital and sexual counseling in medical practice, ed. 2, New York, 1974, Harper & Row, Publishers, Inc.

Annon, J.: Behavioral treatment of sexual problems: brief therapy, vol. 1, New York, 1976, Harper & Row Publishers, Inc.

Barbach, L.: For yourself: the fulfillment of female sexuality, New York, 1975, Doubleday & Co.

Barnard, M.: Human sexuality for health professionals, Philadelphia, 1978, W.B. Saunders Co.

Bass, M., and Gelof, M., editors: Sexual rights and responsibilities of the mentally retarded, revised ed., Ardmore, Pa., 1975. (Available from Medora Bass, 1387 East Valley Rd., Santa Barbara, Calif. 93108.)

Becker, E.: Female sexuality following spinal cord injury, Bloomington, Ill., 1978, Cheever Publishing Co.

Blank, J.: Good vibrations: the complete woman's guide to vibrators, Burlingame, Calif., 1978, Down There Press.

Bleck, E., and Nagel, D.: Physically handicapped children: a medical atlas for teachers, New York, 1975, Grune & Stratton, Inc.

Bors, E., and Comarr, A.: Neurological disturbances of sexual function with special reference to 529 patients with spinal cord injury, Urol. Surv. 10:191-222, 1960.

Bullard, D.: Sexual enhancement in physical disability and medical condition, Int. J. Ment. Health. (In press.)

Bullard, D., Causey, G., Newman, A., Orloff, R., Schanche, K., and Wallace, D.: Sexual health care and cancer: a needs assessment, Front. Radiation Ther. Oncol. 14:55-58, 1980.

Bullard, D., Knight, S., and Rodocker, M., editors: Special issue on spinal cord injury, Sex. Disabil. 2(4):entire issue, 1979.

Bullard, D., Knight, S., Rodocker, M., and Wallace, D.: The sex and disability training project, final report, 1976-1979, unpublished manuscript, 1979.

Bullard, D., Mann. J., Caplan, H., and Stoklosa, J.: Sex counseling and the penile prosthesis, Sex. Disabil. 1(3):184-189, 1978.

Bullard, D., and Wallace, D.: Peer educator-counselors in sexuality for the disabled, Sex. Disabil. 1(2):147-152, 1978.

Buscaglia, L.: The disabled and their parents: a counseling challenge, Thorofare, N.J., 1975, Charles B. Slack, Inc.

Chigier, E., editor: Special issue: sex and the disabled, Isr. Rehabil. Ann. **14:**entire issue, 1977.

Chipouras, S., Cornelius D., Daniels, S., and Makas, E.: Who cares? A handbook on sex education and counseling services for disabled people, unpublished manuscript, 1978.

Cole, T., and Cole, S.: The handicapped and sexual health, SIECUS Rep. **4**(5), 1976.

Comarr, A.: Sexual concepts in traumatic cord and cauda equina lesions, J. Urol. **106:**375-378, 1971.

Comfort, A., editor: Sexual consequences of disability, Philadelphia, 1978, George F. Stickley Co.

Daniels, S.: Sexual health care services for the disabled, unpublished manuscript, 1978.

Diamond, M.: Sexuality and the handicapped, Rehabil. Lit. **35:**34-40, 1974.

Dickman, I.: Sex education and family life for visually handicapped children and youth: a resource guide, New York, 1974, SIECUS and American Foundation for the Blind, Inc.

Dunn, M.: Psychological intervention in a spinal cord injury center: an introduction, Rehabil. Psychol. **22**(4):165-178, 1975.

Dunn, M.: Social discomfort in the patient with spinal cord injury, Arch. Phys. Med. Rehabil. **58:**257-260, 1977.

Dunn, M., Herman, S., and Van Horn, E.: *Social skills and the spinal cord–injured individual,* education videotape, 1976, Washington, D.C., National Audiovisual Center, (30 minutes).

Dunn, M., Lloyd, E., and Phelps, G.: Sexual assertiveness in spinal cord injury, Sex. Disabil. **2** (4), 1979.

Edwards, J.: Sara and Allen: the right to choose, Portland, Ore., 1976. (Available from Jean Edwards, P.O. Box 3612, Portland, Ore. 97208.)

Exceptional Parent: a magazine devoted to the needs of children with disabilities. Subscription information available from Room 708, Statler Office Building, 20 Providence Street, Boston, Mass. 02116

Gagnon, J.: Human sexualities, Glenview, Ill., 1977, Scott, Foresman & Co.

Geiger, R.: Sexual implications of spinal cord injury. In Cull, J.G., and Hardy, R.E., editors: Physical medicine and rehabilitation approaches in spinal cord injury, Springfield, Ill., 1977, Charles C Thomas, Publisher.

Geiger, R. and Knight, S.: Sexuality of people with cerebral palsy, Med. Aspects Human Sex. **9:**70-79, 1975.

Gendel, E.: Hearing conservation of children: a special five year project in Kansas, Am. Public Health Assoc. **58**(3):449, 1968.

Gendel, E., Cozad, M., and Schloesser, P.: Deafness case finding—hearing conservation for Kansas children: a cooperative project in preventive medicine, J. Kans. Med. Soc. **68**(9):363-366, 1967.

Gochros, H., and Gochros, J., editors: The sexually oppressed, Wilton, Conn., 1977, Association Press.

Gordon, S.: Living fully: a guide for young people with a handicap, their parents, their teachers and professionals, N. Scituate, Mass., 1975, Duxbury Press.

Green, R., editor: Human sexuality: a health practitioner's text, ed. 2, Baltimore, 1975, Williams & Wilkins Co.

Greengross, W.: Entitled to love: the sexual and emotional needs of the handicapped, London, England, 1976, Malaby Press Ltd.

Hale-Harbaugh, J., Norman, A., Bogle, J., and Shaul, S.: Within reach: providing family planning services to physically disabled women, New York, 1978, Human Sciences Press.

Heslinga, K., Schellen, A., and Verkuyl, A.: Not made of stone, Springfield, Ill., 1974, Charles C Thomas, Publisher.

Hite, S.: The Hite report: a nationwide survey of female sexuality, New York, 1977, Macmillan, Inc.

Horenstein, S.: Sexual dysfunction in neurological disease, Med. Aspects Human Sex. **10:**6-11, 1976.

Johnson, W.: Sex education and counseling of special groups: the mentally and physically handicapped, ill, and elderly, Springfield, Ill., 1975, Charles C Thomas, Publisher.

Kaplan, H.: The new sex therapy, New York, 1974, Brunner/Mazel, Inc.

Kempton, W.: Sex education for persons with disabilities that hinder learning: a teacher's guide, N. Scituate, Mass., 1975, Duxbury Press.

Kempton, W., and Foreman, R.: Guidelines for training in sexuality and the mentally handicapped, 1976. Planned Parenthood Association of Southeastern Pennsylvania, 1200 Sansom Street, Philadelphia, Pa. 19107

Kentsmith, D., and Eaton, M.: Treating sexual problems in medical practice, New York, 1979, Arco Publishing Inc.

Knight, S.: What you always wanted to know about sexuality and handicapped people . . .

now you can ask! Disabled U.S.A. 3:11-13, 1979.

Labby, D.: Sexual concomitants of disease and illness, Postgrad. Med. 58(1):103-111, 1975.

Lenz, R., and Silverman, M.: *Active partners*, 16 mm. film, San Francisco, 1979, Multimedia Resource Center (sound, color, 18 minutes).

Like other people, 16 mm film, Northfield, Ill., 1973, Perennial Education, Inc., (sound, color, 37 minutes).

Luria, Z., and Rose, M.: Psychology of human sexuality, New York, 1978, John Wiley & Sons, Inc.

Masters, W., and Johnson, V.: Human sexual response, Boston, 1966, Little, Brown & Co.

Masters, W., and Johnson, V.: Human sexual inadequacy, Boston, 1970, Little, Brown & Co.

Medical Aspects of Human Sexuality, Hospital Publications, Inc., 609 Fifth Avenue, New York, N.Y. 10017

Money, J.: Phantom orgasm in the dreams of paraplegic men and women, Arch. Gen. Psychiatry 3:373-382, 1960.

Mooney, T., Cole, T., and Chilgren, R.: Sexual options for paraplegics and quadriplegics, Boston, 1975, Little, Brown & Co.

Moos, R.: Coping with physical illness, New York, 1977, Plenum Publishing Corp.

Nordqvist, I.: Disabled persons—relationships and sexuality. Swedish Central Committee for rehabilitation, Fack, S-161, 25 Bromma 1, Sweden.

Nordqvist, I.: Life together—the situations of the handicapped, Stockholm, Sweden, 1972, E. Olofssons Boktryckeri AB.

Nowinski, J.K.: Becoming satisfied: a man's guide to sexual fulfillment, Englewood Cliffs, N.J., 1980, Prentice-Hall, Inc.

Oremland, E., and Oremland, J.: The sexual and gender development of young children, Cambridge, Mass., 1977, Ballinger Publishing Co.

Robinault, I.: Sex, society and the disabled, New York, 1978, Harper & Row, Publishers, Inc.

Rodocker, M., Bullard, D., and Knight, S.: Films in sex and disability, J. Sex Marital Ther. 3: 285-286, 1977.

Rubin, I.: Sex life after sixty, New York, 1976, Basic Books, Inc.

Selvin, H.: Sexuality among the visually handicapped: a beginning, Sex. Disabil. 2:192-199, 1979.

Sexual Medicine Today, International Medical News Services, Inc., Suite 405, 600 New Hampshire Avenue, N.W., Washington, D.C. 20037.

Sexuality and Disability, a quarterly journal, Human Sciences Press, 72 Fifth Avenue, New York, N.Y. 10011

Shaul, S., Bogle, J., Hale-Harbaugh, J., and Norman, A.: Toward intimacy: family planning and sexuality concerns of physically disabled women, New York, 1978, Human Sciences Press.

Stoklosa, J., and Bullard, D.: Talking about sex: suggestions for the health professional, Front. Radiation Ther. Oncol. 14:79-82, 1980.

Stoklosa, J., Bullard, D., Rosenbaum, E., and Rosenbaum, I.: Sexuality and cancer. In Rosenbaum, E., and Rosenbaum, I., editors: A comprehensive guide for cancer patients and their families, Palo Alto, Calif., 1980, Bull Publishing Co.

Stubbins, J.: Social and psychological aspects of disability, Baltimore, 1977, University Park Press.

Taggie, J.M., and Manley, M.S.: A handbook on sexuality after spinal cord injury. Unpublished manuscript available from M.S. Manley, 3425 S. Clarkson, Englewood, Colo. 80110.

Tarabulcy, E.: Sexual function in the normal and in paraplegia, Paraplegia 10:201-208, 1972.

Trieschmann, R.: The psychological, social, and vocational adjustment in spinal cord injury: a strategy for future research. A. Executive summary. B. Final report. RSA 13-P-59011/9-01, Washington, D.C., 1978, Rehabilitation Services Administration.

Weiss, H.: The physiology of human penile erection, Ann. Intern. Med. 76:793-799, 1972.

Woods, N.: Human sexuality in health and illness, ed. 2, St. Louis, 1975, The C.V. Mosby Co.

Zilbergeld, B.: Male sexuality, Boston, 1978, Little, Brown & Co.

Zilbergeld, B.: Sex and serious illness. In Garfield, C., editor: Stress and survival, St. Louis, 1979, The C.V. Mosby Co.

INDEX